Awakening Spirit

WISE Seminary
First Year Certification Course
for Wiccan Clergy

Belladonna LaVeau, HPs
Illustrations by **Keslevar Teague**

Awakening Spirit

Order this book online at www.trafford.com
or email orders@trafford.com

Most Trafford titles are also available at major online book retailers.

© Copyright 2003 Donna M. Thompson.
All rights reserved. No part of this publication may be reproduced, stored in a retrieval system, or transmitted, in any form or by any means, electronic, mechanical, photocopying, recording, or otherwise, without the written prior permission of the author.

Print information available on the last page.

ISBN: 978-1-4120-1229-4 (sc)

Because of the dynamic nature of the Internet, any web addresses or links contained in this book may have changed since publication and may no longer be valid. The views expressed in this work are solely those of the author and do not necessarily reflect the views of the publisher, and the publisher hereby disclaims any responsibility for them.

Any people depicted in stock imagery provided by Getty Images are models, and
such images are being used for illustrative purposes only.
Certain stock imagery © Getty Images.

Trafford rev. 08/17/2018

Trafford PUBLISHING   www.trafford.com
North America & international
toll-free: 1 888 232 4444 (USA & Canada)
fax: 812 355 4082

This book is dedicated to my loving husband, Keslevar Teague, who at the tender age of 18 thankfully had enough sense to recognize his soul mate.

Acknowledgements

As we are all eternally connected, every spirit on earth is somehow responsible for bringing this information to light. In addition to thanking each one of them, I would especially like to thank:

My husband, Lord Keslevar who, as the Goddess pointed out to me many years ago, before I could understand what She meant, is the greatest teacher I will ever know.

My children, Luaxanna, Tatiana, and Ramsey, who have taught me that good energy always loves everything, even the bad stuff.

My teacher, Paul, who awakened, challenged, nurtured, and empowered me to know my true self, and taught me the Old Ways with skill and patience.

My mother, Patricia, who kindled my imagination and my love for reading, taught me how to write, and shared with me the mysteries of being a Priestess of Venus, even if she didn't have a name for it.

My father, Danny, who taught me that spirituality comes from within and that magic is real.

My students and the many seekers whose paths I have crossed, for giving me a reason to write all this down.

Table of Contents

In Service of the Goddess — vi
How to Use This Book — viii

Initial Activation

Chapter 1 – Initial Root Chakra Activation
- Relative Truth — 1
- Grounding — 5
- Religion v/s Spirituality — 10

Chapter 2 – Initial Sacral Chakra Activation
- Personal Responsibility & Karma — 19
- Sacred Energy — 24
- The History of Wicca — 27

Chapter 3 – Initial Will Chakra Activation
- Creating Your Reality/Manifesting Your Will — 39
- Shielding — 46
- Understanding Thought-forms — 51

Chapter 4 – Initial Heart Chakra Activation
- Connecting with Your Patron Deities — 63
- Channeling — 67
- The Power of Myth — 74

Chapter 5 – Initial Throat Chakra Activation
- The Human Energy Field — 79
- Seeing Auras — 97
- The Nature of Dis-ease — 108

Chapter 6 – Initial Third Eye Chakra Activation
- Reincarnation, Space, Time & the Eternal Now — 113
- Past Life Regression — 119
- Utilizing Past Life Information — 122

Chapter 7 – Initial Crown Chakra Activation
- The Wheel of the Year — 129

Chapter 8 – Initial Transpersonal Point Activation
- The Trials of the Goddess — 177
- Lineage and Service — 182
- Spells and Magic — 189

Second Activation

Chapter 9 – Second Root Chakra Activation
    Creating Your Personal Temple — 199
    Clearing Negative Energy & Making Incense — 203
    Mars – Warriors — 209

Chapter 10 – Second Sacral Chakra Activation
    Sacred Tools — 213
    Blessing & Consecrating — 223
    Venus – Maidens — 227

Chapter 11 – Second Will Chakra Activation
    The Power of the Circle — 231
    Casting the Circle — 234
    Sun - Oak Kings — 239

Chapter 12 – Second Heart Chakra Activation
    The Four Elements — 245
    Calling the Quarters — 251
    Moon – Mothers — 264

Chapter 13 – Second Throat Chakra Activation
    The God & The Goddess — 269
    Balance & Polarity — 273
    Mercury – Scholars — 276

Chapter 14 – Second Third Eye Chakra Activation
    Invoking Deity — 281
    Drawing Down the Moon — 286
    Saturn – Crones — 288

Chapter 15 – Second Crown Chakra Activation
    The Eight Paths of Power — 295
    Raising Energy & Directing Power — 301
    Jupiter - Holly Kings — 304

Chapter 16 – Second Transpersonal Point Activation
    Letting the Magic Work — 309
    Cakes & Wine and Banishing — 312
    Pluto – Priest Kings — 316

First Year Certification Requirements — 320
About the Cover — 323

In Service of the Goddess
Preface

I have walked in the footsteps of the Goddess for many years now. I have sought Her, served Her, adored Her, cried out to Her, and been irrevocably changed by Her. Looking back at my path, I can see that She was always leading me here. She sent me to this lifetime with all the gifts and talents I needed to achieve my greatest potential, though I did not know it. I set out looking for Her as a bitterly confused young woman caught between the establishment of Mormonism and the fetters of Patriarchy. I remember the rage in my heart as I sought self-actualization.

It brings me comfort knowing that many things have changed in the years I have served Her. It is no longer difficult to find books about Her. Today, I can't go to the supermarket without running into another follower of the Goddess. Our beliefs may vary, but our hearts are tuned to Hers. I can feel Her spirit echoing through the veins of my sisters as I see the women of my culture rejecting the burdens previous generations have tried to place on us.

I see the Goddess awakening in the brothers whose paths I cross. Their power exudes from embracing the balance of mother wit with father-wisdom. There is an undeniable strength in a Priest empowered by the realization that he is neither above nor below, but equal to the creative potency of a Priestess exalted.

I know our world is changing. I was Wiccan when teachers were few and none dared risk doing a ritual outside, much less in our own backyard. I have been personally persecuted for my faith, by strangers and loved ones alike. I have witnessed the pain of mothers being separated from their children in custody battles over their love of the Goddess. And I have seen the results of fanatical religious persecution.

I know the love and fear of serving her in private, and in open community. I realize the human desire to be validated. We all want to believe we have the one right answer. We all want to make our voices heard, and our ways understood. We want to be One.

Yet that is the challenge of the physical universe, to daily see the illusion of separateness and in the face of evidence to the contrary, remember who we are. We are children of Goddess, God, Allah, Diana, Zeus, Jesus, Isis, Shiva, Jehovah, Yahweh, Demeter, by whatever name you call, by whatever face you place, Spirit will come to you, because It loves you.

So, in reading the words that the Goddess has given me to pass on to you, remember: It is not the religion that enlightens you, or the face you place on God. It is not your gender, your bloodline, your IQ, or the color of your skin that gives or denies you the right to divine truth. It is your ability to be open-hearted, open-minded, and flexible in what you call reality. It is your willingness to suspend your disbelief, and your desire to pursue the knowledge. It is your motivations to study, pray, meditate, and listen. It is your ability to give love as well as receive it. It is your capacity to see yourself as a child, and realize that no matter how much you think you know, or how far you think you've come, new information can completely change your world and open you up to ever growing dimensions of truth that are not based on fixed, tangible, physical realities.

God/dess is all that is and everything that isn't, and without the adaptability to pursue Spirit with childlike, flexible innocence, we are no different than the dogmatic oppressors that forbid the Hebrews to pray in Egypt, tortured the Jews in Germany, and burned the Witches in Europe. God/dess is without limitation, and so is love.

Introduction

How to Use this Book

There is a place where one day we all stand. A threshold when something inside us knows there is more to this life than we had previously thought, but we don't know where to look to find it. It's a place that floods us with the desire to seek answers and truths. It's the call of our spirit, as it awakens from the Piscean slumber that has enchanted us all to sleep and forget.

Now is the time to remember.

Within the pages of this book, you will discover a co-directed journey into spiritual awakening. I say co-directed because somewhere along the pages you will realize that something else is happening. Something beyond the pages you hold in your hand. Spirit creates things; situations, circumstances, challenges and rewards, in conjunction with the journey that personalizes it, transforming your world with the power of your own magic. At some point, usually within the first four Activations, you realize that Goddess is there, nurturing you, loving you, and giving you what you need to wake up, remember, and be consciously One with Her again.

Awakening Spirit empowers and activates the Human Energy Field, so that you can more fully participate in the physical universe as a magical and spiritual being. It spirals around in the appropriate cycles for you to grow and mature magically through a natural process that awakens you to the unseen world of spirit and energy. Similar to the artist that paints the entire picture at once, this process layers thought upon thought and principle upon principle, bringing you astounding awareness while protecting your natural balance. As you integrate cosmic principles, and learn foundational energetics, it clears and matures your chakras, creating an energetic evolutionary transformation that allows you to feel, move, interpret and understand energies and thought-forms in a way you never knew anyone could. It teaches you how and when to use the powers

Introduction

created in your energy centers, and begins opening your being to the possibility of truly walking the sacred path as an incarnation of God/dess.

Raising your awareness nurtures your spirit, educates your mind, cleanses your heart, activates your passions, and stabilizes your world. For those things to happen, change must take place. Those changes start with letting go of the things that weigh you down, cause you grief, fear or sorrow, and prevent you from embracing love.

This process takes time. Change cannot occur too drastically, or it will upset your connection with reality. Therefore it is recommended that you spend one week with each Activation, so that you can work with the energy and fully integrate it into your field. Take your time. Rushing can cause you to miss something important. Pray, meditate, and reread the Chapters. Ask Goddess to help you understand and integrate the information.

Each Activation is set up with corresponding material from three interrelated subjects. This three-dimensional perspective creates an energetic shift in your awareness that awakens the connections within yourself, the universe, and your oneness with Spirit. Each Power Activation builds on the previous work, allowing you to gradually and comfortably grow in power and awareness. *Awakening Spirit* is the Freshman Course in the WISE Seminary and contains the first two attunements. These attunements allow you to transform your reality and reshape your world from the inside out. As we know in magic, 'third time's a charm,' therefore *Empowering the Sacred Self*, the WISE Seminary Sophomore Course, consists of the Third and Final Master Activation, fully maturing your chakras and enabling you to participate in your spiritual path as a consciously aware, actively empowered, magical being.

Take time to fully understand and work with each principle. Color and meditate on the symbol provided at the beginning of each section. These symbols speak to the subconscious mind and work with the information, meditations, and exercises to help facilitate the energetic activation process. Be creative, and enjoy the process. Pay attention to patterns, cycles, dreams, and feelings. Write down realizations, and epiphanies as they come to you. Every step you take is so sacred to Goddess. Take time to honor your sacredness by recording your path on paper in a personal journal.

There are layers upon layers of understanding within these pages. Part of the fun of this path is making the connections as you unravel the mysteries. It is the same within this book. A first glance will show you a simple awakening. The second and third time you read it you will uncover truths you didn't see previously. Turning to it again and again over the years will refine and tune your perspective to the magical, allowing you to transcend the illusion of a fixed, inalterable reality and giving you the tools to redefine your world. Finding the connecting mysteries of how this information is put together teaches you how to find and connect the mysteries on your path. Seek with an open heart, and let Goddess reveal the answers to you. Refer back to the book whenever you are stuck, pray for understanding as you read these words, and you will be amazed at the answers you will discover between these lines.

The WISE Seminary, College of Wicca, provides you with full-color mandalas, along with graphics, animations, color photos, and sound files that correspond with each chapter. These are complimentary and available for you on-line to use as often as you like at www.wiseseminary.com. But if possible, do spend time coloring the ones in the book. Coloring is relaxing. It suspends the conscious mind, moving you to that 'tween place where magic happens. It takes you back to your childhood, when your mind was open to the world of faerie, and dreams were real. It gives your consciousness something to do, so you can be open to hearing the words of spirit. It reminds you that you can create something very beautiful, even with the simplest of tools.

Enjoy your journey.

1

Initial Root Chakra Activation
Relative Truth
The Alchemy of Perspective

Red

Color Me Red!

Many of us have been taught all our lives that truth is absolute fact. "Truth is truth, and you can't change the truth." "The truth shall set you free." And "It's always important to tell the truth." But in Metaphysical studies we find truth to be changeable, and mutable. It is a perception of the facts, based on our views and opinions. We understand that truth is relative to each individual based on how he sees the world, what he believes is real, and what he tells himself about what he believes he has witnessed.

We are convinced that our version of the world is a tangible reality that everyone experiences in the same way. But, what is reality? Reality is *your* perceptions, feelings, understandings, and beliefs about *your* day-to-day experiences. Perceptions, feelings, understandings, and beliefs change depending on which facts *you* feel are most important. Therefore, *your* reality is based on a truth that is a unique blend of conclusions based on selected facts, and what *you* have told *yourself* those facts mean.

Your reality is different from everyone else's. Your reality may mean that the world is an abundant place that always fills your needs. Or, your reality may be that the world is filled with lack and there is never enough. Your reality may have proven to you that men are controlling, self-serving and disrespectful of women. Or, your reality may have proven to you that men are capable of being loving, nurturing, supportive partners. It may seem that your reality is real, tangible, and factual. But in truth, your reality is only *your* perspective of the world based on conclusions *you* have drawn from *your* experiences.

Your expression of reality is nothing more than an illusion that you have created to support the world in the way you believe it to be. If you believe the world is an abundant place, you will look for reasons to support that belief. You will automatically discount any evidence to the contrary. In fact, the evidence may never even enter your field of perception. If you believe that there is not enough to go around, you will look for reasons to support that belief. You will notice every example available to prove that people don't have enough. You will notice the rich and famous person, who just filed for bankruptcy. You will identify with the poor and afflicted. You will unconsciously sabotage your opportunities for prosperity because you believe; the world is not an abundant place, there is not enough for everyone to have plenty, and that you do not deserve to have your needs met.

Embracing this first principle is key to unlocking the mysteries of the universe. Recognizing the illusion of mundane reality is foundational to being able to change it.

Relative truth means that your view of the universe is relative to your prospective, your outlook, what you expect to happen. As well as your perspective, what you tell yourself about what did happen. If you don't like what you are seeing, look at it in a different way. Unless, of course, you don't believe that you can. Then your reality will be that truth is tangible fact that you cannot change, and you will be locked into validating your version of truth. This process feeds your fears and perpetuates stagnation. Without accepting that you have your own truth, you cannot create change. If you cannot create change, there is no point to believing in God, having faith, or even expecting results when you pray.

We see relative truth in action through the beautiful portrayal of humorously conflicting stories cast by our wonderfully talented sitcom writers. I'm relatively sure everyone has seen at least one sitcom, where a person tells her version of the truth, and another person tells his version of the truth. Each person tells a similar story, but changes certain variables in favor of himself and his ego, thus making the other person look as much to blame as possible. This is a very humorous situation, but it's also the root cause of most conflicts. It is daily routine in the lives of humans and the stories they tell themselves about who they are, what they do, and why they do it.

It's easier to see and understand Relative Truth when you see it in action. When you believe something is one way, and someone else sees it completely differently. You should not have to go far to find such an example. Take hair color for instance. Julie's hair is red. No, it's brown. Which one is it? Well, it depends who is looking at it. Apparently it's red to some, and brown to others. Another good example can be found at the movies. When you watch a movie with your significant other and then discuss the meaning. If you watched the movie for the pure entertainment of it, but your significant other saw underlying symbolism that related to an abstract concept, what was the movie really about? Again, it depends on whom you are asking. This demonstrates the concepts of Relative Truth.

Relative Truth literally means that truth is relative. If you believe it, then it is true for you. If your neighbor believes something else then that is true for him. Is either one of you wrong? No, but you could both *choose* to believe the other is wrong. You could argue your points, and try to convince each other of the validity of your own truth. OR, You could respect each other's truth, honor that every person has a right to their own truth, and accept that every one sees the world differently.

Letting go of your need to force others to agree with your perception of truth, so that you can feel validated and right in your world, frees your mind to think outside the illusion of tangible reality, and restructures your world to a malleable medium with which you can create change.

When you choose to accept that everyone has a right to their own truth, then you can ascend to the next level, and realize that everyone is right in their personal realm of reality. You do not need to validate your truth through any one else's approval, or by making any one else wrong. You can stop building walls between you and those who think differently from you. You can come to accept that we are all connected, and you begin to move back into a state of love with your fellow human beings.

When you no longer have to defend your concepts as true, right, and correct, you are free to listen to the conclusions others have drawn based on their experiences. You can allow the rich variety of understandings to permeate your existence, and enrich your experiences as well. Through the recognition that everyone expresses their reality through their perceptions of their experiences, you no longer need to feel threatened by others expressions of reality. You are free to open your mind to new ideas and concepts. You can connect with the flow of the universe and open yourself to the overwhelming unconditional love of God or Goddess, whichever way you choose to see it.

If it is possible for everyone to be right, then it is also possible for you to be able to change the way you look at something, and therefore completely change your world. When you stop looking for lack, and begin looking for evidence of abundance, you automatically begin to see abundance in your life. By recognizing the abundance you create more abundance, which validates that the universe is an abundant place, and allows you to find comfort and safety in the knowledge that all your needs will be met. This allows you to release your fear, and move into love. Everyone has already established their own concept of what they believe is true. You don't have to accept it. It has already happened. All you need to do is recognize it. Sally believes the leaves are green, and Bill believes the leaves are shades of a bunch of different colors. They are both right. And so is everyone else, about everything else. It is very freeing to realize that you no longer have to argue with someone else. You can make room in your reality for both of you to be right. You can choose unconditional love. You do not need to convince anyone of your reality to make it true for you. You can give yourself and everyone else, permission to think freely. You can let everyone else work out his or her own truth, while you are free to work out yours in whatever way suits you best.

This week, work on freeing your mind of the illusion of absolute truth, by validating the various truths expressed by others, that conflict with your conclusive truth. Confused? That's ok, it's a difficult concept to bridge when all your life you have thought that truth was absolute. Just remember that others have drawn conclusions based on experiences that have been different from yours, not better, not worse, just different. They have different lessons to learn, and their reality is reflecting that for them. You need to only notice the different perspectives, and how that perspective changes the way that persons sees his or her reality.

Grounding
Plugging in to your Power Source
Red

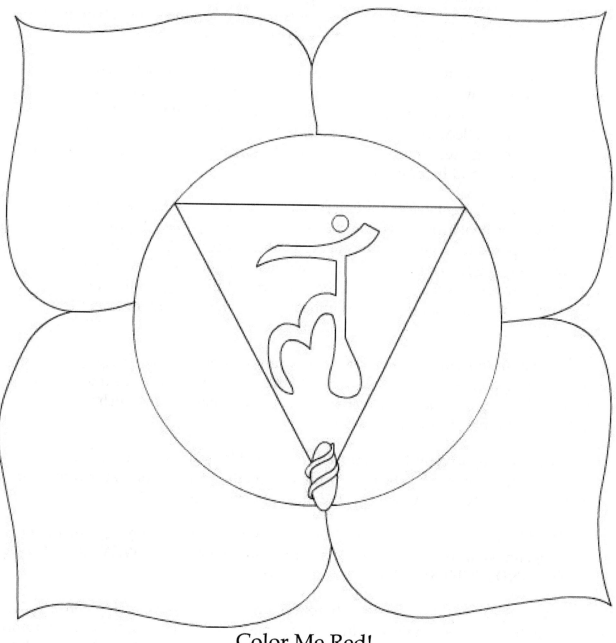

Color Me Red!

The most important skill for anyone to utilize, especially someone who is actively working with energy, is grounding. The point of grounding is to open a full energy channel that is constant, and abundant. The better you can ground the more energy you can receive and direct. Grounding should be done consciously as much as possible, until you can maintain the energetic connection without needing to consciously focus on it, like breathing.

Grounding allows old, stagnant energy to be replaced by clean, new energy. It is the difference between taking a fresh, new shower and using the same tub of dirty water that you have bathed in every day since you were born.

Grounding is a vital component in keeping us healthy and balanced. You may notice some people, who work with energy, become very sick over time. Grounding is often misunderstood and avoided. People tend to believe that it is only for draining away excess energy. Because the goal of spiritual growth is more energy not less, draining away energy seems undesirable and therefore it is not something at which many people study and become adept.

The physical, mental, and/or emotional strain on a person, who is trying to increase their spiritual awareness, can cause a wide variety of health problems. This is from being exposed to large amounts of energy and not properly recycling it through the earth. It is possible to receive energy from other living things as well as the earth. Some of this energy is beneficial, such as food sources. But using the life source of another living being is undesirable and unhealthy, much like drinking water from a stagnant pond.

Each of us individually generates a finite amount of personal energy. However, when you are grounded, you are connected to the infinite energy of the universe. The only thing that regulates how much energy you can channel is how much you have conditioned your physical vehicle to handle.

The only way to condition your self to channel large amounts of energy is to practice, as often as possible. The more you practice, the more adept you become, the greater your capacity to move energy, the more effective your magic.

*********A word of caution here. You are responsible for the energy you direct and the repercussions of that energy. Be careful, and remember, ALWAYS ACT TO THE BEST AND HIGHEST GOOD OF ALL CONCERNED.

The magical world is a vastly different place from mundane reality. Once you have begun living in the magical realm, you can never totally leave it behind. Therefore, you should respect it, and learn to use your tools in every day situations. If you wait to use them only in a magical setting, you will never become adept enough to truly use them at all.

Initial Root Chakra Activation – Grounding

Magical training is something that should be practiced every moment of every day. A Priest or Priestess should incorporate their knowledge and apply it to the way they live their life, in all its wondrous aspects. Do not save this discipline for meditation or ritual. Do it as much as you possibly can, until you have mastered it and made it a part of you.

There are many different ways to ground. On the following pages, you will find examples and exercises designed to help you ground. Practice these different methods or other methods that appeal to you until grounding has become second nature. Whatever you can imagine, you can create. Trust your imagination, visualize the grounding, and have faith in your abilities. You are your only limitation.

Whenever you feel nervous, upset, agitated, irritated, angry, or any other unpleasant feeling, if you will think to ground you will immediately improve your sense of well being, and be better prepared to deal with any issue at hand.

Earth Visualization

The Tree

Sit up straight, put both your feet on the ground, and breathe deeply. Breathe into your belly, as low as you can. As you focus on deep, rhythmic breathing, begin to imagine that roots are growing out of your feet and creeping down into the earth. Allow the roots to split off from each other, and multiply as they continue reaching deeper into the earth. As the roots continue to establish themselves, envision your body becoming a tree trunk, and grow branches that reach up to the sky. Begin drawing nutrients from the earth through your roots, send it up your trunk and through your branches, to the leaves. Allow the energy to be released from the leaves, fall back to the earth, and be recycled. Allow every part of your being to be energized and enriched through the energy you draw up from the earth.

Fire Visualization
The Lightening Rod

Sit up straight, put both your feet on the ground, and breathe deeply. Breathe into your belly, as low as you can. As you focus on deep, rhythmic breathing, begin to imagine a lightening rod, that runs from above your head, through your spine, and down into the earth. See any energy surges coming your way attracted to the Rod and immediately sent into the ground. Allow any negative energy that you have to also be attracted to the rod and carried away into the earth.

If you are moving around you can use this visualization with a ground wire coming out of the base of your spine and trailing behind you.

Water Visualization
The Rain Shower

Sit up straight, put both your feet on the ground, and breathe deeply. Breathe into your belly, as low as you can. As you focus on deep, rhythmic breathing, imagine that you are in a cleansing rain shower. Feel the energy, like water, constantly pouring into your energy field, cleansing your aura of any negative energy, as you are bathed in healing, unconditional love. Feel any negative or excess energy drain away, and release all unhappiness, fear, and unpleasant emotions. Feel your heart lighten, and your mood uplifted. Relax and smile as your aura is cleansed and refreshed to a state of perfect love and perfect trust.

Air Visualization
The Cleansing Breath

Sit up straight, put both your feet on the ground, and breathe deeply, inhale through your nose and exhale through the mouth, blowing the breath away from you. Envision the breath coming into your root chakra at the base of your spine, energizing and cleansing it, as you focus on deep, rhythmic breathing. Visualize breathing in rich, vibrant, red light. When you exhale don't control the color. Allow any negative energy to be released with the breath. Observe the color of the exhaled breath. Blow it far away from you. Continue to breathe in the rich, vibrant, red, until the color you are exhaling is the same color that you are inhaling.

Spirit Visualization
The Abundant Earth

Sit up straight, put both your feet on the ground, and breathe deeply. Breathe into your belly, as low as you can. As you focus on deep, rhythmic breathing, envision your root chakra glowing red. Send a beam of energy from your root chakra, down to the earth. Extend the energy down into the earth's red core, and connect with the power source of the earth. Allow the earth's energy to blend with yours, creating an abundant circular flow of energy into your being. Allow the positive energy to be drawn up into you, energizing and refreshing you. Allow any stagnant, negative energy to be heavy, and fall back to the earth to be recycled.

Awakening Spirit – Freshman Course – www.WISESeminary.com

Religion v/s Spirituality
A Means to an End

Red

Color Me Red!

Initial Root Chakra Activation – Religion v/s Spirituality

I once heard Bill Maher say something about Religion v/s Spirituality that I thought explained it very well. He said, "Religion is the dogma that gets in the way of spirituality". I believe that is a very true statement. Many times I have seen people unable to discover their own spirituality due to the confines of their religious beliefs.

Religions often define our spiritual goals for us, and provide a path for us to reach that goal. If we are not used to thinking this through, and defining our own goals, we do not even realize that we may not want to achieve the goal that has been set for us. We follow along, because that is what we have been taught to do, and that is what we expect.

Many religions use fear to keep us from exploring our spiritual awareness. They tell us things, that if conveyed in a non-religious context would not make sense, such as "learning about other religions is bad". We know that knowledge is good. The more educated someone is about a subject the more intelligent that person's understanding will be. If this is true, then why do many religious leaders tell us not to learn about other religions? Why should we fear education and knowledge about the beliefs of other faiths?

It is not a logical conclusion that theological education will lead us away from our spiritual path. Faith and logic can exist simultaneously, in balance and harmony. One does not preclude the existence of the other. It is through challenging illogical assumptions that blind faith can be transformed into awareness and enlightenment.

Educating yourself is always good. Being able to make an informed decision about your religion is, in my opinion, very important. I would not buy a car without first finding out everything I could about that car, and every other comparably priced vehicle on the market. Why would I not research the fate of my immortal soul? Wouldn't that be more important than the purchase of a car?

Studying the way others relate to God/dess gives us a broader perspective, and a deeper personal understanding of our own relationship to God/dess.

Religion is a tool to connect you with God, in whatever form that takes for you. If your religion isn't fulfilling you, then it is appropriate to find out why. It is possible that your religion is not helping you reach your spiritual goals.

There are many different religions because there are many different people with many different values and needs. There are many different tools in a garage because there are many different jobs to be done. You can't fix everything with a hammer. Nor can everyone be satisfied with the life of a Jewish rabbi. Nor, would everyone want to be a nun. However, there are people who are extremely happy being a rabbi or a nun. They spend the majority of their life dedicated to their spirituality, and they feel that their religion serves them.

Who is right, the Jewish faith, or the Catholic faith? I think I could get a strong argument from both sides, probably ending up with both sides completely frustrated at their perceived ignorance of the other. If, instead, both sides of the argument could accept that both faiths are true in the heart of the worshipper, they could work together to create peace, and deepen the meanings of both of their lives work, and their general understanding of divinity as a whole.

All Religions teach Spiritual truths. All Religions also have man-made customs, myths, and traditions that are intermingled with these truths. Man-made customs and traditions are necessary to relate the concept. But, the truth is found in the concept, not the custom, myth or tradition.

If the nun, or the rabbi, felt unfulfilled in his or her work, would it mean the entire religion was wrong? No, but it could mean the religion is no longer serving his or her needs. It would be inappropriate for the nun to continue to try to serve in her position if her heart was no longer calling her to do that work. It would be counter-productive to her spiritual growth. It is equally counter-productive for you to continue to go to the church that your mother took you to, and to force your children to go, if you aren't feeling fulfilled in its teachings. If you are a member of a religion because you are afraid not to be, then you are doing it for the wrong reasons. You are no longer a church member. You are a cult-member.

Spirituality is something that belongs to each individual, and each individual expresses that spirituality in different ways. It is ok to need something different, and to have those needs fulfilled, as long as it doesn't infringe on the rights and needs of others. Some find deep fulfillment in the Christian faith, while others feel oppressed. Muslim's may embrace their religion as enlightening and freeing, while others only see racism. There are many who find the peacefulness of Buddhism as comforting, while other's find if restrictive. Not every religion fits everyone. It is up to each individual to recognize that they are entitled to their own truth, and that sometimes means that your religion isn't the same as your parent's. It's may be difficult on holidays, but Christmas comes only once a year, and you may not want to be Presbyterian the other 364 days so that everyone can have a Merry Christmas.

Spirituality is an individual's personal connection with divinity. Religion is a tool to help you find and maintain that connection. If your current religion is not serving you in making that connection, then it is your right to find one that does. Your personal search for God/Goddess is a sacred process between you and spirit. It is not up to anyone else's approval. It's not anyone else's business.

Spirituality is a personal path, and religion is a tool to facilitate the process. There are no right or wrong religions; each one has a specific lesson to teach. As long as someone needs the lessons that each religion teaches, it will continue to have a place in our world. When the lessons are no longer needed the religion will cease to exist.

As a Priest or Priestess of the Goddess, it is right and appropriate to honor God and Goddess in whatever way God and Goddess finds to express Him or Her Self to those who wish to worship. This means that it is also appropriate and right to honor all religions and all religious leaders, who are doing their best to serve spirit in whatever way they feel is good and right. You do not have to agree with their methods, or their teachings, but it is appropriate to recognize that they are serving the same deity as you to the best of their ability, and that makes you the same. If you want others to honor your right to have your own beliefs, you have to begin by honoring theirs.

Awakening Spirit – Freshman Course – www.WISESeminary.com

Self Evaluation
Relative Truth

Check which example represents Relative Truth.

_____ Your co-worker just received a promotion at work. She is complaining because while she is making more money she has a lot more responsibility, and being in charge of so many important details makes her uncomfortable. You love to be in charge of details, and wish that you had been picked for the new position.

_____ You and your friend go out for coffee. You both order the same coffee, and laugh about how much you have in common. As you go to the table you spill your coffee and have to go purchase a new one.

_____ You are watching a movie with your significant other. The movie is about a historical figure and you feel a very deep connection to the time period.

Which of the following demonstrates how Relative Truth can be applied to magically transform a situation?

You are broke, your bills are piling up, and you have no money to pay them.

_____ Get a second job, and work as much as possible until you get caught up.

_____ File bankruptcy, and try your best to avoid overextending yourself next time.

_____ Search your home for valuable items that you no longer need or use to sell.

Jerry's wife never has a good thing to say about him. She always notices the things that he neglects to do. Which would be the best way Jerry could apply Relative Truth to change his situation.

_____ Avoid going home until late in the evening, and leave as early as possible in the morning to avoid the abuse.

_____ Listen to his wife and try as hard as possible to live up to her expectations in the future.

_____ Call his wife's attention to the many things he does do for her.

Initial Root Chakra Activation – Certification Requirements

Religion v/s Spirituality

Mark the Following Statements as either a Religious concept or a Spiritual Truth.

R S God is Love.

R S Do what thou wilt, lest ye harm none.

R S What goes around comes around.

R S Thou shalt not kill.

Answers
Relative Truth

Check which example represents Relative Truth.

√ Your co-worker just received a promotion at work. She is complaining because while she is making more money she has a lot more responsibility, and being in charge of so many important details makes her uncomfortable. You love to be in charge of details, and wish that you had been picked for the new position.

This is correct. You perceive the details of the position differently from your coworker.

_____ You and your friend go out for coffee. You both order the same coffee, and laugh about how much you have in common. As you go to the table you spill your coffee and have to go purchase a new one.

This is not an example of Relative Truth. There is no difference of opinion.

_____ You are watching a movie with your significant other. The movie is about a historical figure and you feel a very deep connection to the time period.

This is not an example of Relative Truth. There is no difference of opinion. However, it may be a Past Life Memory.

Which of the following demonstrates how Relative Truth can be applied to magically transform a situation?

You are broke, your bills are piling up, and you have no money to pay them.

_____ Get a second job, and work as much as possible until you get caught up.

This is a possible solution, but it doesn't utilize magic to transform the situation. Working two jobs actually reinforces your subconscious belief that you don't have enough, and aren't worth enough to pay your bills.

_____ File bankruptcy, and try your best to avoid overextending yourself next time.

This is a possible solution, but it doesn't utilize magic to transform the situation. Filing Bankruptcy reinforces your subconscious belief that you aren't responsible enough to manage your finances.

√ Search your home for valuable items that you no longer need or use to sell.

Yes, this is correct. This is one way to find value in your self (through the things you own), and reinforce a state of abundance. It is sometimes appropriate to get rid of the old and make way for the new.

Jerry's wife never has a good thing to say about him. She always notices the things that he neglects to do. Which would be the best way Jerry could apply Relative Truth to change his situation.

_____ Avoid going home until late in the evening, and leave as early as possible in the morning to avoid the abuse.

This is not an example of Relative Truth. This is a clear case of avoidance, and will not do anything except make a bad situation worse.

_____ Listen to his wife and try as hard as possible to live up to her expectations in the future.

This is not an example of Relative Truth. Changing yourself to appease someone's harshness is destructive to both parties, and the relationship itself. It ultimately makes Jerry a victim, and his wife will eventually lose respect for him. In the long run, the relationship will suffer.

√ Call his wife's attention to the many things he does do for her.

Correct. By focusing his wife's attention on the positive things Jerry contributes to the relationship, Jerry is adjusting her perceptions about her husband. As she begins to take notice of the good things about Jerry, her perception will reinforce that Jerry is a loving, helpful, partner, and she will no longer be motivated to find fault with Jerry.

Religion v/s Spirituality

Mark the Following Statements as either a Religious concept or a Spiritual Truth.

R S God is Love

*Conception of God being one certain thing is a **Religious** concept, and a matter of Relative Truth. Some religions teach that God is to be feared, or that God is Truth and Righteousness, which is not the same as love.*

R **S** Do what thou wilt, lest ye harm none.

*The ethical value of not hurting living beings, including your self is a **Spiritual** Truth. It is taught in various ways by many different world religions. In Christianity it is similarly expressed in the Golden Rule; "Do unto others as you would have them do unto you".*

R **S** What goes around comes around.

*The Concept of reaping what you sew, The Law of Consequence, and Karma is a **Spiritual** Truth. All religions believe in some way that we are affected by the consequences of our actions.*

R S Thou shalt not kill.

*The morality of murder is acceptable in some religions. Executing those who transgress against God, and the declaration of Holy Wars are a documented part of history. Thus making this a **Religious** concept.*

Certification Requirements

Complete each grounding meditation, and record results. (See page 303)

Journal Entries

Congratulations! You have completed the first Activation. This week as you practice the techniques and integrate the concepts discussed, pay attention as your spirit guides begin to interact with you. They will give you many opportunities to apply what you have learned here.

As you are blessed with these interactions, you will receive questions, thoughts, and epiphanies. You should record these in a journal. In time, you will forget what today seems unforgettable. It will be very important to you, and others, to be able to look back at the information and ideas you experience now.

2

Initial Sacral Chakra Activation
Personal Responsibility & Karma
Creation is the art of Balance

Orange

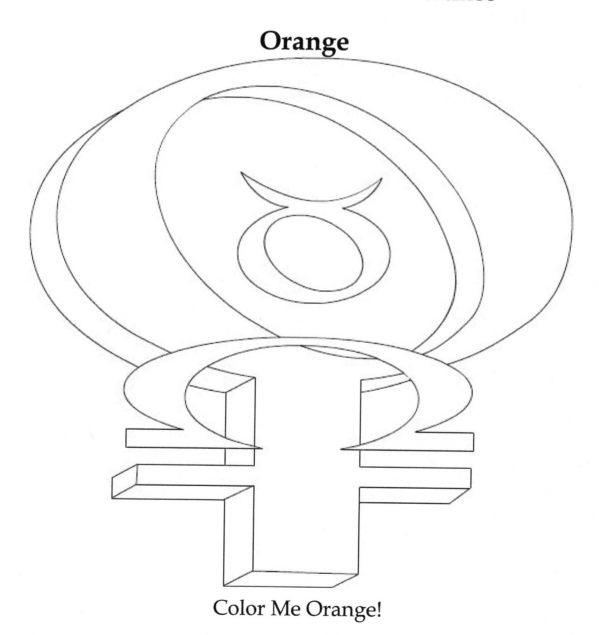

Color Me Orange!

Those of the Wicca are charged with 'keeping the balance'. This means, if we are to live in service of Goddess, we must live our lives in balance and harmony with the universe. This requires living life with consideration for the other people, places and things that are affected by our actions and energy. This is a level of awareness that is unusual for most people. We try not to negatively affect others, but usually are so focused on our own needs that we seldom consider the consequences our actions may have on those with whom we are connected. Especially if it's something we really want, and it negatively affects someone of whom we aren't particularly fond.

However, magically this attitude doesn't work. The power that we call upon to manifest and create our reality operates under the rules outlined in the previous paragraph, if we do not work to manifest our reality in balance with the same rules, our reality will not be allowed to flourish. We may force it into existence for a short period of time, but eventually the balance will find a way to restore itself, and we will incur loss and suffering for our unperceived selfishness. Then we will probably blame God, Goddess and others for not giving us what we want so badly, even if it's not in our best interest to have it.

When we can't make something happen, we have to look at why. There is something in our plan that is counter-productive to the balance. When all is in harmony, then our goals will be achieved effortlessly. That's why we call it magic.

Living in balance means living with ethics, doing the right thing and taking responsibility for our mistakes. A Priest/ess is only as good as her honor. Power is generated within ones self. Those without honor cannot maintain power. They can steal it, but they can't maintain it. Once we choose to act, our Karma will carry us down a path of consequences. If we give love, we will receive love. If we give fear, we will receive fear.

If we use our power responsibly and in balance, we demonstrate to the universe that we are capable of more power and our power will grow. If we use our power irresponsibly, we show that we will hurt our self and possibly others with it, and we will lose it. It's really a very simple concept. It has complexities within it, but the overall concept is truly that simple.

We are all connected. We are all part of each other. We are all individual pieces of God/dess. Just as the first cell that begins at conception is capable of creating an entire human being, each of our spirits contains the entire blueprint of God/dess. Within you is the expanse of all there is, you need only recognize it is there and allow yourself to be it.

We each have a separate physical body. Just like each cell of our body is individual, and functions within it's own world as a separate entity, needing oxygen, water, and nutrients. It also functions as part of a whole, whether it is part of the heart, the kidneys, a bone cell, or a skin cell. Each cell grouped together with other cells make up the body. No one cell being more or less important than the others, each cell being able to completely replicate the entire body with its map of DNA.

This is the nature of God/dess. Each individual person contains light bodies, which group together to make up your soul. These light bodies are pieces of God/dess just like each cell is a piece of our body. Each light body contains within it the ability to become the whole, but functions as though it were an individual.

Since we see ourselves as individuals, not connected to each other. Is it possible that our cells also see themselves as individual entities separate from the other cells? It is not only possible but also probable. In the limited consciousness of a single cell, *if* there is any awareness at all, it is probably as a unique individual, and not as a piece of the greater whole. Is it so hard to make the leap from microcosm to macrocosm? Are we too, in our limited consciousness, incapable of seeing ourselves as one cell in a body of infinite cells, capable of so much greatness, but limited by our own self-absorbed nature?

Each of us, being a part of the whole that is God/dess, cannot act without it affecting the entire being that is God/dess. Just as a cell that becomes cancerous ends up infecting the whole body, whatever negativity we manifest and act out on each other, we do to the whole universe, including our self. Our cells are living in a sea of water. We are living in a sea of energy. You can see it, and you can feel it. Sometimes you can even hear it. It is there, and just like you can make waves in a pool, everything that you do ripples out from you, affecting everything it touches, and eventually returning to you.

It is not an abstract concept. It is a science. It is only because we cannot measure it yet, that it is labeled *meta*physics. Metaphysics is physics that cannot be proven. Gravity is not understood. No one can explain why it works, but we can prove it simply because we are all standing on the earth. Karma is no different. Once you begin to look for it, and recognize it, you will see it is much more fact than theory.

As with everything spiritual, Karma works in simple but complex ways. What you do to others will be done back to you, but in greater capacity. Wiccans have the threefold law. "Ever mind the rule of three; what ye send out comes back to thee." It means that whatever you do comes back to you threefold. There are some who believe the more aware you are of the laws of Karma the more responsible you are for your wrong doings.

I have experienced the threefold effect. I have seen that the more spiritually aware you are the faster your karma comes back to you. I have also seen people experience their Karma, and refuse to recognize it only to repeat the same mistake over and over again. Sometimes you don't experience your karma until the next lifetime. Other times you may experience it immediately. But you can't escape it; you can only refuse to retaliate, choose to forgive and let it go. I think Robin Williams said it best, "Karma, everywhere you are."

If you have killed someone in a past life, you have created a karmic debt. You will die the same way you choose to kill, as the energy you sent out comes back to you. Through your choices you create and connect yourself to a pattern. The person you killed will come back in the next life and be tempted to kill you. If they choose not to commit murder, someone else will fulfill the cycle, so that you can die the death you choose and the balance can be restored. The cycle continues until you decide that murder is not an option, and you choose some other way to deal with the situation. Then you are free from the debt. You have learned your lesson and are ready to move on. You have evolved.

What happens to the other person? They will go on repeating the karmic cycle, with another person learning the same lesson, until they too discover that murder is not an option and evolve out of the cycle. But, what happens to the other person is not yours to fix. You can only be responsible for what you do. The fate of others is in their hands. Your fate is in yours.

What is the meaning of forgiveness? Can you truly forgive and forget? If you forgive only to be hurt again did you learn your lesson?

To seek apologies and forgiveness from another is not necessary; you must forgive yourself, for you are the one who chose to be hurt. For someone else to hurt you, you have to give them the power to do that. For this to happen you have to be attached to the outcome of your relationship with that person, and that involves your own fears, not their actions. For you to attach your fears to their actions is passive-aggressive. It is inappropriate to make someone else responsible for your happiness. Why do you expect someone else to give you what you cannot give yourself?

As the creator of your reality, you are responsible for all your triumphs and your woes. It is interesting that when we succeed we are all too willing to take credit for it. But, if we fail it's someone else's fault. Do not be the victim of someone else's deeds and actions. Change your truth about what you are experiencing. Find the lesson within the suffering and learn from it. Spirit teaches us through making us uncomfortable. It is only when we are uncomfortable that we feel a need to change. You can transform all your sorrows by recognizing the lesson and learning it. Yes, ALL of them, every single one. Nothing happens expressly for the purpose of defeating you. Goddess is by your side, working in your life to protect you, and make you stronger. That doesn't mean giving you what you want. It means providing you with the means to grow and provide for yourself. No one owes you anything. It is up to you to take the resources given and create success or choose suffering.

Our fears can stem from various past traumas. We can be afraid of a great many things. These fears bind us to our pain. It is no one else's fault that we have pain, we choose to cling to it because we are afraid of choosing love. Each of us, knowing all the flaws and faults within us, feel that we do not deserve to be loved. Yet we desperately seek for some kind of external proof that we are worthy of love. The proof will not come from outside our self, for the Goddess tells us gently, "that if that which thou seekest thou findest not within thee, then thou wilt never find it without thee."

All those who cross your path are spiritual teachers for you, some hold more painful lessons than others, but all are to be honored. It is the desire of all humans to have, give, and receive love. It is the instinct of all humans to isolate them selves in fear. It takes enlightenment to move beyond that instinct, to realize that our initial knee jerk reaction is an illusion. The magic is to be able to see through that illusion into the heart of our lesson, transcend our fear, and allow our energy to only flow towards love.

Honor is about love, love for your self. If you love yourself, you must respect yourself, and that means doing the right thing and acting in harmony with the balance. When you do the right thing you know you are honorable, and therefore worthy of love. When you do something dishonorable, even if no one else knows about it, you know about it, and you reinforce your belief that you do not deserve to be loved. You see it every time you look in the mirror. You know who you are, and you cannot escape yourself.

It is imperative that a Priest/ess holds honor in the highest regards, for it is the foundation of perfect love and perfect trust. How can any relationship have perfect love and perfect trust if any member in it does not have honor? We cannot expect to be open hearted enough to connect to others, if we are afraid others will see our dishonor.

Spiritual growth begins on foundational principles. All the greatest mysteries are found in the simplest of places; honor, love, truth, and respect are some of them. All of these things must first come from within, for our external world is merely a physical manifestation of our spirit. If our life reflects pain, misery, poverty, and the like, look within, because that's where it came from. If we had the power to create that through fear, imagine what we can create through love.

Sacred Energy

Color Me Orange!

Sacred Energy is the energy generated by your sacral chakra. I call it the Sacred Chakra because there is where we find the soul of our sacred selves. If we feel unworthy or debased in some way, this imbalance will manifest in our sacred chakra.

Our society is not conducive to integrating the concept of sacred sexuality into our consciousness. Many women have menstrual problems, cancer, and other gynecological disorders, due to the fact that they have not learned to hold their

Initial Sacral Chakra Activation – Sacred Energy

sexuality as sacred. Now, with the onset of feminism, and the popularity of male bashing, we are suddenly hearing more and more about male sexual disease and dysfunction, a topic that rarely entered our realm of consciousness ten years ago.

Wicca is a matriarchal religion. Many women, who have been traumatized in this area, are drawn to Wicca so that they can be empowered, healed, and appreciated for their femininity. Wicca is a very good place to find that sort of healing. But, it is extremely important for women to recognize that taking back our feminine power does not require the emasculation of our men. To be whole and healthy we each need to be a balance of both.

Placing blame does not solve the problem; it only gives us a target for our anger, which then serves to turn us into that which we fight against. Becoming the oppressors of men will not heal women. Women will be healed when they recognize their own sacredness and begin to utilize that power in an appropriate way that serves the best and highest good of all, and so will men. What many women do not recognize is that men have been disempowered in our society in a different way. Men have been sexually, emotionally, and spiritually repressed as well. We have all been damaged by the lack of sacredness in our culture. We all need to be healed, and we must work together to accomplish this task. Balance is the key to wholeness.

We each have a male and female side within us. They must work in balance for us to be effective, healthy, whole, and happy. Equal ity does not mean the same; it means being *valued* the same. Men and Woman are different. Priests and Priestesses are different. They have different jobs, and fulfill different needs. Mothers and Fathers, sons and daughters are different. These differences are the result of social conditioning, and hormones. Understanding and appreciating these differences are important to our spiritual growth. One's strengths are another's weaknesses; by working together we can achieve more than we can alone. We are equally valuable for our contribution to the perpetuation of the species. Neither one of us can exist without the other.

We have lessons to learn from the balance and harmony of working interdependently with each other. Connecting with an external polar opposite helps us work out the lessons we have with our own internal polar opposite. Connecting with one other person, and finding wholeness within the union, is the first step towards connecting with the greater consciousness of God/dess

This is not a simple task. It involves increasingly challenging degrees of releasing the ego's need to be recognized as a special and unique individual, while accepting that spiritually you are a part of a much greater whole. Much of the squabbles and battles in our day-to-day routines, have to do with ego and the need to be validated. Allowing yourself to experience perfect love and perfect trust through a relationship, where you become truly vulnerable, honest, open, and connected, is in and of itself a spiritually enlightening experience.

Sacred energy is shared in relationships. Our relationships are direct reflections of the lessons we are trying to learn. In dream interpretation, we understand that everyone in our dream is a reflection of our self. Everyone represents a different aspect of our personality. This is also true in the waking state. We can learn about ourselves and the lessons we are learning, by analyzing our relationships, and those to whom we have chosen to connect ourselves.

Sharing sacred energy with someone, who honors and empowers you, is a wonderful experience that fills you with love, and motivates you to fulfill your greatest potential. Sharing sacred energy with someone, who doesn't love and respect you, leaves you feeling used, abused, worthless, unlovable and unsacred. It is the interplay of your sacred energy (that energy which is generated by your sacral chakra) with someone else's that reinforces your sacredness or lack thereof, and empowers you to realize your greatest potential in this lifetime, or not.

Relationships are formed when one person seeks to establish a relationship with another person. Person A extends energy towards Person B. If Person B accepts the energy from Person A and reciprocates by sending an equal amount of energy back, then a balanced relationship is established. A balanced relationship empowers both parties to operate at a greater capacity, enriching both parties' lives with a greater degree of success, joy, love, and happiness.

If for any reason one stops sending energy to the other, the person who stops receiving the energy will begin to feel the effects through lack, sorrow, pain, or unhappiness. For balance to be achieved both parties need to be equal in the amount of energy shared. There is no way for one person to give enough energy for both people. This is called co-dependency. If one person is putting in more energy than the other, it is destructive to both parties. It is human nature to want to be loved. It is difficult to admit that you may not be. But, if you truly love someone, and they aren't giving back to the relationship, it is unloving and destructive to the balance on both sides for you to continue putting energy into the relationship. It causes guilt, remorse, karmic debt, and all kinds of dishonorable attachments. If you love someone, set him or her free. If he or she comes back to you, then you know he or she loves you as well.

If someone loves you more than you love him or her, and you continue to receive his or her energy without giving in return, you are creating a cycle for you to fall in love with someone, who will use you in return. Karma works both ways. Be mindful of your selfishness, and always try your best to do the right thing.

The History of Wicca

The Origins of Wicca

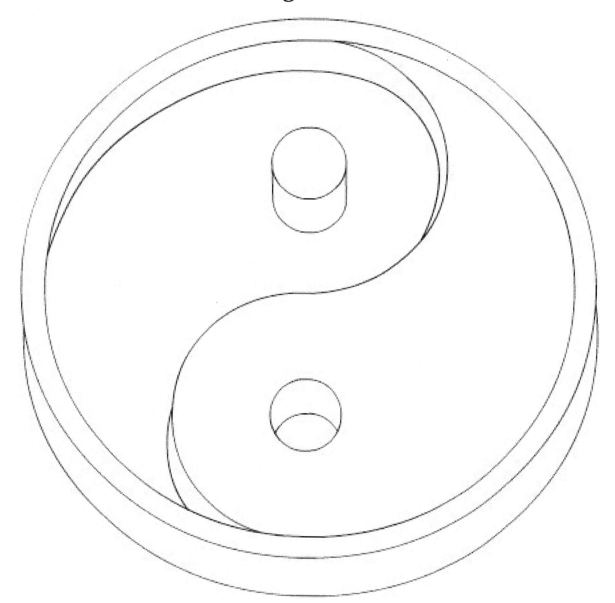

Color Me Orange!

There are many different books about the History of Wicca. Just about every beginner's book has a section on it. I will not go into detail about the history here. I do not claim to be a historian. However, I do believe that studying the history of our religion and all religions is an important part of the path. I encourage all students to study the history and have an intelligent understanding of it.

One of the reason's why it is important to know the history of Wicca is because it's history is in dispute. There are arguments that Wicca is the original religion of the Goddess that has been secretly taught and passed down from ancient times. There are those who say Gardner invented modern day Wicca and took many precepts from his friend Aleister Crowley, who was a Ceremonial Magician.

I see no point in arguing the matter, either way. I don't think either argument validates or invalidates the religion. If anything it shows us Wicca's greatest strengths.

Wicca is a religion that encompasses all religions. Wicca makes room for every religion to have truth, and draws from the collective truths of all of them. It is flexible enough to evolve with the rising consciousness of the current times, and supports all paths to enlightenment.

For one to argue that a religion is more valid just because it's older than another religion invalidates the whole concept of spiritual evolution and rising consciousness. Religion is a tool that helps us expand our consciousness and connect with spirit. Whatever method used to attain spiritual fulfillment and connection with the divine is valid, as long as it is to the best and highest good of all concerned. Age is not a factor.

Wicca is the best tool for me. It may not be the best tool for everyone and I feel no desire to convince anyone that my way is right for him. While I enjoy talking about spiritual and religious matters, it is not my place to try to recruit or convert members. I trust that the Goddess will make the path clear for those who seek her.

In my opinion, we owe a debt of gratitude to Gerald Gardner for the work that he did in service of the Goddess. He brought Wicca into the public eye, and made it possible for us to have access to the wealth of information available today. Whether we agree with his teachings or not, he paved the way for everything that we have today. If nothing else, we can honor his courage, and the results of his efforts.

The Reflections of the Ages

As spiritual awareness increases, religions evolve. Sometimes new religions are formed. Sometimes old ones are revived. Religions change as spiritual needs change. Spiritual needs change drastically from one astrological age to another. It's not spiritually beneficial to blame the decline of Goddess worship on men or Christianity. It is an equal waste of time and energy to try to convince people that because Goddesses were worshipped a long time ago it's ok to worship them now.

Religion is a combination of cultural and social values; physical, emotional and spiritual needs, and divine inspiration. As early man became spiritually aware, he developed religion from his own personal observations and experiences. Religion changed and evolved with the evolution of man, and the changing of the astrological ages.

During the Age of Taurus, ruled by the glamorous and affectionate energy of Venus, we reference the Golden Calf images, the sacred cows of Hinduism, and a loving, motherly reverence for all life. During the Age of Aries, influenced by the forceful and aggressive, passions of Mars, the sacrificial lamb was a popular way to appease the warring God of Abraham.

The Age of Pisces was heralded with the birth of Jesus, who encouraged fisherman to become his Apostles and fishers of men. The mother of Jesus, a Virgin represents the polar opposite sign of Virgo. The Christian church holds faith above all else, and encourages you to escape the pain and suffering of this world through the salvation of Jesus. Pisces loves to escape from the harshness of reality. It's difficult for their dreamy, sensitive, empathic nature to be exposed to so much external stimulation. Pisces envisions a surreal, serene, peaceful hideaway, where she can relax. Coincidentally, Pisces' key words are "I believe", and the Christian symbol is a fish. How does a fish represent Christianity? The Christians have a story about it, but it makes perfect sense to me when you look at Astrological history and recognize that Christianity is the religion of the Piscean Age.

The Sleeping Goddess

Let's dwell on Pisces, and explore the astrological reasons why Goddess worship may have lost popularity during this Age.

To truly understand a cycle that reaches beyond the bounds of recorded history, we must first explore similar cycles that we can see clearly. The Goddess cycles with the moon, and the seasons, as well.

We see the maiden in the waxing moon, the mother is the full moon, and the crone is the waning moon. But who is the Goddess during the dark moon? How does she miraculously go from crone to maiden?

The seasons are similar. The Goddess is maiden in the spring, mother in the summer, and crone in the fall. Who is she during winter, when she spends time in the underworld, during the time of introspection, and inner growth?

If the Goddess reawakens in the spring and at the new moon, why do we not celebrate her sleep? I know that as a mother, it can be very unsettling for my children for me to be asleep and unavailable to them. Could we be denying the sleeping

Goddess, because we do not wish to be without her?

If it is possible for the Goddess to sleep during the dark of the moon, and during winter, then it is probable that this cycle would extend to all cycles. As above, so below.

Pisces is the last age of the Astrological Wheel, putting it cyclically in the same place as winter, and the dark moon. Pisces is ruled by Neptune, and is the sign of dreams, illusion, mystery and deception. Those ruled by Pisces are the most susceptible to drug and alcohol abuse because of a strong desire to escape the harshness of mundane reality.

Pisceans are also known to love their sleep and private, alone time. It is the sign of eternity, reincarnation and spiritual rebirth. More than any other sign, Pisces would be the most likely sign to embrace the Goddess in her slumber.

Of course, it may empower those who feel victimized to believe that Dad killed Mom, and he should be punished for it. But, if Mom was really just taking a nap, and now she's awake, then we really don't have anyone to direct negativity at, and in retrospect owe Dad a bit of gratitude for doing the best he could under the circumstances.

Through understanding the Law of Karma, we know it is a normal and natural process for the Goddess, and possibly the entire matriarchy, to rest in Pisces and be reborn in the Aquarian Age. We can stop looking for external validation and let go of any hatred towards men, Christians, or any other group that has been blamed for responding to the spiritual vibration of Pisces.

Is there any wonder the world is in the state it is in today? Do you remember when you were a kid and your mother went off to see relatives for the weekend? What became of the house while she was gone? The God aspect is vital and necessary for a great many things, but neither can function properly without a balance between the two.

Each Age has powerful lessons for us to learn.

Awakening to the Age of Aquarius

Wicca is currently noted as being the fastest growing religion. Considering that we have just entered the Aquarian Age, I expect as much. Gardner was called to bring Wicca to the world in the 1950's. Wicca embodies the very essence of Aquarius, which is described in "The Only Astrology Book You Will Ever Need" by Joanna Martine

Woolfolk[1] as "assertive, independent, progressive, analytical, original and inventive, has strong dislikes and firm opinions." Yeah, on a whole, I think that's describes us pretty well.

When studying the history of Wicca, or any area of study about religion, remember, you are studying to be a Priest or Priestess of the Gods, not a Religion. All people are all connected as brothers and sisters. We have all suffered at the hands of injustice. We have all experienced defeat and success. We will all grow, heal, and evolve, together. The apparent injustices of the past happened to teach us, and to help us grow stronger. Those, who are our strongest opponents, are the most dedicated to our growth. Those who place obstacles in our way jeopardize their own Karma, so that we can be strengthened by adversity. Honor them, for their sacrifice is great.

Remember all those who have suffered for spiritual knowledge in the past. Many people have died over religious persecution, and although not all of them were burned, Wiccans tend to associate religious persecution with being burned at the stake. Most religions have at one time or another been persecuted. Those trying to escape from religious persecution founded this country.

Religious Freedom is a constitutional right, but persecution still runs rampant. Hate crimes abound. People are afraid to let their relatives, employees, school authorities, or even the police know that their religion may be different from the accepted norm. People have died for religious beliefs, from Judaism, to Christianity, to Witchcraft. People of faith have suffered so that others could have the right to worship in the tradition of their chosen religion.

Honoring and respecting all religions is very important for Priests and Priestesses of the Goddess. You are the keeper of all spiritual knowledge, and that is spread out among the various religions on the planet. Spiritual knowledge is what religions are based on, and every religion has something important to teach. By shunning any one religion, you are perpetuating the persecution. By protecting and respecting them all, you ensure that the mysteries are safe and honored. No one is free, unless we are all free.

---

[1] Woolfolk, Joanna Martine: The Only Astrology Book You'll Ever Need, Scarborough House Publishers, 1982 p. 43

Initial Sacral Chakra Activation – Certification Requirements

Self Evaluation
Personal Responsibility & Karma

You have been promoted to a new position at work. This new position brings with it a big salary increase and some great benefits. You have been trying to get this promotion for a long time, and are very happy to finally have it. You discover that your new supervisor asks you to represent untruths to your co-workers, his wife, and your clients.

_____You tell your supervisor you will not lie, and quit.
_____Lying in this case is ok because professional ethics are different from personal and spiritual ethics.
_____In a private conversation with your superior, you explain that you are uncomfortable with misrepresenting the truth.
_____You silently decide to yourself, that while you won't volunteer any information, if asked you will tell the truth regardless of your instructions.

Your girlfriend of nine months just broke up with you. She has a job, but has basically been financially dependent on you, because you make considerably more money, and are generous by nature. She claims that she needs more space, and is too young to get into a serious committed relationship. She asks you to pay her bills for the rest of the month until she gets back on her feet.

_____You agree to pay her bills for one month.
_____You refuse to give her any money.
_____You agree to pay her bills if she doesn't leave.
_____You agree to pay her bills, but don't.

Sacred Energy

Your spouse is occasionally physically abusive. You have noticed that this only happens under certain situations, and your spouse is always extremely apologetic afterwards, and promises never to do it again.

_____ You do your best to avoid the circumstances that provoke the violence.
_____ You refuse to listen to excuses, or apologies and leave the relationship.
_____ You recommend counseling for you and your partner, and do your best to work

out the problem without disrupting the family.

_____ You make a plan that the next time it happens you will be able to appropriately defend and protect yourself.

Indicate if the action demonstrates an equal (=), less than (<), or greater than (>) relationship between the two subjects.

Julie = < > Robbie

Julie promised to call Robbie at noon to decide on what to do for lunch. Julie had an unexpected rush and can't go to lunch till after 1:00. She knows that Robbie will wait on her, so she hurries to finish her work and calls him at 1:30.

Carol = < > Mike

Mike and Carol just had a new baby. They both agree that it is more important for Carol to stay at home to take care of the baby than to go back to work. Mike and Carol have previously had their own income, and did not mingle their finances. Mike is uncomfortable with having Carol on his checking account and feels that he should have the right to decide how his money is spent. Since she no longer makes any money, Mike assumes all the responsibility for the family finances.

The History of Wicca

T or F - Gerald Gardner is considered the founding father of Wicca.

T or F - Religion is no longer needed once someone achieves spiritual enlightenment.

T or F - All spiritual lessons are painful.

T or F - Because Wicca encompasses all religions, it is the best and most accurate religion to practice.

Answers
Personal Responsibility & Karma

You have been promoted to a new position at work. This new position brings with it a big salary increase and some great benefits. You have been trying to get this promotion for a long time, and are very happy to finally have it. You discover that your new supervisor asks you to represent untruths to your co-workers, his wife, and your clients.

_____ You tell your supervisor you will not lie, and quit.

This is one way to go. However, this is an extreme action and will cause an imbalance in

Initial Sacral Chakra Activation – Certification Requirements

your Karma, leaving you without a job, and an unattractive employer reference. This should be used only if all other attempts to amicably solve the situation have been explored to no avail.

_____Lying in this case is ok because professional ethics are different from personal and spiritual ethic.

This is incorrect. Professional relationships are different from personal and spiritual relationships in many ways. But, you should never compromise your honor and integrity. Agreeing to lie makes you untrustworthy. Even the person you are lying for will see you as a person, who lacks integrity and honor.

√ In a private conversation with your superior, you explain that you are uncomfortable with misrepresenting the truth.

Correct. Tactful, straightforward, direct, clear communication is always the best policy. If this conversation does not bring resolution, then you have grounds to take it up the chain of command. If this is a reputable company, someone along the line will appreciate your honesty and integrity.

_____You silently decide to yourself, that while you won't volunteer any information, if asked you will tell the truth regardless of your instructions.

Lying by omission is still lying. You are also putting yourself in a position to betray the trust of your supervisor. This is devious and passive-aggressive. It will not establish balance or protect your honor.

Your girlfriend of nine months just broke up with you. She has a job, but has basically been financially dependent on you, because you make considerably more money, and are generous by nature. She claims that she needs more space, and is too young to get into a serious committed relationship. She asks you to pay her bills for the rest of the month until she gets back on her feet.

_____You agree to pay her bills for one month.

No. While this would be a nice thing to do, it does not bring balance. She has just added insult to injury, to agree to give her more money only reinforces the feeling that you are being used.

√ You refuse to give her any money.

Correct. It is not your responsibility to pay her bills. It was nice of you to be generous during the relationship, but you were not married, and do not owe her financial support. She created this situation; it is her lesson to learn.

_____You agree to pay her bills if she doesn't leave.

Incorrect – This is encouraging her to use you financially, and exploiting her because she is financially unstable.

_____You agree to pay her bills, but don't.

Awakening Spirit – Freshman Course – www.WISESeminary.com

Incorrect. This is a game tactic. You are manipulating her by lying, with the intent to cause her pain, and to mess up her credit.

Sacred Energy

Your spouse is occasionally physically abusive. You have noticed that this only happens under certain situations, and your spouse is always extremely apologetic afterwards, and promises never to do it again.

_____ You do your best to avoid the circumstances that provokes the violence.

Incorrect, someone who is physically abusive will continue to find ways to physically abuse. It is not your fault, nor do your deserve to by physically abused. Your partner needs to be responsible for his or her own energy, and should be your greatest source of strength and support, not someone you need to protect yourself from.

√ You refuse to listen to excuses, or apologies and leave the relationship.

Correct. Abuse of any kind is not appropriate under any circumstances. Your partner needs help, but you cannot be responsible for them seeking, or getting it. You must be responsible for protecting yourself first and foremost.

_____ You recommend counseling for you and your partner, and do your best to work out the problem without disrupting the family.

While this does seem like the nice and understanding thing to do, this perpetuates your role as victim. It is more important for you to remove yourself from the role of victim, than to concern yourself with helping the offender. This is an enabling tactic, which allows the offender to become the victim of an earlier trauma, and encourages them to become even more co-dependent and attached to you, their victim. This also allows you to be in denial about your own need to be in this imbalanced and disruptive relationship. You cannot avoid disrupting the family by staying in the relationship. The family has already been disrupted and traumatized by the physical abuse. This action will escalate the situation, and create opportunities for you to be subjected to future, and possibly more destructive abuse.

_____ You make a plan that the next time it happens you will be able to appropriately defend and protect yourself.

No, Resorting to using the tactics that you find unacceptable will only bring you down to the same level as the abuser. Fighting back would have been the appropriate thing to do the "first" time, not the "next" time. This is not an appropriate way to defend or protect your self.

Indicate if the action demonstrates an equal (=), less than (<), or greater than (>) relationship between the two subjects.

Julie = < > Robbie

Julie promised to call Robbie at noon to decide on what to do for lunch. Julie had an unexpected rush and can't go to lunch till after 1:00. She knows that Robbie will wait

Initial Sacral Chakra Activation – Certification Requirements

on her, so she hurries to finish her work and calls him at 1:30.

Greater than - Julie > Robbie

Julie should have called Robbie at noon as promised, giving him the right to choose to wait on her or go ahead and eat. By not calling him, she assumed power in the relationship, by making him wait around, and wonder why she hadn't called.

Carol = < > Mike

Mike and Carol just had a new baby. They both agree that it is more important for Carol to stay at home to take care of the baby than to go back to work. Mike and Carol have previously had their own income, and did not mingle their finances. Mike is uncomfortable with having Carol on his checking account and feels that he should have the right to decide how his money is spent. Since she no longer makes any money, Mike assumes all the responsibility for the family finances.

Less than - Carol < Mike

Carol has just received a real strong message that Mike doesn't trust her to make appropriate financial decisions, and that her work as a stay at home mom has no value. Mike just took Carol's independence and power away from her. All of Carol's future needs will be decided by Mike from this point forward, making Carol basically powerless in the relationship.

The History of Wicca

T or F - Gerald Gardner is considered as the founding father of Wicca.

True – Because of his work to bring Wicca to the public, he is considered as the father of Wicca.

T or F - Religion is no longer needed once someone achieves spiritual enlightenment.

False – Spiritual Enlightenment is not a final destination, but a series of epiphanies as you spiritually evolve. There is always something new to learn. Religion is the path through which spiritual enlightenment is achieved.

T or F - All spiritual lessons are painful.

False – You must choose to suffer. You can choose not to suffer by choosing to walk in balance with the universe. If you can learn to recognize when you are not in balance, then you can choose to restore balance. None of this requires pain or suffering. It is only through our inability to see the imbalances that pain and suffering manifest.

T or F - Because Wicca encompasses all religions, it is the best and most accurate religion to practice.

False – This is subject to opinion, and falls into the category of Relative Truth. All religions serve a valid purpose, and none can be judged as either the best or most accurate for everyone. Each religion serves a unique and individual purpose, and should be valued for its contribution.

Certification Requirement

Chapter 2 - Write a one-page biography about an historical Wiccan.

Chapter 2 - Write your story of how your came to Wicca.

Journal Entries

This week remember to practice the techniques and integrate the concepts discussed. Try to walk gently in balance with the Laws of Karma. Notice the relationships you have chosen to create in your life, and how the connections bring you joy or pain.

Record your relationships below, noting if you are an equal (=), less than (<), or greater than (>) partner. Ask yourself what these relationships are trying to teach you and how they enrich your life. Try to look at the relationship from a third party perspective and from the other person's point of view to get a broader understanding of the dynamics.

3

Initial Will Chakra Activation
Creating Your Own Reality

Yellow

Color Me Yellow!

As above, So Below

"As Above, So Below" is a fundamental belief and a common phrase in Paganism. Simply put, it means that what is true and functioning on the macrocosm (the Greater Universe, such as the solar system) is true and functioning on the microcosm (the smaller universe, such as an atom). From this theory, we can unravel many mysteries of our universe by simple observation.

"As within, so without" is another way of stating the same truth. Just as every cell in our body has the DNA blueprint to recreate our entire body, each person on the planet has the same relationship to God/dess. You are a microcosmic hologram of God/dess, the all of everything that is. Everything in the universe is an extension of you. All the mysteries are contained within you, and all the answers are there for you to discover. You need only ask the right questions, and be truly open to receiving the answer.

This means that as a part of God/dess, you have at your disposal all the power of God/dess. But, you are also subject to the will of God/dess. Nothing can happen that is outside the will of God/dess. She is the collective consciousness of all that is, and everything that exists. Everything that comes to pass does so by Her command, to serve Her in some way. We may not always understand the will of Goddess, nevertheless, we cannot manifest anything nor act in any way that is not in accordance with Her will.

It is our own inability to see the big picture, our limited awareness, that makes some things seem bad, and other things seem good. Just as we sometimes enforce unpleasant situations or limitations on our children, so that they may learn a lesson, all that happens within our world teaches us something valuable. The more horrible the experience, the more important the lesson, the greater is our resistance to learning it. When you understand that all that comes to pass is for the best and highest good of all concerned and the will of Goddess, then you can attune to the magic that permeates our universe. That is the essence of Goddess.

The role of the Priest and Priestess is to bring themselves into harmony and awareness with the Will of Goddess. From this place of attunement and oneness with Her, your desires are Her desires, and Her will is your will. It is the duty and responsibility of a Priest or Priestess to work in Her service, as a physical vehicle from which She operates, to manifest what is divinely destined to come into being. It is through this connection that the Priestess can be one with the Goddess and act on her behalf. This is doing the work, to allow your self to be a willing, receptive conduit from which the Goddess can manifest her will. When you work to manifest the divine will of Goddess, you cannot fail.

Recognizing Divine Will

To find your divine will, you must take away all the self-imposed restrictions. Remove all the reasons why you think you can't do something. If there were absolutely no obstacles in your way, what would you choose to do, just for the sheer love of doing it? That is your contract. That is divine will.

We all have a divine contract. Your impulses may vary drastically, but your deepest heartfelt dreams, the burning desire that brings you the most joy, that thing that you love to do so much that you can't NOT do it and be happy, that is the will of Goddess.

When you look for answers, look for the simple answers. Don't try to make it hard. The greatest mysteries can be so simply explained. It is our belief that it's difficult, that makes it so.

As *"The Charge of the Goddess"* teaches us, "And thou who thinkest to seek for me, know thy seeking and yearning shall avail thee not unless thou knowest the mystery; that if that which thou seekest, thou findest not within thee, then thou wilt never find it without thee. For behold, I have been with thee from the beginning; and I am that which is attained at the end of desire."

All those obstacles in your way are put there to help you learn a lesson, to teach you a skill that you will need in fulfilling your contract. If you will need to learn to have strong boundaries, in order to protect something, the universe will present opportunities where you will learn to establish strong boundaries. Whatever you will need to know to fulfill your contract will be information that is available to you. The Goddess will provide for you everything you need to learn and grow in your path. Struggle comes from not manifesting your true joy.

Manifesting True Joy

The reason you have the desires, talents, and instincts that you have, is because you have a contract with the divine. As a part of Goddess, you have manifested on the physical plane with a burning desire to complete your contract. Over the years you have been subjected to various stimuli to prepare you for the completion of your contract. The choices you have made have determined whether you move closer or further away from the completion of your contract. Unhappiness, lack of fulfillment, all suffering, comes from not seeking to fulfill your divine joy.

We are taught to deny ourselves, be sensible, go along to get along, be responsible, follow the rules. Get a job, any job, so that you can pay your bills. Job's aren't supposed to be fun, etc. What purpose would it serve for humans to live an existence of misery? Why would Goddess put us in a place where there was never enough, and every day of your life you were forced to deal with things that made you miserable? What possible sense could that make? None. It doesn't make sense. And the ways of Goddess always make sense. We don't always understand it, but somewhere if you keep looking you will find a pattern that fits in perfectly with everything else.

Because a life of perpetual misery is not what we want for our children, it cannot possibly be what the Goddess wants for us. If we constantly provide everything we possibly can for our children to be happy, why then do they continue to fight, argue, and struggle? Why can't they just be happy with the paradise we provide for them?

Why can't we humans see that Goddess provides everything that we need to be absolutely blissful? Why can't we achieve our bliss? Is it because we always want more than we have? Is it because we are always denying ourselves what we truly want? Is it because we see the world and it's resources as limited? Or is it simply because we do not recognize that we are living in a paradise of plenty, where all our needs will be met and cared for, if we just choose to follow our joy?

We desire to learn to manifest a reality where there is abundance, yet we have refused to accept the abundance that has already been offered us. We act as a hungry child who will not eat off the red plate, because she wants to eat off the blue plate. The red plate is her favorite plate, but her brother likes the blue one, and so she is afraid that the blue one may be better.

For you to manifest your reality, you must stop comparing your successes to what other people believe is success. Success is not measured in material wealth. It's measured in the ability to do what you love. It's measured in the joy, and happiness that you have in your heart for yourself, and those you love. All the physical comforts of this world are insignificant if in your heart you are not happy. Rice and beans make a great meal if you are sharing it with people, who make your heart sing.

So before you start burning money candles, and doing prosperity spells, rethink your situation. Maybe you should sell that comic book collection in the attic, and start your own business. Maybe what you really need to do is be a stay at home mom. Maybe your greatest joy is writing poetry, but your scared to submit anything for publication because the rejection would break your heart. Is the possibility of rejection worth living a life of drudgery? Should you never risk loving anything, because one day it may leave you? Do we lack the courage to embrace our greatness?

Each of us is here for a purpose, to do something important. Most of us will choose not to do it. Most of us will live our lives in struggle, and suffering, always wanting something that we think we cannot have, allowing others to tell us what we want and need, and never being true to our inner self.

So, before you use the power of manifestation, make sure you really want what you are asking for. Examine and re-examine your priorities. You have heard the saying, be careful what you ask for because you just might get it. Before you work magic, explore the ripples. What are the consequences? What will you get in addition with what you think you want?

With fame, goes the inability to make a casual trip to the grocery store. Elvis was a prisoner of his fame. Do you want money? Do you want to have to deal with your broke relatives begging you for cash, and then hating you if you don't give it to them? If someone showed up on your doorstep tomorrow with $1,000,000.00, would that serve to make you a better person?

Accepting Success

If you have truly researched your desires, and you have explored the ripples and believe that if this thing were to come to pass, it would be for the best and highest good of all concerned. Recognize that through the perfection of the universe and through the love of the Mother Goddess, that you already have all the resources that you need to achieve it. You have only to agree to accept it, and begin taking the steps necessary to integrate that into your life.

Setting Goals

Manifesting your will is a matter of setting goals, and working towards those goals. There is no separation between the magical and the mundane. Your life will manifest according to your dreams and desires, if they are clearly defined. You must decide exactly what you want, and how you are going to go about getting it, for you to employ all the tools in your magical bag.

If you do not have a plan, you will go about your day responding to upcoming stimuli. You will not work towards achieving your goal, because you don't have one. You cannot tell the subconscious "I want things to be better", because that is too abstract. There are no defined parameters. Better than what? The subconscious will reject that command. It will pick up on the fear motivating the command, and create more of whatever is causing the fear.

Your subconscious is adept at manifesting your reality. It is so good at it, that it does it without your awareness. You don't need to learn to manifest. You are already doing it. What you really need to learn is how to master your conscious thoughts, so that your subconscious mind will receive the correct messages to manifest the reality you want.

Your subconscious is most easily reached by the uncontrolled thought. The abstract wish that you throw into the wind without a thought is the one that will manifest the quickest. The one that you sit around and focus on for days on end will have the greatest trouble finding its way into your reality. This is because you are putting doubt and fear into it. You are spending so much time focusing on it, because you need it so badly. Your desperation has already created an atmosphere that is opposed to that reality, and you are validating that you don't think it will happen by devoting that much energy to it.

Your Will Chakra is like a sharp dangerous power tool, and your subconscious is like a child. Without direction, boundaries, and constant supervision, it will see how many things it can destroy for fun, because it doesn't have to deal with the physical consequences of it's actions.

The subconscious doesn't eat, sleep, drink, wear clothes or have any desires or judgments. It just exists. We can learn to direct our subconscious minds. We can set goals and make conscious choices. But, as long as we allow ourselves to be motivated by fear, we will continue to create situations that do not serve us.

To be adept at creating your reality you must first consciously identify your goals, and consciously work on a mundane level to make that happen. That act alone will stimulate your subconscious to begin working in coordination with your conscious mind.

Writing this information down is vital to the creation/ manifestation process. It will bring into conscious realization the steps necessary to make your dreams a reality. Once you are able to clearly define what it will take to achieve your goal, you may find that you are unwilling to do what it takes, or possibly that the goal is not what you really want, and therefore choose to change your goal. Writing the information down brings your magic into tangible reality that you can relate to on a mundane level.

Defining the Goal

This is an easy spell that helps clearly define what you want. Draw a circle in the center of a piece of paper. Write what you want in the center of the circle. Draw a line from the circle, like you would a ray of sunshine, and write on that line a detail describing what you want. Continue to do this deosil around the circle, until you can't think of any more details. Now take this paper, fold it up, put it where it will not be disturbed or discovered, and leave it. Don't think about it, or go back to look at it, until you have either received what you asked for, or decided you don't want it anymore.

Example of Sun Spell:

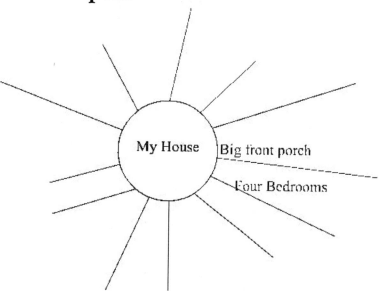

Get another piece of paper and write out what you need to do from where you are now, to achieve that goal. Get detailed in your steps. If you want a house, you may need to call a Real Estate Agent, go look for houses, get Real Estate guides, save money, work on credit issues, etc. If you want a job, you need to put in applications, send out resumé's, etc.

Do not focus on your final goal, as this may seem out of your current reach, and you may undermine your ability to achieve it. Focus on completing the next step toward your goal, as you have outlined for yourself. This will be something that you can accomplish, and you will be able to keep your thoughts positive. Before you know it, you will have that what you asked for.

Shielding

Color Me Yellow!

Shielding is the act of protecting yourself from the negative energies in your surroundings. It is as important as eating, just as grounding is as important as breathing. Shielding protects you from the constant energetic frequencies coming out of the various other energy sources on the planet. Everyone, everyday, is trying to achieve goals. They are working to make money, go places, do things, and their thoughts are radiating from them, working to affect their will. To avoid being manipulated, confused or compromised by the will of others, you must establish and protect the boundaries defining your reality.

Boundaries

Setting boundaries is the foundation of shielding. What is ok, and not ok in your world? You have the right to make those decisions, and expect the people who interact with you, to respect those decisions. When someone compromises your boundaries, whether intentional or not, they are disrespecting you, and they are imposing their will on you. It is appropriate for you to stand up for yourself, and not be controlled by others. It is vital to your self-respect, self-worth, sacredness, and personal power, to be able to define your own reality.

This includes all aspects of your life, physically, emotionally, mentally, and spiritually. It is very easy to spot physical abuse. If someone hits you, you know it. But emotional, and mental abuse is more difficult to spot. Spiritual abuse is almost impossible to recognize until the damage has already been done. Here is your baseline: If someone does something to you that you do NOT like, enjoy, feel comfortable with, or that causes you pain or anguish you have the right to stop that person from doing that. If someone is controlling you, manipulating you, or forcing their will on you, even if they are doing it in a nice way, they may as well be attacking you physically. You have as much right to protect yourself from emotional, mental, or spiritual abuse, as you do physical abuse.

Setting Boundaries is very important in creating your reality. Without appropriate boundaries, you are not safe to select or reject which things you are willing to have in your reality. You must be clear on what you will and will not accept in your life. If someone crosses a boundary, you must be willing to defend your boundary. If you are not willing to defend your boundary, then you are giving permission to another to exert his or her will onto yours, and therefore giving them the power over your reality.

It is important to realize here that they are not taking power from you. You are giving it to them. As an adult, you are always *capable* of defending your boundaries, however unwilling you may be to do so.

Many of us have unclear and compromised boundaries, because of our cultural and societal rules, such as:

It's important to be nice.
Don't hurt someone's feelings.
Saying no makes us a bad person.

We will stand by and allow someone to take advantage of us, and not say anything, because we don't want to be thought of as mean. Or, we will take advantage of someone else, and not even recognize it. When they stop us from harming them, we get our feelings hurt and cry foul.

This behavior stems from not being allowed to establish proper boundaries as a child. Our culture often refuses our children's right to say no. We take away our children's right to make decisions about many things that directly affect them. Now that we are adults, we don't know what proper boundaries are, because we have never had them.

You may be afraid that your boundaries are unreasonable or that you have no right to set them. If we have created a reality where our boundaries were not respected in the past, we will begin to believe that we have no right to establish them. This could be from a past life trauma, and/or recreated in childhood. We all have a right to boundaries, and we all have some boundaries. People, who have compromised boundaries, will try to compromise the boundaries of others. The best way for you to help someone with compromised boundaries is to maintain your own.

You may feel that defending yourself is rude. We are taught that it is important to be polite. Therefore, many times we find that instead of protecting ourselves from unwanted behavior, we try to ignore it, overlook it, rationalize it, or put up with it. We may have incorporated it into our belief system that it is more important to be nice, than to stop them from imposing their will on others.

In truth, when you are put in a position to have to defend yourself, the social transgression is on the part of the offending party. However, defending your boundaries does not mean that you have to be rude or aggressive. You can simply remove yourself from the person's immediate presence. You can say "No". You can ask someone to stop. You do not have to react with anger, or any other emotion. Just respectfully point out the boundary, and expect it to be respected in return.

You may believe that you will not be liked if you have healthy boundaries. This is a common belief, and simply not true. People like those whom they can respect. They will not like those, whom they feel they can manipulate or control. They may use someone like that to accomplish their agenda, but they will not care about them personally. Trust and Respect are foundational to human relationships. If you cannot trust someone to honor their boundaries, you cannot trust them to honor yours. You cannot respect someone whom you cannot trust, and you can't love someone whom you can't respect.

Healthy boundaries make someone a whole person. It is not up to anyone else to decide what boundaries you should have or to enforce those boundaries. It's a personal choice based on your goals, priorities, and aspirations in life. No one else can live your life for you, and no one else can decide what is best for you. They can give you advice, and offer a different perspective, but you have to make your own choices

Priorities

We all have priorities in life, and everything has a price. Sometimes we have to do things we don't want to do, to get something that we do want. I hate to wash clothes, but I do it because I want to wear clean clothes more than I don't like washing them. It's a trade off. I check with my husband before I make plans, because I want him to afford me the same respect. I pay the electricity bill; because I would rather have electricity than the $100.00 it costs a month. But, I would feel taken advantage of if asked to pay $1,000.00 a month for electricity, even though I need it. I would buy a generator, or make some other arrangements to provide electricity in my life.

It seems simple when put in those terms. But, what if all your life you have lived paying $1,000.00 a month for electricity, and you don't know everyone else only pays $100.00 a month. You don't know you are being taken advantage of until you become educated to that fact.

It is no different than if you grew up being called fat, lazy and stupid. If you have come to believe that you are fat, lazy, and stupid, how can you argue against someone treating you badly? After all you're fat, lazy, and stupid, right? Until you stop allowing people to tell you who you are, and decide for yourself, you are going to continue being exactly who they tell you to be.

What does not enter your reality does not exist. You control what happens in your world. You allow everyone in your life, to do whatever it is they do. You get something in return for each relationship you have. If someone does something you don't like, examine why you have chosen to deal with this behavior. What is it teaching you? Is the behavior serving you? Does it uplift you? Does it betray your self-respect?

Magic is not some airy-fairy intangible thing. Every element of your being must work in harmony to perform magic. If you visualize a shield, while you stand there and allow yourself to be slapped in the face, you're wasting your efforts. You need to move, put your hands up, and do something to protect yourself. Shielding happens on all levels at the same time. You can measure your ability to shield by the negativity that permeates your existence.

Healthy boundaries keep you safe. Once you are safe, you are free to focus your energy in ways other than defending your will against the will of others. You are free to begin consciously manifesting your will.

Shielding involves using the power of your will to create a force-field barrier around your aura that prevents negative energy from reaching you and affecting your reality. Visualize a bubble around you; make the bubble out of something strong, and impermeable like concrete or steel. Whatever you can visualize will work. You should practice maintaining this energetic in various situations. The goal is to be able to maintain a gentle filter at all times, and to be able to pop up a hard shield when you are in contact with negative energy.

Eventually, your shields should come up automatically whenever there is negative energy present, even if you aren't consciously aware of it. Many times my shields come up before I am aware that I am in danger. I can then physically respond, because I have been alerted. The first time I noticed this happen was in my car. Another motorist was driving recklessly and endangering my safety. I was able to get out of the way, and avoid an accident. With practice, your shields will protect you in the same way with an automatic or autonomic reflex.

Shielding Meditation

Place your feet on the ground. Sit up straight. Begin deep breathing, and relax. Send your energy down, deep into the earth. Connect with the power source of the Earth Mother at Her center, Her deep, red core. Feel any excess, nervous energy drain away. Feel the revitalizing, red, powerful energy coming up into your being, empowering you. Focus your attention on your solar plexus, above your belly button, right below your rib cage. Focus the energy there, and see it glowing a bright, hot, yellow, like your inner sun. Expand that energy. Make it bigger. Allow it to explode into a ball of energy surrounding you in all directions, protecting you. Feel the power of your personal shields. Remember to maintain your grounding. Breathe deeply. Feel yourself surrounded by the vibrant, yellow light, protecting you, empowering you.

When you are ready open your eyes, and try to maintain these energetic connections. Work on this all week until you can pop up your shields just by thinking "Shield!".

Understanding Thought-forms

Color Me Yellow!

Thoughts are powerful forms of independent human generated energy that exist in our environment. We receive thoughts and generate thoughts. There is almost a constant flow of incoming and outgoing thoughts that permeate our reality, every moment of our existence.

Thoughts vary from raw elemental energy, to well developed, organized, and meticulously planned thought-forms. Each of these thoughts trigger a chemical interaction within our physical body, and somehow affects our reality. How these random flows of thought affect your reality is based on how you process them.

Thought-forms are spiritual manifestations of our thoughts. We are constantly creating thought-forms. Every time we have a thought we create a thought-form, and whether or not that thought-form materializes on the physical plane is up to us. As the thought-form is our creation, we are its God or Goddess. This is a microcosmic, consciously directed example of the ability that we have, and use subconsciously, to create the reality within which we live.

Manifesting a thought-form on the physical plane requires the same action as manifesting anything in your life. You already manifest things in your life, you are just unaware of the process. It is our goal to bring to the conscious mind, the subconscious actions you are taking to manifest your current reality. We are creating a link between the conscious and subconscious, so that you can train your consciousness to direct your subconscious mind to create the reality you desire.

The subconscious mind has no reasoning ability. It cannot, and will not, differentiate whether or not you need, want, or can benefit from what it creates. It simply responds to stimuli. It creates what you tell it to. If you tell it to create lack, poverty, unhappiness, jealously, or betrayal, it will. If you tell it to create abundance, happiness, or loyalty, it will.

The subconscious mind is incapable of discernment, and will not judge right from wrong. It is the void into which your conscious mind inputs the spark of creativity. From that connection everything in your world has manifested.

The subconscious mind is your Goddess-self, and the conscious mind is your God-self. Your conscious mind is constantly providing your subconscious with material to create. You are continuously being subjected to stimuli designed to invoke a response from you. When you watch television, commercials are broadcasted to persuade you to buy products. When you go to the store, there are advertisements, specials, and impulse items, all designed to entice you to purchase something that you may not have intentionally set out to purchase.

Your family members have learned how to interact with you in ways that produce reactions from you to get the results they desire. Your employer has developed skills that result in your work behavior. You are constantly at the mercy of your surroundings. Yet, you alone hold the power over these surroundings.

You choose where to shop, what television programs to watch, or not to watch,

Initial Will Chakra Activation – Understanding Thought-forms

who you interact with on a day-to-day basis, and where you work. You have created all the relationships in your life, and you are in choice whether to continue to subject yourself to those relationships. If they are positive or negative, however they affect your life, you have the power to continue, change, or terminate them.

The energy exchange is constant. You cannot stop the input, or the output. Even in a meditative, restful state, you are receiving stimuli. The temperature of the room, the abstract noises of the universe, the posture of your body will all affect you. The messages you send out and receive will continue. It is your responsibility, as a priest or priestess, to monitor this energy, and recognize it's ebb and flow. It is your right, as a God or Goddess, to direct this energy and make it work for you.

Creating Thought-forms

When I think of thought-forms, I think of the story "The Sorcerers Apprentice". Disney did a Mickey Mouse version of it on "Fantasia". It's the one where the broomsticks are brought to life to carry buckets of water, and they won't stop. The Sorcerer comes home to find his house flooded and his apprentice in quite a big mess. Take this story to heart, as there is a very valuable lesson about thought-forms that apply here. You are responsible for whatever you create, and you may not have a Great Sorcerer to come home and bail you out. So, BE CAREFUL! But, more importantly EXPLORE THE RIPPLES!

There are many thought-forms throughout my home. From the moment you enter the property there are many eyes upon you, each doing a different and clearly designed task. There are protectors, messengers, guardians, helpers, secret keepers, teaching assistants, baby-sitters, and informants. I even have a wake-up fairy, who unfortunately was not programmed to recognize weekends, but I appreciate her efforts just the same. The only limit to the type of thought form you can create, is how well you can define them. Boundaries, and goals are the very heart of a thought-form.

Thought-forms can occupy statuary, magical tools, paintings, furniture, cars, and virtually any inanimate object. They can do whatever you can program them to do. They can live as long as you tell them to live. They can be as simple or as complex as you design.

The rules are simple:

1. Give it a physical place to manifest, an inanimate object.

2. Program the thought form with the four elements, and establish its goals and boundaries. This will take some serious thought and planning. Do NOT forget to write this down, years later you will not remember everything your programmed into

your thought form.

- ✓ Earth gives it substance, strength, and establishes a length of time it exists.
- ✓ Fire gives it a purpose, goal or mission.
- ✓ Water establishes its ethics, and social attachments.
- ✓ Air narrows its focus and intent.

3. Then breathe life into the thought-form, and release it to do its work.

The varieties of ways to create a thought-form are numerous, and a talented Priestess will continue to discover new and better ways to accomplish this task. You can incorporate herbs, oils, crystals, statues, talismans, runes, incense, jewelry, potions, photographs, paintings, and the list could go on and on. But, the technique is the same.

I'll explain it again in a different way. Another perspective may deepen your understanding.

Start with form, foundation, earth. Give the thought-form a place to manifest, a physical thing into which the thought-form can attach itself, a home, so to speak. This can be as simple as a pentagram drawn on a piece of paper, or as elaborate as a hand carved statue. The amount of work you put into each element, will be directly proportionate to the results of your spell. When creating the foundation, be sure to speak into being why you are creating it, and what you expect it to do. Speak to each element, of the properties you wish that element to offer.

Then move to consciousness, fire. What is the thought-forms' mission, it's instinctual desire. What do you wish it to be driven to accomplish, against what odds? What talents does it need to have? Feel this desire within yourself, and project it into the thought-form, you can place a candle on top of your piece of paper, and write the goal or mission on the candle, hold the candle in your hands and empower it with your desire. Or, for the more detailed spell, you can infuse an oil, using essential oils, with the correct properties to carry your spell into the thought-form. Remember to charge the oil with your desire, just as you would the candle. Then anoint the form with the oil, telling it what you want it to do.

Then move to ethics and attachments, water. What are the parameters within which you want this thought-form to operate? I usually say "to the best and highest good of all concerned," because I am aware that in my limited consciousness I am not able to foresee all the possible consequences of my actions, and wish to stay within the bounds of "harm none". Do you wish this thought-form to only act at certain times, under certain conditions, towards certain vibrations? Consider the issue, think through the ethical decisions, and be clear. Use water, or an appropriate potion to anoint your thought-form. Another thing you can do is write all the instructions that you have, or will be giving the thought-form, down in an appropriate ink, and place it under the pentacle or statue, or whatever form you have chosen.

Now we are at focus, intent, skill and intelligence, air. Remember this thought-form is not capable of thinking in any terms other than those you provide. You must program the correct intelligence to complete the mission. It may be that its intelligence can be limited. You may not need it to think beyond a small, simple scale. Or you may need it to do something complex that requires skill, such as "be able to pick a lock". Now, if you don't know how to pick a lock, you certainly can't give that information to an elemental. Be aware that you cannot give a thought-form a "skill" that you are not capable of doing yourself. However, you can give it the magical power to open locks, if you have a spell that will open locks. All obstacles can be overcome with some ingenuity and cleverness. You just have to learn to think outside the limitations of mundane reality, while still working within them.

To empower it with air, you can give it a metal talisman, with runes or appropriate language written upon it. If you want to create an elemental that will be effective in healing you may want to carve a caduceus onto it since that is the symbol Medical Professionals use. Carving, or writing symbols and language is a very appropriate use of air; you can also speak the instructions to the elemental while smudging it with appropriately charged incense, or both.

To complete the spell you want to breathe life into it. If you were creating a full thought-form, then you would want to name it. As you breathe life into it, say something like "from my breath, I give you life, and name you _____".

Things to remember about thought-forms:

*You need to preordain a time for it to expire, and/or care for its upkeep. Such as honor it for its service by giving it an appropriate gift.

*You created it, and you are karmically responsible for anything it does.

*It is irresponsible to leave a thought-form uncared for, just as it would be to neglect a pet or a child. Keep up with your magic, and if you no longer have use for a thought-form, release it into the west quarter.

*Always write down your spells, especially the ones that will carry into an unknown future. You will be amazed at what you can forget in time.

Following is a sample ritual from which you can get a more detailed insight into how to go about creating your own elemental.

Creating an Owl Totem Elemental Protector

Circle is cast, quarter's called, gods invoked.

Raise Power.

Part I – Creating the Elemental

Statue of an Owl - Earth - Place your hands on the statue and bless it. - "I call upon the power of Owl; predator of the night, he who has vision through the darkness, deliverer of justice. Elemental, from my hands of earth, I create thee to defend and protect me from malevolent energies."

Dragon's blood oil - Fire – Anoint the statue with Oil – "I call upon the power of Owl, ferocious predator, skilled hunter, loyal mate. Elemental, from my hands of fire, I create thee to defend and protect me from malevolent energies."

Potion - Water – Anoint statue with an appropriately brewed potion – "I call upon the power of Owl; keeper of mysteries, omens, silent wisdom, knower of dreams. Elemental, from my hands of water, I create thee to defend and protect me from malevolent energies."

Incense - Air – Smudge with an appropriately blended incense - "I call upon the power of Owl; knower of secrets, with keen vision, and sonar hearing, wise judgment and wisdom of the ages. Elemental, from my hands of Air, I create thee to defend and protect me from malevolent energies."

Part II – Programming the Elemental

Pentagram or Amulet – "I present to you this pentagram. As I wear this sacred symbol to represent my connection to Goddess, so shall you wear the same symbol to connect you to me and me to you."

Red Tail Hawk Feather & Perch – "I give you the power of Red Tail Hawk to balance out your nocturnal nature, and give you equal strength during the day time hours. With it, I give you this perch. May it keep you grounded in your center, and help you stay ever able to defend when necessary."

Black Tourmaline & Pyrite - "I give you the power of black Tourmaline that you will be able to repel and protect against all negative energy that comes my way, you will have the power to break all negative spells that may be cast against me and you will be protected from harm when acting on my behalf."

Initial Will Chakra Activation – Understanding Thought-forms

Rabbit Pelt – "I give you Rabbit to renew your strength after battle, to make you invisible to those who would harm me, and lightening fast in your actions."

Carnelian Eye – "I give you the power to see with Carnelian, that your eyes may see the suffering of my attackers. While protecting me you can return love to those, who are trapped in their fear."

Angelite – "I give you the power of angelite that you may surround me with protective light, that you may communicate with me when necessary, be able to dispel all anger and remove unnecessary obstacles from my path, so that I may be able to do the work of the Goddess in love and light."

Botswana Agate – "I give you the power of Botswana Agate that you may remain ever vigilant in your task of watchfulness over my safety and protection."

Basil – "I give you the power of Basil, that you may be able to immediately sooth the tempers of all those who confront you."

Citrine Eye – "I give you an eye of Citrine that you may see with wisdom, into the heart of the situation and bring a swift and wise conclusion to struggle, strife, and misunderstandings."

Sunflower Seeds – "I give you Sunflower seeds to attract any, who would do me harm, to you, so that they may find the wisdom to release their anger and fear."

Shield – "I give you this shield so that you may use it to deflect any evil intent."

Singulum – "I weave this singulum for you that it binds me to you and you to me, making you a part of my family, my totem, my elemental; a defender and protector, green for earth, red for defense, yellow for offense only as a last resort.

Raise Power and Chant – "**Strength, Protection, Wisdom, Justice**" repeat until power peaks.

Send your life's breath into the Protector, see it breathing into being – "I call your soul into being and name you _____." Chant the name over and over until the Protector responds to it and recognizes it as its name.

Release it to do its work – "Go forth and fulfill you mission as vigilant Protector and Defender. So mote it be!"

Cakes and Wine, Release Quarters, Close Circle.

Notice that nowhere in the spell was the protector given the power to hurt, cause harm, or inflict pain on anyone else. Nor was it programmed to protect its master from lessons that he needed to learn. Everything was focused towards reducing hate, malevolence and hostility. Remember to keep all your magic focused on the best and highest good of all concerned. Using magic to control your life and avoid your lessons is counter-productive, and will not work.

Initial Will Chakra Activation – Certification Requirements

Self Evaluation
Creating your Reality

You want to have a baby. You have tried and tried and you have been unable to do so. You have been to doctors. You've tried everything, and still no luck. You have considered adoption, but really want to have a child that is your flesh and blood. Which one of the four answers could possibly be the spiritual lesson motivating this issue?

_____ Your contract requires you to be free from the responsibility of parent-hood.

_____ You wouldn't be a good parent, and therefore Goddess won't trust you with a child.

_____ You are being punished.

_____There is something that you need to learn about yourself, before a child can manifest in your life.

"As Above, So Below" means:

_____ Everything that happens on a large scale, also happens on a small scale.

_____ The Universe teaches us by example.

_____ Your ceiling should be the same color as your floor.

_____ All energy is the same.

Shielding

You should shield from:

Yes or No - A co-worker that comes in late, and is worried about getting in trouble.

Yes or No - Your child when he's hurt and crying.

Yes or No - A friend asking advice about a personal issue.

Yes or No - A friend expressing anger about a personal issue.

Thought-forms

A good foundation for a thought-form is:

_____ A cat

_____ A statue

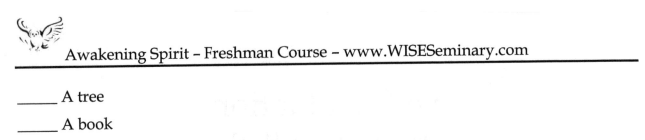

_____ A tree

_____ A book

Answers
Creating your Reality

You want to have a baby. You have tried and tried and you have been unable to do so. You have been to doctors; you've tried everything, and still no luck. You have considered adoption, but really want to have a child that is your flesh and blood. Which one of the four answers could possibly be the spiritual lesson motivating this issue?

_____ Your contract requires you to be free from the responsibility of parent-hood.

Possibly, but if this were the case, I would think that you would not feel such a driving need to have a child.

_____ You wouldn't be a good parent, and therefore Goddess won't trust you with a child.

Probably not, being a parent is a difficult task. But, people who really want to have a child, and ache to share that love and experience, usually try their best to be good parents. No one parents perfectly; it's a trial and error endeavor, at best.

_____ You are being punished.

Probably not, many people want to beat themselves up or blame God when things don't go their way. God does not punish us. We punish ourselves. Choosing this answer would indicate that you have issues of self-worth that need to be cleared.

√ There is something that you need to learn about yourself, before a child can manifest in your life.

Correct, having a child is a life-transforming experience. Until we have completed phase 1, we cannot enter phase 2. There are major life changes, and lessons that are learned through pregnancy, childbirth, and raising a being that is completely dependent on you. For whatever reason, you're not ready to enter into that phase yet. Release your attachment, search your heart, pray, and meditate, and the lesson that is blocking you will emerge. When you have integrated the lesson, you will be able to either conceive, or the desire to conceive will no longer be there.

"As Above, So Below" means:

Initial Will Chakra Activation – Certification Requirements

_____ Everything that happens on a large scale, also happens on a small scale.

Sort of, maybe not everything, but, this is one way of expressing the relationship of Macrocosm to Microcosm.

√ The Universe teaches us by example.

Correct.

_____ Your ceiling should be the same color as your floor.

No.

_____ All energy is the same.

Incorrect. Energies have a wide variety of frequencies, although similar energies do act in similar ways.

Shielding

You should shield from:

Yes or No - A co-worker that comes in late, and is worried about getting in trouble.

Yes - they are emitting negative energy that you do not want to affect you.

Yes or **No** - Your child when he's hurt and crying.

No – Your child depends on your for emotional, and spiritual support. You would want to hold your child and ground the negative energy, while you are comforting him.

Yes or **No** - A friend asking advice about a personal issue.

No – Someone who is asking your advice is receiving energy from you, not projecting towards you. You would not need to shield in this situation

Yes or No - A friend expressing anger about a personal issue.

Yes, if someone is venting to you, even though they are not necessarily directing energy at you, they are releasing negative energy. You can listen and allow them to vent, and still shield your self from receiving any negativity.

Thought-forms

A good foundation for a thought-form is:

_____ A cat

No – A cat has a spirit. Projecting a thought-form into a cat would be detrimental to the health of the cat.

√ A statue

Correct – A statue would be a very good place to manifest a thought-form.

_____ A tree

No – A tree has a spirit. Projecting a thought-form into a tree could be detrimental to the health of the tree.

_____ A book

No – A book is already programmed with someone else's thought-form, and would be in conflict with anything that you projected into the book. However, You can influence the thought-form already present and re-program it, to an extent. Or you can project a thought-form into a book that you have written.

Certification Requirements

List some boundaries that you have established in your life that you defend at all costs, and how these boundaries serve you. Example – "I don't drink and drive, because I don't want to hurt someone or go to jail." List some boundaries that you would like to be more established, and how these boundaries could serve you.

Practice shielding. Record your experience.

Journal Entries

This week remember to practice the techniques and integrate the concepts discussed. Try to notice the interplay of your will with those who interact with you. Notice when you try to impose your will on others, or when others try to impose their will on you.

4
Initial Heart Chakra Activation
Connecting with Your Patron Deities

Green

Color Me Green!

Before we get started in this chapter, I want to clarify a point about gender roles. Anything that is manifested in physical form has a balance of male and female, God and Goddess, within it. While humans do have a dominant gender, that determines whether we are male or female, we are not limited to function within that gender role.

Please recognize that Priest and Priestess are both capable of manifesting their energy as receptive, projective, or both. I use genders interchangeably within the coursework. It is not my intention to exalt, limit or disrespect either gender.

Our Goddess calls to us across space and time in a way that sings to our soul in an unknown, but deeply recognized tongue. It is the language of symbols; pictures, signs, dreams, visions, coincidence, gut feelings, and messengers.

You will hear her calling in your deepest childhood memories; a favorite cartoon, or TV show, a special story, or character, someone you remembered gently tapping you on top of your head, and then disappearing, a comforting hand in a moment of need. You will recognize her song in your most vivid dreams, and undeniable obsessions.

Her's is the call you cannot resist. She is the siren, whose voice enraptures and entrances you. She is the force greater than yourself, whom you long to be one with. She is the one with the most fascinating stories, the greatest powers, the one you can't find enough information on, nor read enough about.

The Priestess is the bridge between the two worlds. She is the interpreter through which the messages of the Gods and those, who are on the other side of the veil, flow to the physical plane. She communicates the needs and wants of those on the physical plane to the other realm. She represents the Goddess to the people, and the people to the Goddess. She helps to make connections between the two, and reveals the path for those who seek it. She teaches those who wish to join her in doing the sacred work.

The Priestess' role is to serve both worlds by keeping them in balance. To monitor the energies of both realms, and be the doorway through which love, truth, understanding, and harmony can flow.

We often have difficulty finding our self-worth in the face of our greater purpose. An overwhelming feeling of insignificance stands in the way of our ability to accept that the Gods would actually speak directly to us personally. I struggled for years with recognizing my Patron's. I knew which Gods and Goddesses I liked the best. But, I thought they were way to magnificent to be bothered with me.

In my early training, I always thought Cerridwen was so awesome with her Cauldron, far too powerful a Goddess for someone as powerless as me. But, oh how I wish I knew what was in that potion she made! How I longed to know the secrets of immortality.

I was always fascinated with Pan. He was so carefree, so powerfully male, so intimidating, and exciting, so sexy and romantic with his flute music. I had a statue of him and everything. It wasn't until my High Priest pointed out that Pan was one of my patron gods that I realized it myself.

I have always loved the story of Persephone's abduction. I know we studied other Myths in school, but I can't remember them. It always amazes me when people don't know who Persephone is. How can anyone NOT remember the story in High

Initial Heart Chakra Activation – Connecting with Your Patron Deities

School? It was so romantic. Is it such an odd coincidence that my husband's patron god is Hades?

Once I began studying the mysteries of Persephone, it became very clear to me that she had directed my life. Many of the situations I was confronted with in childhood were to prepare me for my duties as her Priestess.

These were the gods and goddesses to whom I called. It never occurred to me that while I was calling them, they were calling me as well. As above, so below!

Hecate and Demeter, both aspects of Persephone, came to me as well. Cerridwen, Aphrodite, Kwan Yin, Oshun, Kali, even Mary came to me early in my practice. But, even after well over a decade of daily worship and practice, I am discovering Hathor, Bast, Isis, and Sekhmet. Egyptian Expressions of my familiar and beloved Greek deities.

Each Goddess has shared a special individual message for me, which has helped me along my path. But together they have woven a tapestry, upon which communicates a clear, unified message of my calling, which has given me understanding of my service as Priestess. As I look back over the years of epiphanies, coincidences, messengers, and lessons learned, I can see that my training as a Priestess began long before I knew it. I can see that Goddess was directing me, moving me along my path, placing opportunities before me, and strengthening me with hard-learned lessons.

It wasn't until I was ready to accept the path before me that I could also see clearly the path that I had walked to arrive here.

The nuances of my path are amazing to me, as I am sure yours are to you. I have been finding the connections between different spiritual disciplines all my life. When I was 16, I wrote a paper in high school comparing Aphrodite to Venus, Hathor, and Freya, looking for cross-cultural similarities within similar manifestations of each culture's pantheon. I had no idea that I was beginning what was to become my life's work as a Priestess.

As a teenager, I was so frustrated with my future. I didn't know what I wanted to be. Priestess wasn't even a word I used, much less a viable career choice. There was no category that fit my unique talents and interests. When I took the career counselor's standardized test, my score placed me right in the smack middle of nothing. The closest thing they could recommend was secretary or nursing. While I enjoyed both, I still longed for something more.

My Grandfather's best advice was to learn how to type. Today, I can type 100 words a minute. That's just about fast enough to take dictation from the Goddess. Thanks Grandfather, I didn't know it at the time, but that was really great advice. I'm glad I did it, even though at the time I thought it was terribly sexist.

This is the path; a meandering, twisting, turning, confusing, around your elbow, over your head, just up that hill, and around the next corner, and then.... There you are! All the pieces suddenly fit into place and you realize that she was holding your hand, leading you through the darkness, all along. The million faces of the Great Mother, showing up in the most unexpected people, places and things; quietly, subtly, gently, sometimes quite loudly and not so gently, providing all the right circumstances for you to do exactly what you need to do. Your unawareness of it doesn't mean it's not happening.

The greatest obstacle between you and the Goddess is your willingness to accept that she is there, and that you too make a difference. It is so difficult to believe that I am important enough to be singled out to be her voice. But, in truth, I am not being singled out; I am just listening, and doing what I am asked to do. I am willing to serve the Goddess and do the work. That doesn't make me special, great, or more important than anyone else, it is just who I am called to be.

Every one of us is capable of listening. Every one of us is being guided by spirit. We are the physical manifestations through which the Gods operate. It's a symbiotic relationship. We need them and they need us. It is a balance. Without us they cannot evolve, and without them we cannot evolve. There is no "them" and "us". We are all one.

You were born into this universe for a specific reason, to do certain things, important things. Your spirit guides, and patron deities are working through you to help you complete your contract. They are already speaking to you, guiding your footsteps, sending you messages, and leaving you clues. You only have to stop and notice, to get in the loop.

Who are you drawn to? Who do you have statues of? Who do you pray to? These are your clues. Search out the stories of your childhood. Was Robin Hood your hero, or Wonder Woman? This tells you something about your patrons.

The answers to all your questions are literally being whispered in your ear right now. All you have to do is be still and listen.

Channeling

Color Me Green!

"Listen to the Words of the Great Mother; she who of old was also called among men Artemis, Astarte, Athene, Dione, Melusine, Aphrodite, Cerridwen, Dana, Arianrhod, Isis, Bride, and by many other names." *The Charge of the Goddess*

Understanding Channeling

Channeling is the act of attuning yourself to be a physical vehicle through which the Gods speak. It is a talent and a skill. This means some people will be naturally more open to the process, but all can learn how to do it. Gifted channels are those of pure intent, who are dedicated to listening, recording, and sharing what they receive.

Preparing Your Physical Vehicle

It is possible to reach a state of awareness where you are constantly in connection with Goddess, and available for Her to speak through you at any time. It is when you have reached this place that you are able to walk the bridge between the worlds, and consciously serve as a voice for Goddess.

This requires selfless, committed devotion to serving Goddess, daily prayer, reflection, and meditation. It also requires a certain amount of physical work as well.

Preparing Your Mind

You will only be able to reach information that you are comfortable with, or able to understand. If you don't know what the Elusinian Mysteries are, you cannot channel very much information about it. So you have to study. Study the sacred texts, and sacred sciences. Read all that you can. People ask me which books to read. I answer "all of them". Is this a big task? Yes, it is. Being a Priestess, or clergy of any religion is a huge endeavor.

Use your intuition to guide you. Ask Goddess to lead you to which books are best suited for you. If you find you are having trouble getting through a book, put it down and try again in six months. Maybe you're not ready for that information yet. But read. Read everything you can. Be educated about the subjects in which you are interested. Place value on scholarship. Build a personal library.

Preparing Your Body

Toxins and impurities within the body, mind and spirit interfere with the ability to connect with deity. By clearing one, you simultaneously clear the others. Physical impurities are the easiest to identify, so I recommend starting here.

When I began my training, I was an avid meat eater. Then suddenly I couldn't eat any meat. The smell or sight of meat made me sick. I quit eating meat and became a militant vegan for a while. I now eat meat occasionally, but I recognize that it has a very grounding effect and can definitely interfere with one's ability to channel. You may have different experiences. I am not advocating vegetarianism for everyone, but that did work for me.

If you are a substance abuser, drink excessively, or have significant weight issues, your ability to receive divine inspiration will be impeded. Sometimes these issues are accompanied with a feeling of being detached from spirit. Balance is the key. Over indulgence of any kind causes an imbalance.

It is difficult for spirit to manifest in a body that has a toxic vibration, until it gets so toxic that it is faced with death. That's called 'hitting bottom'. There isn't really a bottom. Everything is a circle. It's just very close to the negative end of the veil. A lot of people find spirit there, but I don't recommend taking that path. There are easier ways.

Taking care of your physical form is a basic need. Proper nutrition, exercise, and hygiene are necessary for personal pride, self-confidence and physical health. Your body is a temple of Goddess. Care for it, and treat it with sacredness.

Preparing Your Consciousness

Preparing your consciousness involves getting your subconscious and conscious mind into the habit of working together. Remember that your subconscious mind is like that of a child. It needs structure, order, habits, props, symbols, etc. Create a schedule. Decide that you are going to worship, pray, and meditate every day at a certain time, and do it.

Incorporate things that make you feel magical, burn incense, light candles, and play appropriate music, whatever makes you feel like connecting with deity. Guided meditations are good if you don't know how to meditate, and are having a hard time with it. But, really it's just a matter of praying, addressing and calling to deity, and then listening to what they have to say to you. Prayer is when you are talking to Goddess. Meditation is when Goddess is talking back to you. Just listen.

Preparing Your Emotions

You will often dismiss really valid information, and feel like you are making it up. Try not to be over-skeptical. It is possible that you are making it up, but if that's true, you haven't lost anything. It's best to not be overly attached to the outcome. Let the information flow, and see where it takes you. You may start out making something up, that turns into channeled information somewhere in the process.

Be focused, and make sure you state your intention. Remember that this is only difficult for people who don't know how to do it. Once you get over your own fears around it, it will be easy for you as well.

Fear is your biggest obstacle. It is ok to be afraid, but it is not ok to let your fear stop you from accomplishing your goals. Fear stems from ignorance. People are afraid of the unknown. Find out what you are afraid of, and educate yourself about it. Ask questions, read information, find out everything you can about what you are afraid of; explore that unknown thing until you know so much about it that you can find love for it. Come to the understanding that the universe really is a safe place.

The astral realm is not a place for someone who is afraid. Do not practice magic with fear in your heart. Stop. Deal with your fear. Find the courage to face it and defeat it.

Recognizing the Connection

It is difficult to allow your self to recognize the difference between your voice, and the voice of deity. From inside your own head they often sound very much the same. The best advice I can give you is to begin by writing those words down. Journaling gives your own fears a voice, and place to process them. But, it also allows you to get the surface chatter out of the way, so that you can get to the deep information that you seek.

Automatic writing is a great process that really works, and is very easy. Get your journal and a pen. Write down your question at the top of the page, and then just write whatever thoughts you hear. Even if the first 10 minutes are about how stupid the exercise is, just keep writing until the words stop coming.

I have written 10 pages of horrible, self-destructive things about myself only to find that once that fear was allowed to speak it's peace, there was some really enlightening information on the other side. It was very much worth it for two reasons. While the self-destructive things that I wrote out used to plague me often, I haven't thought of them since that day. But, I remember quite clearly the epiphany that I received, and it changed my life.

When you are writing down what you hear inside your head, you will notice that different voices speak. These are different personalities, or different aspects of your self. Just as the Gods and Goddesses have different aspects, and wear different masks with different cultures, we do the same thing. My different aspects look like this: wife, daughter, mommy, teacher, counselor, high priestess, writer, friend, lover, confidant, consumer, etc. I act and speak differently to my children than I do to a telemarketer, or to my husband when we are making a date for Saturday night. These different voices represent different aspects of yourself. Some of them will be hateful, and some will be loving. But, all of it will be therapeutic, as long as you don't do anything hurtful with any of the information.

Many people believe that channeled information results from a being entering your body, taking possession of your physical form, and speaking in a funny accent. This makes for a great dramatic floorshow, but doesn't necessarily mean that someone is channeling. They could be acting. Weigh the value of the information. Pray about everything you learn. Always ask for guidance. Spirit will guide you to truth.

Once you start looking for them, Spirit will give you clues of how to tell your voice from Theirs. When I use to receive information They would speak to me in rhyme. This was my signal that I was receiving guidance. Even though I have poetry that I have written, it is always something that springs forth from me, or rather through me, and not generated within me. I have a difficult time trying to rhyme. So it was easy for me to recognize when information was coming through in rhyme, that it was not my own thoughts.

Other common symptoms are goosebumps, tingling sensations, yawning, facial ticks, warm sensations, or your hair standing on end. This is called confirmation or validation. However, you may not recognize any of these symptoms at first.

I have been practicing as an active channel for many years now. I do it all the time. Whenever information needs to come through, I get it. It happens in the car, in the tub, making dinner, whenever, wherever. You may recall similar situations, when you have been praying for an answer to a question, and suddenly you realize your prayer has been answered.

Warning signs

OK, now let's get real.

Hearing voices in your head is often considered a symptom of mental illness. Schizophrenia is a disease that includes auditory hallucinations. Additional symptoms include paranoia, inability to start or complete simple tasks, inability to carry on a conversation, speaking in short nonsensical bursts, moving slowly, disorganized thinking, belief that people are monitoring your thoughts, plotting against you, or that you can control the thoughts of others. People with mental illness, who have auditory hallucinations, often interpret the voices inside their head as coming from demons. They are afraid, and live in a constant state of fear.

This is extremely different from channeling. However, as a Priest or Priestess functioning in this religion, it is important to be able to determine the difference. Schizophrenia most commonly occurs between the ages of 16 and 30. This is also the most common age range of people joining the craft. Many people within the craft do have borderline personality disorder, manic depression, bi-polar disorder, and other diagnoses of mental or emotional disturbances.

It is important to take these things into consideration. If you have been diagnosed with an emotional or mental disorder, or are teaching someone, who has symptoms of a disorder, the symptoms need to be brought under control and supervised by a medical professional. Spiritual leaders should be aware of their limitations, and encourage students to seek proper medical attention, should the need present itself.

Deciphering Information

True spiritual information will never tell you what to do, such as "get a divorce". It will be loving, gentle, enlightening information that opens windows in your mind to new insights. It will uplift you, and feel like a light bulb going off in your head. It will never be judgmental, or encourage you to get revenge, steal, kill, cheat, lie, or do anything that you think is wrong.

Divinely inspired information will strike you as something that is "too good for you to have thought of yourself", or uses words you don't find common. It will be so simple that it is genius, or concepts that are pure and humble, never full of ego.

While deity will challenge you to grow, it will never push you to do something, or shame you into action. It will inspire insights that are about soul growth and concepts that are much bigger than winning lottery numbers. You will receive only what you need to help you learn your next lesson, not tell you in which stock to invest.

Lower Astrals, and other entities on the astral plane, can and will speak to you if you open the door for them. They will attach to your aura, feed off your energy, and influence your thoughts, if you create a space for them to do so. Therefore, it is important to always be sure that you are grounded and shielded. Establish some sort of safe space in which to channel until you are adept at it.

Holding your athame, or wand is a great way to connect with deity and protect your self from lower astrals at the same time. But, you could also cast circle, grid your space with crystals, burn incense, wear protective jewelry, and many other things. It is not important how you create safe space, as long as the safe space is effective.

Safe space is created when a force field of some sort is established between you and undesirable energies. Lower Astrals do not have physical form, nor do they have a strongly established astral form. Many of them are disembodied spirits or man-made thought forms. Either way, any reasonable shield is good enough to send them on their way, and keep them from disturbing your space.

Initial Heart Chakra Activation – Channeling

When a lower astral, or any entity that is not physical, or God/dess, hits an energetic force field its energy is suddenly and quite alarmingly dissipated over the expanse of the force field, both frightening and confusing it. In years past, I have accidentally astral projected myself into someone's shields, and walked through the boundaries of a cast circle. It was a very disorienting and disturbing experience for me as a physically manifested entity. I can fully understand why a lower astral would be sure to avoid any such tragedy.

The Power of Myth

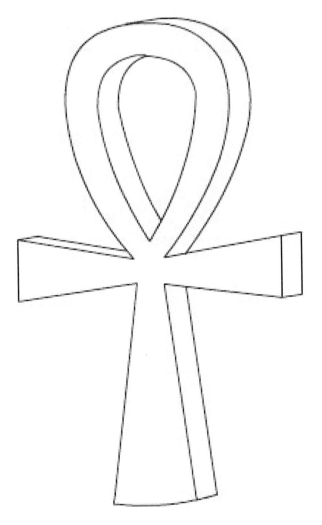

Color Me Green!

People often ask me how I know all these Gods and Goddesses. Whenever I am asked this question it takes me back in time to when I asked my teacher the very same question. His response was the same as mine usually is, "Just from working with them over the years", accompanied with a shrug.

I remember my response to his answer was not voiced aloud. I thought about all the different cultures, and all the many different Gods and Goddesses over all the different pantheons, and it seemed very overwhelming. How was I going to learn all the many different things about Wicca AND all the different Gods and Goddesses as well? Couldn't I just pick one? Wasn't there just a catchall God and Goddess that would listen to everything, or did I have to pray to different ones? What was the purpose of all the different Gods and Goddesses?

He explained to me that I could just pray to Goddess, and that she would hear all my prayers. That made me feel better, and at the time relieved my sense of urgency to tackle the world of mythology. As different Gods and Goddesses called out to me, I began studying them. It's a body of work that has grown over time.

I have reference books to refer to when a new deity calls to me that I need to learn about. I have never set out with the intention of learning an entire cultural pantheon. I have never read the Iliad by Homer. I have never completely read the Egyptian Book of the Dead, although I keep a copy of it on my desk for reference.

Knowledge isn't about what you have stored in your head, as much as the ability to access the information when you need it. A person can be a walking encyclopedia of mythology, but if they cannot put the pieces together, they cannot unravel the mysteries. Memorizing raw data does not make you intelligent, it means that you are good at memorizing. Processing the information, and integrating it into your life demonstrates intelligence. You do not need to know everything to be a Priestess, but you do need to know how to utilize what you have to accomplish your goals.

Myths are stories that relate spiritual concepts. They teach you a spiritual lesson that transcends the limits of language. Myths use symbols to speak to your subconscious to open doors that will lead you to the mysteries. Each time you explore a myth you will discover a deeper truth within it. These truths are 'the mysteries'. If you were color blind you could be surrounded by color, and not see it. It is the same with the mysteries. It can be right under your nose, but if you aren't in the right spiritual place to understand you won't see it.

This is important; because it shares with the seeker only what he is ready to receive. It shields the information from those who would misuse it, and it preserves it for those who's hearts and minds are open to enlightenment.

Acting out Myth is called Psychodrama. A Psychodrama is a mystery drama. It uses the science of symbolism to explore the 'truth' by dramatic methods. Psychodramas are utilized in ritual to reveal mysteries. The beauty of this technique is that it speaks to each person individually, relating truths that they are ready to receive at that time. Each time you witness a psychodrama you learn more and more about it, spiraling you deeper into awareness, creating relationships with deities, and archetypes that guide you on your own path to enlightenment.

Mythology is sacred text. The mysteries have not been lost, destroyed, or bastardized and stolen. They are still very much here to discover. They may be scattered a bit. But they are alive and hidden within the pages of myth, fables and fairy tales. This has always been the way of our ancestors. Even in the unbroken traditions, the mysteries are safely hidden within the sacred texts, camouflaged in symbolism, available to those who seek it, but protected from those who would use it for harm. Spirit reveals to us what we need to know based on our intentions, goals and purpose.

As we move into the Aquarian age, the myths will reveal different truths that speak to our time. We evolve spiritually as well as physically, consciously, emotionally, and intellectually. And as we spiritually evolve our needs are different. We can see that the stories are symbolic, and not literal or historical. We can understand that the Goddess can manifest as one great force, or we can focus our attention on one certain aspect about Her. Just as we can appreciate the whole of whom we are, or focus on one specific characteristic.

In the past we have seen the Gods as something outside ourselves. But as you grow in your relationship to deity, you will find that the Gods and their stories manifest in your life. You will find that your patron Gods and Goddesses not only influence your astrological chart, but manifest themselves within the events of your life. It is through this relationship, and the realization of the interdependence between the Gods and us, that we ascend to our next dimension of awareness.

The Psychopomp is a soul guide, often referred to as the Greek God Hermes, or Thoth, of the Egyptian pantheon. The Romans called him Mercury, the messenger of the Gods. He guides you through the lessons of life. The Hermit is another character that lights your way through the darkness of the unknown, through the 'tween land of fairy and illusion, into the light of conscious awareness. These archetypes can be very helpful when trying to understand these mysteries.

The key is your pure intent. Search with patience, and diligence. Remember that the answer today is only a layer that will continue to reveal depths as the years spiral into the past. Ask Goddess to guide you to the answers you seek. You will receive the answers that you need if you listen.

Certification Requirements

Collect wood and light a sacred fire, either inside or outside, without using man made accelerants. Tend the fire and keep it burning for 24 hours. Record your experience.

List the names of Gods and Goddesses that stand out to you and why.

Journal Entries

This week establish a time when you can sit down and devote a minimum of 30 minutes to your spiritual growth. It is most effective if you choose the same time every day, and preferably not on a full stomach. Before breakfast, lunch or dinner is an ideal time.

You can incorporate as many elements as you feel you need to, but it's important that each element be for a specific purpose that adds intent to your devotional. Example: You may want to light a candle because you are a fire sign and it helps you get in a magical mood to have a candle burning. You may choose a white candle to represent your pure intent.

Burn some protective incense that includes one or any combination of the following:
- frankincense,
- myrrh
- mugwort
- rosemary
- sandlewood
- lavendar
- sage

Have your pen and journal ready.

To begin, light the incense, and breathe deeply of the aroma. Allow it to be a catalyst that shifts your focus from the mundane to the magical. Place the incense close to where you will be so that it will fill the space that you are in. Sit either on the floor or in a chair, with your back straight, and your chin lifted slightly, have your book open in your lap or on the table in front of you, with your pen in hand.

Ground, shield, and send your energy up like a fountain through the top of your head.

Now say a prayer:
- ✓ Address the deity (Mighty Isis, Great Cerridwen, Mother of the Moon, Mother Goddess, whoever)
- ✓ Express your gratitude (thank you for my blessings, my children, my job, etc.)
- ✓ State your Intent or ask your question (please help me understand …, or whatever)
- ✓ Write down your intent or question in your journal, and then write whatever you hear in your head, for as long as the words come, or until you run out of time.

When you are done, say loudly and with conviction "So Mote It Be!"

Get up, stomp your feet, and

GO EAT!

5

Initial Throat Chakra Activation
The Human Energy Field

Blue

Color Me Blue!

The Human Energy Field is made up of major and minor vortexes of energy and connecting meridians or pathways that encompass and permeate the physical body. This energy must be in harmony and balance for the body to exist in a state of well-being.

Whenever disharmony or imbalance exists within this energy field, malfunction or disease manifests within the body. Whatever affects the spiritual body, affects the physical body, and vice versa. If something happens to your physical body, it also happens to your spiritual body. They cannot exist separately from each other.

Spiritual healing begins with the Human Energy Field. Healers should have a good understanding of the anatomy of the spirit and how it works to be dependably effective in a ministry that includes counseling and healing.

It is through understanding this subject matter that you will be able to isolate specific areas of imbalance, and be able to restore health in yourself and others.

Chakras

The Chakras are energy vortexes in the Human Energy Field, and are multi-dimensional spheres. These spheres exist on many levels and manifest in many ways. There are seven personal chakras, two generational chakras, and one transpersonal chakra. We will be exploring the seven personal chakras in this chapter.

Chakras are whirling energy vortexes that interact with dimensional awareness in a unique way, connecting us to many levels of existence at once. Most humans are only acutely aware of 1 or 2 dimensions of awareness and vaguely aware of 3 or 4. Some humans have extended their awareness to multidimensional and it is through development of the chakras that this is made possible.

To ascend to multidimensional awareness, we must first fully utilize our current awareness and establish balance in these dimensions. As with all spiritual matters this sounds very complex, but is really very simple.

Most people are not consciously utilizing of all five layers of existence that are currently available to humans. They are usually in touch with only one or two layers of themselves. These layers can be defined as physical, mental, emotional, spiritual and instinctual.

Initial Throat Chakra Activation – The Human Energy Field

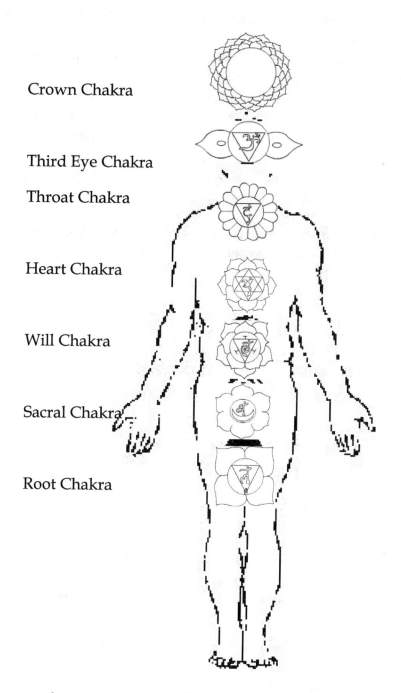

- Crown Chakra
- Third Eye Chakra
- Throat Chakra
- Heart Chakra
- Will Chakra
- Sacral Chakra
- Root Chakra

Some people are very aware of one of these levels, and ignore the rest. Such as:

- ✓ Athletes, who put great emphasis on the body, but do not make time to exercise their mind, or emotions
- ✓ Intellectuals, who can tell you all about anatomy, but can't do a pushup, and are closed off from their feelings
- ✓ Emotionally driven individuals, who spend so much time making friends in college, they forget to choose a career

- ✓ Instinctually driven people, who live for instant gratification, day to day, making no plans for the future
- ✓ Spiritually focused people, who escape reality through pondering the wonders of the cosmos, to the detriment of their credit

Please note; I can find elements of myself in each of these. I don't exercise as much as I used to. I could stand to make better plans for the future. I would like to devote more time to personal education. I am sometimes too focused on spirit, and I am often very emotional. This is similar to reading through a mental illness book and recognizing symptoms of yourself in everything, and then freaking out because you have convinced yourself you're nuts.

Being in balance means you CAN and should relate to every category, as there is always room for growth. An imbalance is identified if when reading through the list you could only relate to one or two categories.

Being able to balance mind, body, emotions, instinct and spirit are essential to healing. If you are constantly ignoring, pacifying, or avoiding the needs of any of these levels of existence, you are not fully reaching your potential. As long as you are not fully reaching your current potential, you will not be able to ascend to new levels of awareness.

Think about your daily routine. Are you good to yourself? Do you pay attention to and care for your aches and pains? Do you provide for your own needs, or do you deny them? Is your underwear drawer full of holey, stretched out garments that you would be embarrassed to let others see? Do you gorge on junk food? Do you spend hours on autopilot in front of the TV? Do you deny yourself sleep? Do you drink or take drugs to avoid dealing with your emotional needs?

As a spiritual healer you will be called upon to help people sort out their problems. Unless you have identified the imbalances manifesting within your own being, you cannot be effective in helping bring about balance in another.

A Healer's training begins within

Before we explore each chakra individually, let's take note any areas that you have identified for improvement. As we discuss each chakra, see if you can find where this imbalance is located within your energy field.

Also note any new imbalances you may identify and which chakra it relates to as we work through the chakra system.

Initial Throat Chakra Activation – The Human Energy Field

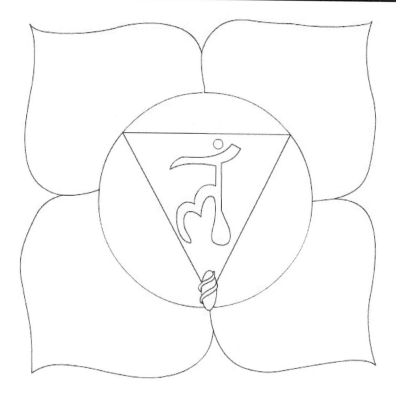

Root[2]

- ✓ Sanskrit Name/Meaning – Muladhara/Root
- ✓ Location - Base of spine, coccygeal plexus, legs, feet, large intestine
- ✓ Main Issue - Survival
- ✓ Goals - Stability, grounding, right livelihood, physical health, security
- ✓ Malfunction - Obesity, hemorrhoids, constipation, sciatica, eating disorders, knee troubles, bone disorders, frequent illness in general, frequent fears, inability to focus, "spaciness", inability to be still
- ✓ Color – Red
- ✓ Right – to have, to exist
- ✓ Planet – Mars

The Root Chakra manifests at the base of the spine and is your connection with mother earth. This chakra matures from birth to age seven, and operates similarly to an umbilical cord.

If someone has a blockage in this area, it most likely originated during their early childhood, and affects their feeling that they have a right to have their basic needs met, like clothing, food, shelter, etc.

---

[2] Chakra reference information compiled from but not exclusive to correspondence tables in The Sevenfold Journey, by Anodea Judith & Selene Vega, The Crossing Press, 1995.

Many root chakra issues manifest in the physical body as colon problems, male sexual dysfunction, impotence, frigidity, external genital disfigurement or disease, weak muscles, and leg problems.

If you think about child development at this age, this is a time when we are very "now" oriented. Everything is "me first"! If a child doesn't get his needs filled immediately, he will cry until the issue is resolved. A child of this age doesn't understand any reason why the parent cannot provide for his needs. This is the mentality of the root chakra.

If basic human needs are not fulfilled at this age blockages occur that will manifest as disconnectedness with the universe. As in an unwillingness to ground, insecurity, lack mentality, fear of being noticed, and disconnection to mother and/or Goddess.

List any issues, obstacles, or health problems that may be root chakra oriented:

_____
_____
_____
_____
_____
_____
_____
_____
_____
_____

Initial Throat Chakra Activation – The Human Energy Field

Sacral

- ✓ Sanskrit Name/Meaning – Svadhisthana/Sweetness
- ✓ Location - Right behind belly button
- ✓ Main Issue - Sexuality, emotions, sacredness, self awareness
- ✓ Goals - Fluidity of movement, pleasure, connecting with others
- ✓ Malfunction - Stiffness, sexual addiction or sexual anorexia, isolation, emotional instability or numbness, inability to connect with others, fear of being alone, infertility, diseased or dysfunctional reproductive organs.
- ✓ Color - Orange
- ✓ Right - To create, to feel, to be sacred
- ✓ Planet – Venus

The Sacral Chakra manifests behind the belly button and energetically establishes or blocks your connection with other people. This chakra matures from age seven to age fourteen, and operates similarly to an umbilical cord but in relation to others and not the earth.

Psychic Vampirism is a result of utilizing this connection to suck energy from others. Some people use this chakra to ground, but unintentionally are grounding through other people and not the earth. This energetic is a learned behavior, usually passed on through the family, and should be corrected. Those grounding in this way do not intend harm. However, this is harmful to those to whom they are connected. Energy connections involving the sacral chakra must be an equal give and take for a healthy balance to occur.

If someone has a blockage in this area, it most likely originated during his or her late childhood and preteen years. Affecting his or her feelings of worthiness to be sacred, respected, loved, appreciated, and accepted.

Many sacred chakra issues manifest in the physical body as gynecological problems, female sexual dysfunction, infertility, diabetes, and STD's.

If you think about child development at this age, this is a time when we are very attached to our friends, and how well we get along with others. Popularity is a focus, and how others react to you is extremely important. If a child receives the message that she doesn't fit in at this age, it creates a trauma that cannot be shrugged off like it would have been at an earlier age. Children of this age are learning social rules, and become very self-critical if they feel that they do not measure up to societies expectations.

If social needs are not fulfilled at this age, blockages occur that will manifest as disconnectedness with the community and humanity. This could possibly manifest as intentional cruelty to animals and other children, in adults we see an unwillingness to connect, commit, form relationships, open up to others, or function within society.

List any issues, obstacles, or health problems that may be sacral chakra oriented:

_____
_____
_____
_____
_____
_____

Initial Throat Chakra Activation – The Human Energy Field

Will

- Sanskrit Name/Meaning – Manipura/Lustrous Gem
- Location - Solar Plexus, between naval and base of sternum
- Main Issue - Power, energy, shields, manifesting, courage
- Goals - Vitality, strength of will, sense of purpose, effectiveness
- Malfunction - Excessive: Inability to slow down, need to be in control, rage addiction, stomach ulcers, excessive weight around middle. Deficient: Timidity, low energy or chronic fatigue, addiction to stimulating substances, submissive approach to life, digestive troubles.
- Color - Yellow
- Right - to act, to shield
- Planet – Sun

The Will Chakra manifests at the solar plexus and is the expression of your will. This chakra matures from ages fourteen to twenty one, and is responsible for manifesting your physical world.

If someone has a blockage in this area, it most likely originated during his teens, and impedes his ability to manifest his true purpose.

Many will chakra issues manifest in the physical body as digestive disorders, addictions, back problems, and obesity.

This is the time that you rebel against the structure of your parents and begin relating to the world on your own terms, establishing your own ideas, identity and sense of self. This is a very selfish, domineering, forceful, willful, reckless time of your life. This age group feels immortal, and often generates much destruction and chaos. The Will Chakra has grand, immature, and oftentimes unrealistic dreams of changing the world for the better, and lacks the resources to bring these dreams into reality. This can be the most difficult stage of development. Inexperience limits the ability to make good decisions, and an over-inflated sense of self, limits the willingness to listen to anyone else's advice.

The Will Chakra makes you feel immortal, capable, and unstoppable. It's driven, motivated, focused, and very projective. Just as the Sun controls the boundaries of the universe, and it's gravitational pull regulates where the planets in the sky orbit around it. The Will Chakra is the center of life, desire, intent, and gusto. It knows what it wants, and knows how to get it. It manifests and protects your reality and everything in it.

Blockages that manifest at this time will directly affect the ability to operate within acceptable societal limits. It will inhibit the ability to manifest abundance, realize potential, handle finances, manage personal power, or maintain a sense of basic joy and happiness.

List any issues, obstacles, or health problems that may be will chakra oriented:

_____
_____
_____
_____
_____
_____
_____
_____

Heart

- Sanskrit Name/Meaning – Anahata/Unstruck
- Location – Heart
- Main Issue - Love, self love, relationships
- Goals - Balance in relationships and with self, compassion, self acceptance
- Malfunction - Excessive: Codependent care taking, clinging behaviors. Deficient: Isolation, low self-esteem, collapsed chest, shallow breathing, melancholy.
- Color - Green
- Right - to love, to be loved, love of self
- Planet – Moon

The Heart Chakra manifests in the same location as the physical heart and facilitates your ability to give and receive love. This chakra matures from age twenty-one to age twenty-eight. The heart chakra operates in a pumping motion; receiving energy, processing it, and sending it back out.

If someone has a blockage in this area, it most likely originated during his or her early adulthood, and affects the ability to function as a member of a team or partnership, or to trust and depend on others.

Many heart chakra issues manifest in the physical body as heart disease, depression, circulatory disorders, respiratory disorders, and problems with the arms and hands.

This is the time in one's life when lasting partnerships are formed. People want to marry, establish families, and commit to long-term employment, etc. There is a strong desire to become part of something greater.

If love and trust was violated in a way that caused trauma, the blockage will manifest at this time in an inability to identify as a team member. Fearing the loss of identity will present itself as an inappropriate need to dominate or control the team, disrupting the balance of equality. This most usually manifests in love relationships, since employment situations do not require emotional input. However, these issues will manifest in any partnership where one is emotionally invested, including employment.

One of the most common problems in the heart chakra is the inability to receive love. Giving love is usually easier, as we all want to love and be loved. But, feelings of unworthiness cause us to not want to impose on another. This manifests as the inability to accept compliments, receive gifts, or be publicly acknowledged for accomplishments. Sometimes we see this blockage when people don't want to let others "do" for them. Simple things like getting someone a drink, fixing their plate, or rubbing their feet will make someone with this blockage uncomfortable or feel that they are imposing, rather than accepting the care-taking of another as an expression of love or friendship.

List any issues, obstacles, or health problems that may be heart chakra oriented:

_____
_____
_____
_____
_____
_____
_____
_____

Initial Throat Chakra Activation – The Human Energy Field

Throat

- ✓ Sanskrit Name/Meaning – Visuddha/Purification
- ✓ Location - Throat
- ✓ Main Issue - communication, self expression, examining, details, classifying, recording, cleansing
- ✓ Goals - self expression, harmony with others, creativity, good communication, resonance with self and others, forgiveness
- ✓ Malfunction - Inability to express truth, blocked creativity, sore throats, stiff shoulders, tight necks
- ✓ Color - Bright Blue
- ✓ Right - to speak, to speak the truth, to have clarity
- ✓ Planet – Mercury

The Throat Chakra manifests at the throat and affects your ability to express yourself. This chakra matures from age twenty-eight to thirty-five, and operates as a detailing factor or an extension of your will and sacral chakra. Your will expresses a need, your throat chakra defines the details of how that need is filled. Your sacral chakra expresses creativity. Your throat chakra defines the creativity, and communicates it to others through art, music, and other forms of creative expression.

Blockages in this area affect the ability to clearly define your needs and desires to yourself, or anyone else. Blockages originate from being stressed, rushed, criticized or verbally abused.

Many throat chakra issues manifest in the physical body as thyroid imbalance, endocrine issues, stuttering, or an inability to speak clearly and distinctly.

At this time in your life you should be fully into manifesting who you truly are. You are filling in the details of your world, acquiring property, shaping the minds of your children, expressing leadership within your family, and establishing respect for yourself in your community and social circles.

This is the time in your life when you are no longer a product of your environment. You are the environment. You feel motivated to take the direction of your life into your own hands, stop looking to blame others, and make something out of yourself. This is the time that people will begin to actively start solving problems. People will begin active self-improvement programs, seek therapy, join a gym, or go on health kicks.

At this time you still have the passion and drive of youth, but are gaining the experience of adulthood. People will often choose this time to go back and fix things that were left undone, change careers, or go back to school. It's the time when the priority is to be true to yourself, and become that which you are destined to become.

Blockages manifest as an inability to speak your truth, and self-betrayal. This can be a very constructive as you begin building your dreams. But, it can also be a destructive time if you suddenly realize you have made many incorrect decisions in the path, and must tear down the old to make way for the new.

List any issues, obstacles, or health problems that may be throat chakra oriented:

_____
_____
_____
_____
_____
_____

Initial Throat Chakra Activation – The Human Energy Field

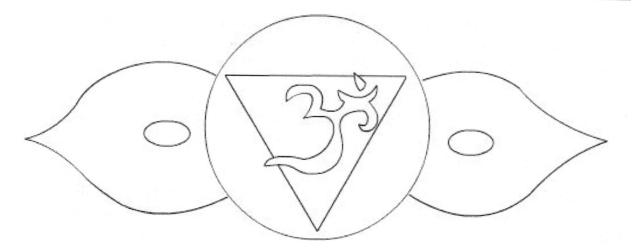

Third Eye

- ✓ Sanskrit Name/Meaning – Anji/to know, to perceive, to command
- ✓ Location - Center of Forehead, behind eyebrows
- ✓ Main Issue - visual perception, imagination, discernment, clairvoyance
- ✓ Goals - Ability to perceive patterns, to "see"
- ✓ Malfunction - Headaches, nightmares, hallucinations, poor visual perception, sinus problems
- ✓ Color - Indigo
- ✓ Right - to see, to see the truth
- ✓ Planet – Saturn

The Third Eye Chakra manifests at the front of the forehead and determines order, space, time, customs, traditions, and ethics. This chakra matures from age thirty-five to age forty-two, and operates similarly to a computer-networking hub, connecting you to universal information.

If someone has a blockage in this area, it occurs from being overly controlled, judged, wrongfully condemned, tortured, ritually humiliated, and mentally abused. Many third eye chakra issues manifest in the physical body as headaches, inefficient eyesight, chronic sinus problems, paranoia, and many mental illnesses.

This is the time in your life when you have most of your personal affairs in order and you begin turning a critical eye on those around you, who have yet to do the same. You begin to feel your age, and can become "set in your ways".

Traditions, customs, family groups, and progeny become important as you begin to cross over into mature adulthood and realize your mortality. Your legacy to the world becomes a focus.

You will begin to see life from a more realistic viewpoint, and have more courage to "call it like you see it". You begin to establish new boundaries within existing parameters, and demand more respect from those with whom you interact.

Your over-all health may take a considerable downward spiral if you are moving further and further away from fulfilling your contract. Arthritis may present itself during this stage, if you are inflexible in your ideas and approach to life. This is the time when most people have their "mid-life" crisis.

New Age texts attribute the third eye with enlightenment, and psychic abilities. Yet, ancient Hindu texts speak nothing of these things in association with the third-eye. While this chakra can be extremely perceptive, it can also result in judgmental attitudes as well. It is dangerous to focus on opening the third eye to the exclusion of the other chakras as it will give you insight, but without the balance and maturity of the other chakras it will make you critical, and disapproving about others. Elevating your personal ideals and conclusions, while condemning the thoughts and values of others.

Intuition is generated within the whole being, as it blends with spirit. I've often found that those who seek power focus on the third-eye, as it does enhance knowledge of the activities of others. But, it also makes them paranoid, and negative towards others, while at the same time overly inflating the importance of their ideas and sense of self. Remember, balance is always the key. It's a spiral path. Learn the basics, and then expand on them as you walk the wheel of the year. Enlightenment comes with patience and wisdom.

List any issues, obstacles, or health problems that may be third-eye chakra oriented:

_____
_____
_____
_____
_____
_____
_____

Initial Throat Chakra Activation – The Human Energy Field

Crown

- ✓ Sanskrit Name/Meaning – Sahasrara/Thousandfold
- ✓ Location - top of head, cerebral cortex
- ✓ Main Issue - Understanding
- ✓ Goals - Expanded Consciousness, to tune into and surrender to divine consciousness.
- ✓ Malfunction - Deficiencies: depression, alienation, confusion, boredom, apathy, inability to learn or comprehend. Excessive: overly intellectual, heady, spacey
- ✓ Color - Violet or White
- ✓ Planet - Jupiter
- ✓ Right - to know, to connect with your divine truth
- ✓ Planet – Jupiter

The Crown Chakra manifests at the top of the head and is your connection with Father God. This chakra matures from age forty-two to forty-nine, and operates similarly to a fountain, sending your energy up and out into the universe, or allowing universal love to shower down on you. This is the time that you realize your deepest connection with God.

If someone has a blockage in this area, it affects their ability to lead, take charge, accomplish goals, or connect with God. Blockages here can significantly reduce your ability to connect with your divine truth and limit your ability to be self-directed, self-motivated, or take initiative.

Most people will feel the call to spirit, and will begin, renew, or deepen their devotion and commitment to their spiritual path at this time. Many find renewal in the comfort of religion and spiritual communities. Priorities are very much in perspective now. Most physical needs are taken care of, children are grown and no longer need nurturing, leaving a great deal of personal time available.

Now is the time to manifest yourself as the wise sage, sharing your vast lifetime of knowledge and experience with the world, putting your energies into your grandchildren, and helping your children become successful in achieving their goals. You are reaping the rewards of your life's work. You have the time and resources available to help those walking the path behind you. By clearing their road ahead for them, you become a stepping stone that helps them achieve more in the next generation.

This is also a time when we can withdraw, feel unimportant, and used up, becoming a closed minded, shallow, shadow of who we could have been. There is still plenty of living left to do, and now is the best time to manifest your purpose. You are fully mature, and your generation is running the world at this time.

Many crown chakra issues manifest in the physical body as Alzheimer's, Parkinson's, and many geriatric diseases. This is the time where you can either be a great source of wisdom and strength to the younger generation, or become so detached from the zeal of youth that people purposefully avoid sharing anything with you that will promote deep conversation.

List any issues, obstacles, or health problems that may be crown chakra oriented:

_____
_____
_____
_____
_____

Seeing Auras

Color Me Blue!

An aura is the measurable field of colored light that makes up your energy field or spirit. It can be seen as different colors in various shades of light and dark.

Each color vibration is a manifestation of a particular type of energy. You can diagnose imbalances within the aura by interpreting what the colors mean and comparing what you perceive to what a healthy aura should look like.

To see your aura use a black or white background, put your hands together in front of you, fingertips touching, palms horizontal, facing straight towards you. You will only be able to touch the two longest fingertips together if you are doing this correctly. Slowly move your fingers apart. You will be able to faintly see threads of auric light between the fingers.

Don't try too hard, relax your eyes, ground, breathe deeply, move your fingers back and forth, and gently ask to see the energy. It is a very gentle, wispy energy.

You can also see the energy of trees if you look out at a tree line, against a blue sky you can see a faint green hue hovering above the treetops. This is an aura.

You already see auras. Your eyes filter out the information, because at some point early in childhood you deemed it as interference, while you were trying to ground your spirit firmly in your physical body. You will be able to see them again as you work with color, and reinstate the information as important and necessary.

Be patient with yourself. It will happen in time, and you will get better with practice. Often I perceive the colors more than physically 'see' them. Allow your intuition to tell you what your eyes will not.

Colors

Colors invoke different energies. We process these energies as emotional responses. The following exercise allows you to explore each color and record the response you have to it. Space has been provided for you too record your experiences.

You are provided with a small symbol that is related to the color. As you color the symbol choose various shades of the color you are exploring. Breathe deeply, relax your eyes, and gaze at the color. Notice how it makes you feel. What images does it bring to mind? You may need to close your eyes and visualize the color. Does it make you comfortable, nervous, impatient, energetic or what? Spend a couple of minutes with each color, and record your experiences while looking at the color. (Colored slides are provided for you on the Internet at www.WISEseminary.com if you prefer not to use the color therapy technique.)

Each symbol will be followed with a few paragraphs giving you basic color therapy properties. Please be assured that your impressions will not be wrong, but they may give you much insight about blockages, or imbalances.

This is an excellent way to really find out what messages your chakras are sending you, and give you an opportunity to balance it. Note which chakra the colors correspond to if you need to clear any imbalances at the end of this exercise.

Awakening Spirit – Freshman Course – www.WISESeminary.com

Red- Root[3]

Red is the right to exist, and the right to have. Red is balance in relation to the physical form. It is survival issues such as; actions, stability, security, self-preservation,

Red is instinctual, grounded, primal, spontaneous, active, courageous.

Red relates the body at the base of the spine. It affects the adrenals, kidneys, bladder, colon, spinal column and legs.

It is the color of beginnings, and new life.

What emotions, thoughts, or feelings came to mind, while you were working with the color red?

_____

_____

_____

_____

_____

---

[3] Color information compiled from Color Therapy Eyewear Eye chart, PO Box 3001, Diamond Springs, CA 95619

Initial Throat Chakra Activation – Seeing Auras

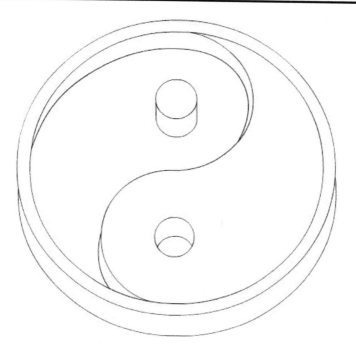

Orange – Sacral

Orange is the right to create, and the right to feel. Orange balance is sensuality, passion, procreation, vitality, optimism, enthusiasm, hospitable, family oriented, tolerant, works harmoniously with others.

Orange relates the body at the sacrum, genitals, hips and lower back. It affects the reproductive organs, prostrate, gonads, knees and spleen.

It is the color of sexuality, sensuality, consciousness, and sacredness. It is change, movement, polarity, desire, lust, pleasure, intimacy and socialization. It is self-worth, and belongingness.

What emotions, thoughts, or feelings came to mind, while you were working with the color Orange?

_____
_____
_____
_____
_____

Yellow – Will

Yellow is the right to manifest, the right to do, and the right to give. Yellow balance is logic, humor, efficiency, organized, warm, radiant, flexible, self-aware, self-control, laughter, will/personal power, inner harmony, and generosity.

Yellow relates the body at the solar plexus, pancreas, liver, gall bladder, stomach, and nervous system.

It is the color of authority, control, and power. It is the ability to metabolize energy and transform it into something you need.

What emotions, thoughts, or feelings came to mind, while you were working with the color yellow?

___

___

___

___

___

Initial Throat Chakra Activation – Seeing Auras

Green – Heart

Green is the right to love, to give love, receive love, have self-love, and the right to give and receive. Green balance is unconditional love, forgiveness, compassion, generosity, openness, contentment, sincerity, understanding, acceptance, harmony, nurturing, assertive, healing loss, and letting go. Green relates the body at the heart, thymus, circulatory system, arms, hands, and lungs.

It is the color of emotions, reactions, and receiving. It is the ability to open up your self and receive the blessings of the universe. It is the ability to balance what you give with what you receive, what you take with what you leave for others, and what you keep with what you return. It is abundance, prosperity, self-confidence, personal value, self-love and vulnerability.

What emotions, thoughts, or feelings came to mind, while you were working with the color green?

_____
_____
_____
_____
_____

Blue – Throat

Blue is the right to speak the truth. Blue balance is freedom to express verbally & artistically. It is integrity, clear communication, honesty, loyalty, peace, reliability, gentleness, kindness, commitment, truth, creativity, and endurance.

Blue relates the body at the neck, throat, mouth, jaw, thymus, and voice box.

It is the color of expression, sending, and sharing. It is the ability to express to the world, creatively, artistically, honestly. It is commitment, honor, reliability and trust. It is dependable, gentle, and steadfast.

What emotions, thoughts, or feelings came to mind, while you were working with the color blue?

_____
_____
_____
_____
_____

Initial Throat Chakra Activation – Seeing Auras

Purple – Third Eye

Indigo is the right to see the truth. Indigo balance is inspiration, intuition, focus, concentration, insight, imagination, devotion, clear thinking, peace of mind, ease in the now.

Indigo relates the body at the Forehead, Pituitary Gland, Left Eye, Sinus, Nose, Ears, and Eyes.

It is the color of dreams, memory, visualization, clairvoyance, intuition, order, reward after hard work, patterns, beauty, royalty, light and darkness, and absorption.

What emotions, thoughts, or feelings came to mind, while you were working with the color indigo?

_____
_____
_____
_____
_____
_____
_____

Awakening Spirit – Freshman Course – www.WISESeminary.com

Violet/White- Crown

Violet is the right to connect with divine truth, the right to know. It manifests in the body at the Top of the head, cerebral cortex, right eye, and central nervous system.

Violet is universal love, spiritual motivation, understanding, open to divine wisdom, idealism, selfless service, physical, mental, and spiritual harmony, unity.

What emotions, thoughts, or feelings came to mind, while you were working with the color violet?

_____
_____
_____
_____
_____
_____

Clearing Imbalances

If you have found an imbalance in your chakras, you need to clear it. Close your eyes and visualize the color, breathe it into the appropriate chakra. Hold it for as long as you are comfortable. As you release the breath, blow it away from you and notice the color. Don't try to control the exhaled color, allow it to be whatever it is. Continue the process until the exhaled color is the same as the inhaled color. This method can be used anytime to restore balance.

Practice

Utilize the techniques that you have learned with your fingertips, and the trees, and apply that to other living things. Look at someone in front of a white or black background and gaze into the area around his body. You should first see wispy tendrils of energy, sparkles or bubbles. You may not "see" the colors the way you "think" you should. Try not to think too hard, or be too attached to how this process develops.

Use your intuition, imagination, and patience with this technique. Don't expect to suddenly see rainbows shooting out of people. Your ability will develop over time with continued practice. However, faith in your self, and validation will help you make fast progress. One of the ways you can get validation is to share your perceptions with the person, whose aura you are reading, and listen to their feedback. Be patient and nice to yourself, while you are learning these techniques. Focusing on your progress will be infinitely more helpful than beating yourself up because you are not doing as well as you think you should.

Be warned, you shouldn't read someone's aura without permission, and sometimes people will purposefully mislead you, because they don't want you to know their hidden secrets. When being confronted with negative feedback, consider the source. At this stage in your development, you are still learning to trust your intuition. Inaccurate or evasive feedback could cause you to inappropriately mistrust your intuition. Be careful whom you choose to help you with this exercise, and be sure that they will be honest with you. But, also be careful revealing things that would make someone want to lie to protect themselves or their secrets. An important rule of thumb for any psychic is NEVER tell someone something bad is going to happen, or is happening to them. ALWAYS find a positive, non-threatening way to communicate potentially destructive information.

*Take note that metal eyeglass frames interfere with the ability to see auras.

The Nature of Dis-ease

Color Me Blue!

Disease is a state of not being at ease. Dis-ease is a state of discomfort, and imbalance. Remove the discomfort, restore balance, and the disease will no longer exist. Healing the body requires being able to detect imbalance and restore balance. It begins with identifying the root cause of the dis-ease or imbalance. This requires talent,

Initial Throat Chakra Activation – Certification Requirements

intuition, unconditional love, and a good bit of education.

Medical science can mask symptoms that are the result of dis-ease. But, healing comes from within. There is no medicine that can heal a fragmented chakra. Medicine is useful because it can help you stop focusing on the discomfort while you find the cause. But it is not a long-term solution.

**Note - As a spiritual healer, no matter how you personally feel about Western Medicine, it is not appropriate to encourage anyone to avoid professional medical treatment. It is true that Western Medicine is lacking in many ways, but by itself so is Spiritual Healing. It takes variety and a combination of many things to bring balance.

Negative and Positive Energy Dynamics

Negative energy is receptive. Positive energy is projective. Negative does not mean bad. It means receptive. Negative energy that is used appropriately is very good. The nighttime is negative energy. It is a receptive time of rest and renewal. Another good example can be found the last time you let someone hug you. You were using your receptive energy appropriately.

Positive doesn't mean good. It means projective. Think of the last time someone was trying to impose his or her will on you, such as a pushy salesman, or a thief. That's projective energy being used inappropriately. Get the idea of good and bad out of your head. Good and bad are labels you choose to put on things based on your perceptions. There is no good and bad energy. All energy is divine.

As a human we often fluctuate between receptive or projective states of being, however a healthy aura is made of predominately positive energy. Positive energy denotes growth, sustained energy, health and motion. Negative energy promotes drawing in, slowing down, less energy, and rest.

Pockets of negative energy in your field are like black holes in space. They are sucking pockets of energy that drain you of the positive energy in your field. Depending on how big, concentrated, and dark they are will determine on how sick you become.

It is appropriate to send positive energy into any dark spot in an aura. As long as your intention is to fill the negative space with positive energy you will be doing a good thing. *Do not try to pull anything out of someone's field or take it into yourself!*

Pulling something out of someone's field is ok to do, IF you are experienced and know how to get rid of it. If you are new to moving energy, you *will* absorb it into yourself and take on the illness. Taking someone else's illness or negativity into you is just never a good idea. There is no one that is experienced enough to do that. It's harmful to yourself and the client.

Spirit moving into physical

Dis-ease comes from a negative force being internalized or caught up in your energy field. The negative pocket attaches itself and begins to feed off your positive energy. If left alone, over time it will grow and eventually affect the physical body.

Negative energy manifests in many different ways. Anything from an unkind word to physical abuse can manifest negatively inside the body. When someone does or says something that you do not resonate with you can choose to own it, or ground it. You choose to own it when you let it invoke a response in you.

An example of this is when someone calls you a name. If someone calls you a dumb blonde, but you are a Red head with a PHD, you will probably laugh it off. But if someone calls you a dumb blonde and you *are* blonde, and quit school in the 9th grade, you may get offended. It doesn't matter what the intent of the other person was, it only matters how you receive it. If you choose to believe it, you internalize it, and it causes you pain, sorrow, or some other negativity.

If you think about language it will tell you a lot about how energy works. As I said before, you already see energy, but your brain deems it interference and doesn't register the information to the conscious mind. So we discuss things in the same way as we energetically see them. 'Let's sit down and work this out', means we have internalized some negative energy, and both of us need to talk about it, until we feed it enough positive energy that it is transformed.

Holding on to a grudge is another way of saying you're holding on to a negative thought form. It will make you sick if you keep feeding it negative energy. It is vital to your health to forgive and find a way to work through the conflicts and traumas that you face along the path.

Healing energy

Healing energy is universal. You can feel the energy coming from your hands by briskly rubbing your palms together. Then relax your hands, cup them (as if you were holding a ball) and move them apart and closer together. You will feel a big ball of energy forming in your hands. It will feel like a slight pressure pushing your hands outward. When you push your hands in, you will feel the density of the energy. It's very subtle. You may also feel tingling, or warmth. Try it, and see if you can see it as well.

Initial Throat Chakra Activation – Certification Requirements

Ground, and pull energy up from the earth. See if you can make the energy between your palms stronger. Can you make it change colors? Experiment and see what fun things you can do with it.

You can use this energy to heal. Make sure you are grounded and pulling energy up from the earth sending it through your hands. Direct it to fill negative space with positive energy.

Do's and Don'ts of Healing

Don't use your own energy to heal someone, channel energy from the earth or from above through you and into the recipient.

Don't take another persons energy into yours during a healing. Either way this is vampirism, and it will harm both you and the person you are working on.

Don't try to heal someone whom you actively do not like. If you can't find love for the person you can't heal them.

Do talk. Moving energy will often encourage someone to discuss the issue, and this, in itself, will help to heal it.

Don't try too hard. Connect with spirit, state your intent, and ask for guidance, then let spirit work through you. Try to be an open channel, like a drinking straw.

Don't try to control the energy. It is divine and knows what to do. Get out of the way.

Don't try to heal someone to impress them with your power. That's abuse of spiritual knowledge and self-serving. That road leads to the left-handed path[4].

Do heal people because you love them, and want them to be well.

NEVER use your intuition to project negative thoughts into someone's head. Recognize the power of suggestion, and people's ability to affect their own reality based on what they believe.

Always state suggestions for solutions to any situations you may see in the positive. "Be very careful when driving, observe all the traffic laws, and make sure you wear your seat belt. Don't drive drunk, or get in the car with anyone driving drunk." is

---

[4] The left-handed path is considered the path of negativity. It is self-serving, and not in concert with divine will. The left-handed terminology is associated with widdershins energy, and is not to be confused with someone, who writes with his or her left hand.

a lot better than saying, "I see you getting into a very bad wreck with a drunk driver."

Assignment
The Human Energy Field

Familiarize yourself with the chakras and colors. This is important to healing. You will refer to this information time and time again.

Seeing Auras

This is going to come with time and practice, practice, practice. Focus on noticing how much information you pick up off someone from your intuition. Where does this information come from? Which part of your body gets the information?

Spend as much time as you can this week practicing on reading people and seeing their auras. ***This is nosey! You are doing this for a class assignment, and your own benefit. Do not make this your Standard Operating Procedure. It is best to keep your observations to yourself. Don't go up and start telling people what you perceive. It freaks them out.

The Nature of Disease

Practice moving energy this week. Experiment with this technique and practice using it every chance you get. Experiment with animals and humans (please get permission first) and see what kind of feedback you get.

Certification Requirements

Record your answers to the Chakra and Color exercises.

Journal Entries

How do you feel about healing yourself, and healing others? What do you tell yourself while you are trying to heal yourself? Notice any self-defeating dialogue you may be having with your self, and explore the validity of it. Give your negative voices a chance to speak their mind to see if there is anything you can learn from them. Negative energy feeds on fear and shadow, getting it out into the light robs it of its power, and it's ability to control you.

6
Initial Third Eye Chakra Activation
Reincarnation, Space, Time & The Eternal Now

Indigo

Color Me Indigo!

Reincarnation, usually thought of in terms of absolute death of the physical body, and rebirth into a new physical body, is the cycle of rebirth, and transformation. It is a method, through which we face our challenges and find balance, of moving through our illusions to our divine joy. It is a cycle of growth and evolution that we see in varying levels of intensity everywhere in our world, everyday.

We reincarnate to learn lessons and grow. We are constantly learning. It may be new tasks at work, interacting in relationships, creating abundance for our selves, or expanding our mind through incorporating new ideas.

Some of these lessons are simple and we assimilate them easily. Some lessons are intense and we may experience struggle, sorrow, or even pain as we work through the experience. But, once the lesson is integrated, we are reborn into new awareness. This rebirth is reincarnation on a smaller scale.

These are the small circles that we walk everyday. We wake up in the morning and face the challenges that await us. At the end of the day, hopefully we can look back upon our day and be satisfied with what we have accomplished. This is a cycle of reincarnation. Death and rebirth are not exclusive to the physical body. You die and are reborn many times throughout your life.

When you learn a lesson that completely changes you, you have experienced a reincarnation. If you wake up to a new awareness that changes everything about your world, then you have reincarnated into the same body. When this experience occurs sometimes people feel motivated to take a new name that reflects who they have become and honors the transition they have made.

Before incarnating, we are in the astral realm. We are disembodied spirits. We have access to the knowledge of the universe. We know what work needs to be done, and make decisions on what we need to accomplish to learn, grow, and evolve. When we have assembled these details, we then have to find a way to provide the right conditions to insure that certain opportunities, circumstances, situations, and environments are provided to bring about the desires results.

Fate

The science that provides these appropriate conditions is Astrology. Astrology is the science by which fate is manifested. Fate is what you receive from the universe. Gaia, our earth, supports certain lessons, and conditions for inhabitants upon this earth. Each planet within our solar system, the constellations or star groups that provide the path that the planets follow, and the planetary houses, all affect the fate of a physical vehicle into which a soul incarnates.

It works much like a software program. So much of a planet in such and such sign, in this house or the other provides a very complex system that determines:

- ✓ How smart you are,
- ✓ What talents you possess,
- ✓ What character flaws you must overcome,
- ✓ How you deal with money,
- ✓ How you communicate,
- ✓ How many children you will have,
- ✓ How your parents will treat you,
- ✓ Your motivations,
- ✓ Your temper,
- ✓ And many other influences.

When you are born, the soul enters the body at the time the baby takes its first breath. This is the moment the Astrological influences are cast in place. This is why it's so important to know the time of birth when casting a natal chart. To the educated Astrologer, a Natal Chart will tell you a person's fate, what they will be faced with in a current incarnation.

Freedom of Choice

Freedom of choice gives us the right to respond to our fate in many different ways. There are jokes about what each sign does in a given situation, like trick or treating or changing a light bulb. A Gemini will think, react, and behave predictably differently than a Leo or a Scorpio. But, all people are free to respond to each situation in any way they deem appropriate, regardless of their zodiac sign.

If you are a Capricorn, you will probably be reserved, skeptical, and concerned about your reputation. However, based on what you have learned over the course of your life, you may have developed a more optimistic view, invest energy into being more outgoing, and spend more time helping people than dwelling on what they think of you. Using the tenacity of Capricorn, to help you overcome the lessons of the sign is how you gain temperance, balance in all things.

Space, Time & The Eternal Now

Space and Time are an illusion to help you process information. We are living in the eternal now. This reality is only a physical manifestation of your design based on what energy you choose to receive, and send out.

There is so much information available for you to process on a day-to-day basis. We humans can only process a certain amount of information based on how much brain capacity we have developed. Scientists know that we can use twice as much of our brain now as we did 100 years ago, but still we are only using about 10%. If we could consciously use our entire brain, we would be fully merged with Goddess.

This means that we have to pick and choose what we are going to process through our consciousness, and exclude that for which we don't have room. I often express my reasons for avoiding certain information by explaining that I currently have developed only so many megabytes, and I don't want those junk files on my hard drive, nor can I anticipate how those files will interface with currently running programs.

I know I have only so much time to comprehend thousands of lifetimes of information. I don't want to waste my time on exposing myself to sensationalism, negativity, or fear-based thinking.

I try to shield myself from anything from image defining advertisements, to negatively motivated individuals. If it doesn't enhance my world in some way, I don't give it my attention. This doesn't mean I avoid problems. I just don't subject myself to those things that rob me of positive energy. I devote my time to focusing on the things and people that bring love and harmony to my world.

Another way of stating this is to say that I monitor my incoming and outgoing energy. I choose what to process and weed out anything that is inherently giving off negativity. If I do not bring in negativity, it is very hard to send out negativity. As I continue on this process I can see how it has changed my reality and my perspective into a happier, more fulfilled and focused existence.

Of course, I am less informed on current events, but I see no reason to expose myself to the reality of someone drowning their children in a bathtub. That is horrific to me. I don't want to know about it. In my reality, mothers love their children unconditionally. If I hold this to be true, and allow no evidence to the contrary into my reality, then I become convinced that this is true for everyone. If I know that this is true it changes my world, and everyone else's world that I affect. If enough people are affected and choose to create that same truth, it will become true for everyone, and motherhood will be instinctually and inherently changed for everyone in the world.

This is alchemy. This is how you change the world. You choose the correct ingredients to create what you want. You change your way of thinking, by monitoring your thoughts, and what you allow into your reality until it gains enough power and validation to move from faith to fact.

You cannot change the world by fighting or trying to convince someone else that they are wrong. You cannot affect positive change by pushing an agenda. You must change your world from the inside out, and let others catch on by your example.

Space and Time

Space and Time are like height and depth; they give your world perspective to process the information. Space lines up 'people, places, and things'. Time lines up 'events'.

Because of the limitations of what we can process we have to line up information in time and space. The physical universe cannot exist on the head of a pin in our minds. Two physical objects cannot occupy the same area, so we have to spread stuff out over space. This begins with the space your physical body occupies, and begins to build from there. You have your body, the clothes on your body, the chair in which your body sits, the floor, the walls, etc.

It's the same way with time only in a different direction. The events that occur are all happening simultaneously, much quicker than we perceive. But, our brain slows them down so that we can process them. If your entire day lasted within the space of one hour, you wouldn't have time to interact with it.

Because we have to interact with each other and share information, we have developed things like maps and clocks so that time and space will seem to be the same for everyone. But still, if you are waiting on a bus, 15 minutes will seem a whole lot longer than if you are engaged in stimulating conversation with some friends. Time is relative.

How does this knowledge affect you? When you come to understand the illusion of space and time, you can transcend it. You have to know the rules in order to bend them. You have to be able to understand what the rules are and why they exist before you can choose to suspend them.

Once you understand that space doesn't exist, you don't need to run over to your friend's house to do a healing on her. You can affect her energy field from where you are, because in reality you are in the same place. If you are late for an appointment, you can alter how long it takes for you to get there, or how bad traffic is based on your understanding and mastery of time and space.

But, even more importantly, you can access past and future information, travel through space and time, and not be limited by the physical perceptions in pursuit of spiritual knowledge.

The ability to travel through space and time is very valuable in discovering our Past Lives. Astral Journeying is not a Shamanic secret; it's available to everyone who understands the illusion of time and space.

Living in the Now

One of the biggest problems with teaching Past Life Regression is that many people are so unhappy with who they are right now, that they will gladly romanticize about past lives living in a castle or palace, having servants, money, power, fame, glory, whatever. This is dangerous, because it can lead you off your path, as you desire to escape from this life by remembering more and more details of a previous existence.

This is the perfect lifetime for you, there is no place better for you to be than right here, right now. The Goddess has protected you and guided you to this place. Find the beauty and wonder of your life now, right now. If you are not appreciated, not respected, not wealthy, not powerful, not loved, or not whatever you think you need to be, it would be the same in any other place. If you are creating the lack here, you would recreate the lack there.

If you are unhappy for any reason, you have become unhappy based on choices you have made. You have acted on your choices and received the consequences of those actions. If you want something else, you have to do something different.

The purpose of doing past life regression or therapy is to recover lessons and knowledge from those times to help you progress now. It's fun work, but it's not just for fun. It has a purpose. Treat it as a sacred journey, and utilize the information for spiritual growth.

Past Life Regression

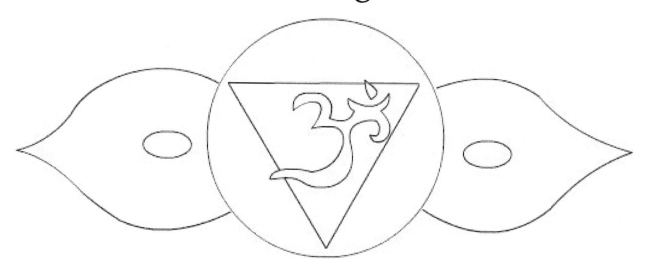

Color Me Indigo!

When you first start working with remembering past life information, it will feel like you are making it up. Many people discount very powerful and relevant memories because they have been taught to ignore or dismiss their imagination.

Imagination comes from the root word Image. Your ability to access and utilize the power of your imagination is very valuable in magical studies. Take every opportunity to exercise and strengthen your imagination. It is the key to the door that unlocks the power of visualization. Anything you can envision, you can manifest.

Get your journal. There is a series of questions coming up. Please record your answers. You will want them later. Answer the questions with the *very first* answer that comes to mind. You don't have to rush through it, but don't over think it, either. Just put down your first impression. You can do this exercise as many times as you like. If you don't know the answer, don't dwell on it. Move on to the next question.

- ✓ If you had a Past Life, where would you have lived?
- ✓ What time period would that have been?
- ✓ Would you have been male or female?
- ✓ What kind of house would have you live in?
- ✓ What kind of clothes would you have worn?
- ✓ What kind of work did you do?
- ✓ What would your name have been?
- ✓ Who would have been in that lifetime with you?
- ✓ Would you have had any children?

Recording and Validating

Recording the information from above, and then exploring that lifetime in meditation is very helpful. You already have a basis from which to go on. Now, all you have to do is close your eyes, begin deep breathing, and focus on that person, in those situations. Information will come to you. It will start out in fragmented memories. But, with practice, you can remember entire lifetimes this way.

Validating historical information is another good way to explore past lives. I have memories of historical people, and it is very exciting to read accounts of these lives. It also gives me confirmation that my path and goals are similar to those persons, and I gain a greater understanding of who I am today, based on the information I have received from my past.

Of course, being able to historically validate your past lives is not something that is overly common to the beginner. I had been digging through my past lives for many years before I found three that I could historically validate. This is why recording the information for future reference is so important. Do not dismiss something just because you can't validate it, yet.

Meditation

Meditation is a key tool to accessing past life information. Sending your intent to explore a past life, and then being able to achieve a meditative state so that the information can be delivered to you is imperative. If you have not yet begun a practice of daily prayer and meditation, now is the time to begin.

Time Line Meditation

Close your eyes and breathe deeply. See a timeline appear before you. Scan back in time across the timeline, until you find a time period that draws your attention. Allow yourself to drop down into your life at that time in history. Allow yourself to imagine who you would have been, and do not discount information because you think you may be making it up.

Specific Interest Meditation

If you are particularly drawn to a certain time period, country, architecture, historical figure, myth, or any other specific thing from the past, close your eyes, and go into a meditative state. Focus on that person, place or thing of specific interest to you, and allow yourself to receive information about how that interest was generated. It may be that you were that person, or you were married to that person, or the child of…. etc. It could be that antique watch that you found was your mothers in a past life, or that really interesting place that you visited on your vacation was a place you had lived before.

Journeying

Open up your mind to the possibilities, and let your mind journey. You can travel through time and space. You can visit other worlds or other dimensions of reality. There is no limit to where you can go. Always ground first, remember to practice in a protected space, shield yourself, and always focus on how the information received helps you overcome the challenges and achieve the goals of *this* lifetime.

Happy travels.

Awakening Spirit – Freshman Course – www.WISEseminary.com

Utilizing Past Life Information

Color Me Indigo!

Past Life Therapy is a very powerful and effective method of healing. It serves to help remove blockages and traumas from past lives that are currently affecting this life in inappropriate ways. It also can help you understand your soul's purpose when you uncover the pattern of your past lives.

Often times we will over-react, or have a gut reaction that we can't explain. We just won't like something, or we will be really drawn to it. We have nothing to base our feelings on and have searched for the lesson, but can't find it. This may be a past life blockage. In Past Life Therapy, the healer goes into your energy field, isolates and removes the blockage, and amazingly you will no longer have the inappropriate reaction.

Removing these types of blockages accelerates your spiritual growth, because you no longer are encumbered with so much baggage that you can't sort out. This frees you to focus on forward movement, instead of keeping you tied to the emotional traumas of the past.

Initial Third Eye Chakra Activation – Utilizing Past Life Information

How often can you do this work?

Healings of this type need a minimum of three days to process. If you are in crisis, three day cycles will be very helpful, anything more than that will cause more and more stuff to surface, and put the patient in more emotional turmoil than necessary, possibly creating new traumas in the process.

It is optimum to get a healing every seven days. This becomes a process that your body, mind, and spirit becomes use to, and you will subconsciously begin to work with the healing process to maximize efficiency.

The next cycle is a twenty-one day cycle. After the seven-day cycle has been maintained for an extended period, the patient's need may decrease. Then it is time to move to a twenty-one day cycle to stay in balance. Anything outside a twenty-one day cycle becomes too sporadic for your being to consider a habit, and you will not get optimum, cooperative results.

What are the dangers of past life regression?

People will have a tendency to want to go into detail and romanticize about certain lifetimes. This is not healthy. Spiritual paths can be completely detoured in this way. This is what I refer to as a Unicorn. Unicorns are magical creatures that lure the innocent away from danger. If you are not ready for more in-depth information, you can become enamored by a Unicorn, and lose your focus. Unicorns often disguise themselves in a romanticized Past Life Regression.

Be careful to remember the reason you are doing the work, and focus on achieving the goals of *this* lifetime. If you uncover a lifetime where you had similar goals that's great, you may have found an interesting parallel, but don't try to relive it.

Don't make life changing decisions based solely on a past life regression. Don't entertain a crush on someone, break up a marriage, have a baby, quit your job, or anything else that will disrupt your balance. Keep the information in its place, as a tool to heal and understand yourself.

Lightbodies

People often want to discount past life information because they receive information about being a historical person. They cannot resolve the conflict of the fact that 150+ different people may believe they were Cleopatra or whoever, in a past life. It is difficult to understand why many people can claim to remember the same lifetime.

There is a reason why multiple people can remember being certain historical figures. The explanation begins with understanding Lightbodies.

We have discussed as above, so below, and how everything that is true in the macrocosm is true in the microcosm. We know that the Goddess is manifest in each person, that our souls are pieces of her. If the Goddess has many souls that make up the whole of who she is, then that concept must also be true on the microcosmic level. Our soul must also have individual sections that group together to make a whole.

Lightbodies are individual spiritual imprints of the goddess, sort of like individual cells. Lightbodies group together to make up a soul. The more lessons a soul learns in a lifetime, the more lightbodies make up that soul. This enables faster spiritual evolution, as more lightbodies can be exposed to needed lessons in order to grow and learn. Lightbodies also impart the strength and power to learn those lessons.

Prior to the astrological attunement of August 11, 1999, light bodies seemed to be fixed within a person, and could not come and go at will unless certain numerological or astrological conditions existed. Now lightbodies seem to be more mutable, and can come and go from person to person as necessary for spiritual progression. This is important, because it can facilitate faster spiritual evolution in those who pursue the knowledge now, than was available in previous times.

Historical figures become historical because they do something that is great, or important, and beyond the expectations of what we consider normal everyday existence. These people are learning powerful lessons. Just as many people will go to see a great Spiritual Leader, Politician, Movie Star, etc; more light bodies will congregate in a physical vehicle that is experiencing more of life.

Lightbodies are attracted to spiritual growth. Therefore, lightbodies will be more attracted to someone who is utilizing their time exploring positive pursuits, and experiencing life to its fullest.

Lightbodies are free to separate and regroup in different combinations with other light bodies. If Cleopatra had one hundred lightbodies, then each of those lightbodies would have a whole and complete memory of her life. Those lightbodies may group together in many different ways with other light bodies over the centuries, and any person doing past life therapy will more rapidly recall a lifetime as Cleopatra than one as a farmer, because her life lessons were more notable. This is similar to your current life memories. Remembering your prom, or wedding, or 16th birthday is more notable than remembering what you had for dinner this date 10 years ago.

Therefore, many people remembering the lessons Cleopatra learned, not only reinforces the theory of Reincarnation, it also validates the concept that we are all microcosmic expressions of Goddess.

You can sometimes notice that you have had a major shift in lightbodies, when you experience a sudden change of personal preferences. If you used to love chocolate, but suddenly prefer vanilla, or you were devoutly Catholic, but suddenly wake up one day and decide to explore Buddhism.

People often experience this phenomenon through spiritual studies. They wake up one morning and no longer want to eat meat, or can't drink caffeine, or suddenly they just can't stand their job. This indicates that there has been a change in lightbodies, and that interesting and possibly challenging times are ahead.

The relationship to the physical vehicle and lightbodies is symbiotic. Lightbodies evolve and grow from learning lessons through the physical experience. The physical vehicle gets more strength and power, and is capable of handling great challenges as more and more lightbodies integrate with the soul.

Someone, who is not seeking greater challenges, will not have as many lightbodies. But, they will not need the extra abilities and benefits that a larger number of lightbodies will bestow, either.

Like everything, it's a balance.

Assignment

List 5 places from History where you would have liked to live, or where you think you have lived before.

_____
_____
_____
_____
_____

List 5 Occupations, Hobbies, or Crafts that you are already good at without training (such as I can cut hair, but I have never been trained to cut hair.)

_____
_____
_____
_____
_____

List 5 ancient cultures with which you strongly identify.

_____
_____
_____
_____
_____

List 5 people, whom you feel you have always known.

_____
_____
_____
_____
_____

Initial Third Eye Chakra Activation – Certification Requirements

Certification Requirement

Record two past life journeys.

Journal Entries

This week devote your spiritual time to past life journeying. Record all the information, especially details, that you discover from your journeys and meditations. After each meditation, record how this information relates to your current life if you can. If you notice parallels from one journey to another note those parallels.

Remember if you get stuck; start asking yourself the following questions:

If you had a Past Life, where would you have lived?
What time period would that have been?
Would you have been male or female?
What kind of house would have you live in?
What kind of clothes would you have worn?
What kind of work did you do?
What would your name have been?
Who would have been in that lifetime with you?
Would you have had any children?

7
Initial Crown Chakra Activation
The Wheel of the Year

Violet

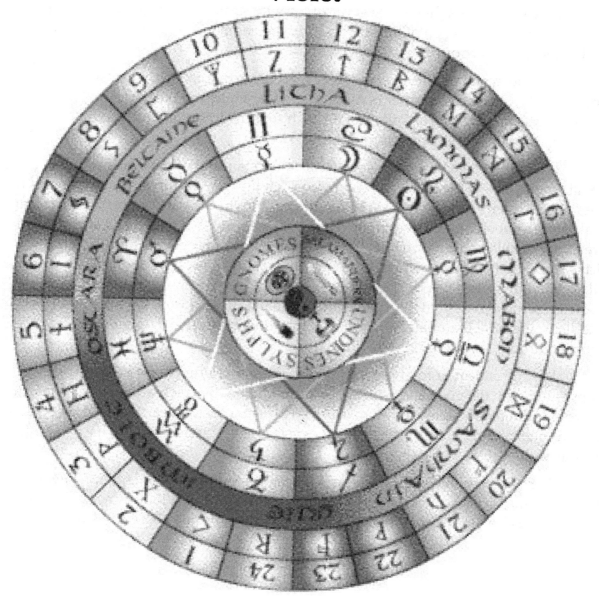

The Sabbats are our Holy Days on the Calendar, with respect to the Sun. They honor the God, and the cycle of birth, death, and transformation of our physical, active, projective God-selves. Through attuning ourselves with the cycles of the seasons, we can transform ourselves from a self-centered, separate identity, to a connected, balanced, entity that lives in harmony with the universe.

Sabbats have layers and layers of depth, and can be celebrated in many different ways. There are myths and psychodramas to celebrate the passing seasons from the prospective of the Gods, and there are personal, inner stirrings that can be ritualized to tune you into the deep, rhythmic movements of the energies of each season.

Any method that helps you connect with the Gods, the energy of the Wheel of the Year, or the procession of the sun through the zodiac, will attune you with these cycles and deepen your connection with spirit.

As Priests and Priestesses, we feel called to harmonize with our Divine Mother and Father so that we can better serve Her and Her children. We gather to "turn the wheel" at the appropriate astrological dates, honor the forces in our lives, and celebrate the oneness and diversity of spirit.

It is sometimes difficult to get a clear understanding of the sabbats and what they are all about, due to the many different interpretations by cultures, who expressed this energy in so many different ways. Getting caught up in the various forms of celebration makes it a difficult puzzle to unravel. I have often found that the rituals of the ancients aren't applicable to life as we live it today. Most of us don't have a herd of cattle to drive through the Beltaine fires. We get our meat at the grocery store, if we eat meat at all. Yet, the mysteries behind the rituals still apply, even if the cultural differences sometimes make the symbology obscure. While the rituals of the ancients make excellent reference material. I never found true understanding and connection to the sabbats through trying to recreate these rites.

It is my endeavor to give continuity to the seasons, and express what is happening with the gods and within you individually. By celebrating the seasons, my understanding of these mysteries matures with each passing year. I expect you will find your understanding of this ever-changing cycle will spiral deeper with each passing year as well.

The Wheel of the Year is a circle, with no beginning and no ending, however, it is easiest for me to begin at Imbolc, as we have finished our previous incarnation and are just past the depth of dark at this time. New awareness is just about to stir into being.

Imbolc – 15° Aquarius
On or about February 2

Waxing light, height of winter, Season of Air
Concerned with establishing a sense of social, mental, and intellectual self-worth
Validation through peers, family groups, social structures
Setting goals for the future
Planting the Seeds that will grow and be harvested

Imbolc – Correspondences

Colors – Red, White
Gods – Holly King, Sleeping Goddess Aspect
Direction – North East
Red Candles
Magic – Bringing back the Light, planning for future

We are at this time in the dark half of the year, not yet born. In the great cycle of reincarnation we are still in the depth of death. We are resting, waiting, contemplating, projecting, and dreaming. We have realized the benefits of merging with the All, and have come to miss our individuality. We begin to assess what we need to continue our evolutionary process and begin setting goals for the future year. Now is the time for serious inner reflection and goal setting. New calendars are purchased, and the ritual of transferring birthdays and important events should be accompanied with detailed goal setting for the coming year.

Imbolc is held at 15° Aquarius. This is the height of winter. Aquarius is fixed air. It is the time of clear, rational thinking, when the energy of the earth is focused on growth, personal and societal evolution. During the time of Aquarius you are most capable of making sound, informed, intelligent decisions based on your future. You have a unique perspective, where you are somewhat detached from what's going on, and able to look at things from more of a bird's eye perspective. You have the ability to see where you have been and project where you need to go and what needs to be accomplished at this time, better than any other time of the year. You can use the energy of Aquarius to help you relate to society as a whole, and understand and work to fulfill your unique purpose.[5]

A wasted year represents a wasted incarnation. Setting New Year resolutions that you have no intentions of keeping is self-defeating and create negative karma. Your personal growth cycle begins here, and what you accomplish over the next year's cycle will make a difference in your mortality, and karma. Great magic should be worked at

---

[5] Astrology, Understanding the Birth Chart, Kevin Burk, Llewellyn Publications, 2001

this time to prepare the seeds you plant. Carefully contemplate what you wish to accomplish in the coming year, through consulting astrologers, spiritual advisors, and dedicated prayer and meditation. How will you use the next year of your life? Will it be the wasted incarnation of an aimless wanderer, or the conscious effort of an advanced soul?

This sabbat is to celebrate the return of the light and is known as the "Feast of the Waxing Light". It is a time of thoughtfulness, and of finding the light that resides within us. The sun's glowing rays begin generating life beneath the soil. Now is the time for the planting of seeds.

Imbolc means "in the belly". At Imbolc we are literally in the belly of the Goddess. In her womb we are waiting to be reborn into our new incarnation of this yearly cycle. Just as we plan our purpose before we are born, we plan our purpose during this part of the year, setting new ideas into motion, and preparing the foundation for our ideas to grow and flourish.

If there is any left over pain or sorrow from the previous year we should let go of it now. Get rid of the old, and make way for the new. A good ritual for doing this is spring-cleaning. Getting rid of the dirt, and throwing out (or giving away) anything that is no longer useful to us, is a great way to physically demonstrate that you are cleaning out the dirt and junk that has collected in your soul as well. Remember to focus on releasing old hurts while you are doing the cleaning, even verbalizing the anger (speaking out loud what you have not let yourself say) if necessary. Do what ever it takes to release (forgive, and forget) anything you are holding onto at this time. You don't want to reincarnate into the new year with a bunch of negative karma to work out.

By the date of Imbolc, we should have our goals and plans for the future clearly set. They should be written down on an astrological chart wheel, a calendar, in a journal, a Book of Shadows, or somewhere that you will have them with you for the coming year. These goals should be presented to the God and Goddess for fertilization. There are many different ways you can do this. Writing them down and planting them under some seeds in your garden is a good way to do it.

Another personal ritual would include planting the seeds of a corresponding herb for each goal you set. I recommend you set a goal for each sign of the zodiac. This is a short easy concise list for your convenience.

♈ Aries – Personal goals, goals about the self, something selfish, just for you.

♉ Taurus – Financial and beauty goals, what you wish to spend your money on.

♊ Gemini – Social goals, goals that involve your interaction with peers and community.

♋ Cancer – Mother and Home goals, how you wish to care for your home, or family, or that involve your relationship to your mother.

♌Leo – Creativity, and Children goals, what you wish to accomplish for your children, or any creative projects that you wish to complete.

♍Virgo – Health or Service (Career) goals, what you wish to accomplish in the way of better health, or service to the universe both charitable and professional.

♎Libra – Partner goals, what you desire to accomplish in regards to your mate or other important partnership.

♏Scorpio – Spiritual goals, what you desire in regards to your spiritual time. Could also be about inheritance or other people's money.

♐Sagittarius – Philosophy, higher education, travel goals, going to college, continued studies or family vacations are planned here.

♑Capricorn – Public reputation and Father goals, goals involving politics, activism, personal pride and appearance, and relationship issues with your father.

♒Aquarius – Wishes and Friends, this is a free wish, something that you don't really expect to get, but want anyway, can also be where you work on issues involving close friends.

♓Pisces – Sleep, dreams, intuition, illusion, here you can plan your nighttime routine, if you have sleep issues, plan dream journals, or dream magic, or access other information that is not currently known to you.

If you need further instruction for each goal, research the zodiac signs for more detailed information. If this is too involved, you can instead set a goal for each element, or use any system that works for you.

Pick a magical herb that represents each one of your goals, and plant the seeds with the intent to incorporate that energy into your life. You may want to plant your seeds in pots and keep them inside until the weather gets warm enough to transplant them to your garden. How well your seeds grow over the coming months will tell you how well your goals are developing.

Imbolc Ritual – The Womb of Goddess

Preparation:

- ✓ Prepare a place to simulate the womb of the Goddess. Fill it with blankets and pillows, yummy foods, good drink, nice music, magical tools. Everything you need for the evening. A fire would be a nice cozy touch. This could be on the bed in your bedroom, a pallet on the floor, a blanket draped over a table, or a place by the hearth. Where ever you feel warm, cozy, safe, nurtured and comfortable.

- ✓ Prepare comfort foods: chocolate, cheese and crackers, hot toddies, and warm herbal tea, yummy snacks that make you feel good and cared about.
- ✓ Have your goals already written out for your records.
- ✓ 12 pieces of paper and pens (you may want to use colored paper and ink that correspond to each goal, or make special herbal paper, layer the intent as you desire)
- ✓ 12 envelops
- ✓ A new calendar
- ✓ Seeds
- ✓ Drums or other music
- ✓ Chalice
- ✓ 12 red Votives (if desired)

Cast, Call, Invoke if desired

Get snuggly and comfortable in the womb, and pour yourself a Chalice full of wine, potion, tea, or whatever you wish to drink. State your first goal over the Chalice starting with Aries, and why this is an important goal for you. Drink to your goal, and pass the Chalice deosil. Write your goal on the paper, with any notes attached, such as which seeds you are planting to represent your goal, and any sacred symbols that will lend power to your spell.

Put the paper in the envelope, add the seeds that you are going to plant for that goal. Label it with the sign for Aries ♈ and then place it under the first red candle. (You may also want to charge the candle, draw a pentacle and other appropriate symbols on each candle.) Light the candle, and envision yourself with the goal accomplished. Leave the candle to burn out completely over the seeds. After ritual, plant the seeds in your garden (or in pots).

If you want to plant the seeds during the ritual, be sure to have 12 pots handy and label them accordingly. Place the paper on which you have written your goal, in the bottom of the pot. Plant the seeds and light the candle (place the candle in the pot over the planted seed or in front of it, whichever you prefer).

When the Chalice circles around to you again, state your Taurus goal. Repeat the process for each goal until you have completed all twelve.

Be sure to eat, and pass food around during the ritual. Be relaxed, and playful. This is about being nurtured, and supported, not about pomp and ceremony. Play music, drum and chant if you want to raise power. Spend time bonding with your spiritual family and dreaming about the future. The womb is such a cozy place. You may want to spend all night in it.

When all the goals are finished, note important dates on your calendar for the coming year. Decide which days you will celebrate the coming moons, and sabbats. If you plan any group outings, gatherings, or birthday celebrations, make those plans now as well.

Remember to release the quarters when you are finished.

Ostara – 1° Aries
On or about March 21

Light and Dark in Balance, Beginning of Spring, Season of Earth
Function is to begin, pioneer, and create new life.
Desires to break away from the collective consciousness, & form the illusion of a separate individual identity.
Birthed into the new cycle, motivated, ready for action

Ostara – Correspondences

Colors – White and Pastels
Gods – Oak King, Maiden Aspect
Direction – East
Decorated Eggs (red for fertility), Rabbits
Magic – Birth, Creativity

Ostara is the time of Birth. It is a time of balance, when light and dark are equal. This is the time when you are ready to burst forth from the womb of the Goddess and begin this year's incarnation.

Celebrated at 1° Aries, Ostara is the first day of spring, bringing warmth, prosperity, and new life into the earth. Aries is fundamentally focused on being first. It is ruled by Mars and carries with it the enthusiastic, blind courage you would associate with the limitless energy of an inexhaustible toddler. As spring fever courses through your veins, encouraging you to get out into the world and kick your heels up, you will notice that your newly sprouting seeds from Imbolc will take off on a growing spurt at this time.

Young plants need nurturing and watering. A personal ritual celebrating this time of year would include tending to these tender shoots. Thin out any crowded plants, as they won't grow well if they have to fight for space. It's better to have one or two healthy plants that you can harvest in the fall, than 15 spindly ones that never really produce anything. If you planted your seeds in pots indoors, now is the time to bring them out and plant them in the ground.

This is the time to celebrate the crossing over into the light half of the year. The usual Easter celebrations that you are used to are applicable now. Bunnies represent the fertility, and the birthing of the season. The colored eggs represent new births.

Ostara is the time for Persephone to emerge from the Underworld, bringing spring, and life back to the earth. Everyone returns from the Underworld with her and is reborn through the eastern portal. It is the beginning of this year's incarnation, your birth into the physical realm of this year. Reading or reenacting the myth of

Initial Crown Chakra Activation - The Wheel of the Year - Ostara

Persephone's return is appropriate at this time. As is opening your outdoor temple, preparing your garden with new herbs, trees, vegetables, and flowers, and moving your Goddess statue to an outside alter decorated with all the symbols of spring.

Divination Spell

Red Eggs symbolize the power of rebirth. An appropriate divination spell for this turn in the wheel would be to insert a folded piece of paper, with a rune or some divinatory message written upon it, into a plastic egg. Or boil the eggs and incorporate decorations on the surface, with symbols or messages that represent the forces that will be blessing your journey this year. While the eggs are being hidden, tell a story about what messages or omens the eggs will bring, so that the egg-hunters will search with the intent of finding that answer.

Personal rituals to do this season include switching out seasonal wardrobes, and buying new seasonal clothes. Just as you would be putting on a new body in the larger cycle of life, now is the time to take care of pampering your physical form with a makeover, or a new hairdo. Start a diet, join a gym, begin a dance or yoga class, anything that helps you get in touch with your body. Of course, you want to keep your yearly goal in mind, and make sure that you are preparing your body in harmony with your long-term goals.

In the interest of renewing pagan drama, this is a beautiful mystery play that tells the story of Persephone's abduction and return.

Queen of the Underworld

A Story of Hades and Persephone

by Lady Belladonna, WolfSong, and Kestral

* Dramatis Personae *

- Aphrodite: Goddess of Beauty and Love, Cupid's mother
- Cupid: God of Love and Desire, Aphrodite's son
- Demeter: Goddess of the Grain, Persephone's mother
- Hades: God of the Underworld
- Haldis: Chorus, that which pertains to the soul, or spiritual concerns
- Hannan: Chorus, that which pertains the body, or emotional aspects
- Hermes: Messenger of the Gods
- Justus: Chorus, that which pertains to the mind, or intellectual pursuits

- Persephone: Goddess of the Underworld, Demeter's daughter
- Styx: The River of Hate
- Zeus: King of Gods
- Stage left is the Underworld. Stage right is Mt. Olympus. Middle stage is earth.

[Demeter and Persephone are dancing, with quiet expressions of love and joy for each other, making the relationship of mother and daughter clear with their banter. Jumping to show how the crops are to grow, they cross the stage at random keeping downstage, middle. Upstage right stands Aphrodite, watches them in deep thought and with consideration. Chorus enters upstage left.]

Justus: Long ago, lost in the yesterdays and tomorrows of time, Aphrodite, Goddess of Beauty and Love, called upon her messenger and son, Cupid.

[Cupid enters upstage left and crosses to his mother. They appear to converse.]

Haldis: Aphrodite's power reached into the hearts of men, and tinkered with the desires of the Gods. But thus far Hades, God of the underworld and his entire domain were untouched by her hand. She feared that Artemis and Athena plotted to be rid of her.

[Hades enter stage left, and watches Persephone and Demeter also.]

Hannan: However, where there is no love, there is no joy; the loss of which would be very great in all worlds. She asked her son to strike deeply with his unerring arrows into the heart of the Dark God, to be befallen to the chaste daughter of the Goddess Demeter, who was called Persephone.

Haldis: This served the purpose of Aphrodite two-fold in that Demeter's daughter would not follow the chaste and loveless ways of Artemis and Athena, and to reach her hand into the underworld through Hades.

Venus: Cupid, Cupid, Come. My dear, my Cupid, my life, my heart, my will, and my right hand, go take your flashing arrows, which never, never fail and fire them straightly into the heart of that dark god to whom the last part of our triple empire came. My dear, your power sways the will of Zeus, Gods of the sea, and even he who rules them. Why spare the lands of Tartarus alone? Why not increase my empire and yours? One third of the whole world shall be your prize. In heaven we've lost prestige and with loss comes the failure of love itself. Surely you know Artemis and Athena are aligned against me. If we allow her, Demeter's daughter will remain a virgin till she dies. For even now her models are the moonlit deities. If you respect the kingdom, which we share, marry the youthful goddess to her uncle.[6]

Justus: Cupid flew, straight and true as his arrow.

[Hades takes pause a moment to watch Demeter and Persephone dancing, showing the crops how high to grow. Cupid sneaks up behind him and just as Persephone comes close to Hades. He shoots him unerringly. A transformation overtakes Hades and he then regards Persephone in a besotted way. He circles them, only having eyes for her, as Cupid rejoins his mother.]

Hannan: [speaking as Hades circles Demeter and Persephone] The arrow felled the heart of the Dark God, King of the Underworld in ways he did not understand, but the joy he felt for Persephone was never again to be undone.

[Satisfied, Cupid and Aphrodite exit Upstage right.]

Justus: He knew that at last it had come to pass that he was in love. He felt for his brother's daughter something he never thought he would. The King had found his Queen, and he knew then what he had to do.

Haldis: Persephone was the daughter of Demeter, who he knew would never give her daughter up. Yet she was also the daughter of Zeus, King of the Gods, his very brother.

[Demeter and Persephone dance off stage downstage left. Leaving Hades center stage looking after Persephone with longing. He suddenly grins.]

[Zeus enters upstage left, scattering the chorus to upstage right and approaches Hades.]

Zeus: [After a time] Hail Brother.

Hades: [Distracted] Hail. [Notices he is joined] Ah! Zeus, my King, my brother, my *dearest* friend. Rejoice with me! At long last my heart has awakened, and I have found my Queen!

Zeus: My brother, this is wonderful news. I am pleased to hear it. Who has quickened your heart and brought such joy to your life?

Hades: Ah yes, about that. You see she is a fair maiden.

Zeus: Yes?

---

[6] The Metamorphosis, Ovid, First Signet Classic Printing, The Viking Press, 1958, p. 150

Hades: Quite beautiful.

Zeus: Go on.

Hades: I am so happy to finally have found my one true love, the dearest of my heart, the joy of my days… and nights, the apple of my eye, the song of my soul, the light of my life, the answer to my question, the….

Zeus: [Amused but with a hint of warning] **Hades**! Who is it?

Hades: [Formally] May I have the hand of your daughter in marriage?

Zeus: Which one?

Hades: [Mutters]

Zeus: What?

Hades: Persephone.

[Zeus looks thoughtful and worried at the same time. Expressions ranging from abject terror, to amusement, to deep consideration as Chorus interjects echoing his thoughts.]

Justus: Demeter will never forgive him if he says yes.

Hannan: Hades is in love. How can he deny his own brother happiness and joy? Of course he will say yes.

Justus: He won't. Demeter… (interrupted by Haldis)

Haldis: He could just not answer. [Zeus appears to like this idea]

Zeus: My brother, my heart is glad you have found love at long last. However, I cannot give [Hades' face falls] *or* withhold my consent. [Stares at him a long time until Hades 'gets it' and starts grinning. They nod to each other having reached an understanding]

[Zeus joins the chorus, as Hades rewards the audience with an award-winning smile. Demeter and Persephone return downstage left, this time dancing in circles with each other. Zeus shoos the chorus away from him, and they join the dancing with Demeter and Persephone as Hades watches. They circle Demeter and Persephone widdershins, Persephone and Demeter weave in and out of the circle deosil, thinking it a game and laughing. Persephone tires and pauses to catch her breath as the circle closes in on

Demeter. The Chorus joins hands, breaking Demeter off from her daughter. Demeter claps and laughs with them as they get closer and closer, distracting her. Hades gives his brother a significant look, and snatches Persephone, running off with her stage right. Her cry is not heard above the laughter of the Chorus. Zeus looks away conveniently, watching the dance]

[One by one the Chorus takes their previous place, waving goodbye and giggling among one another, until at last Demeter looks around for her daughter]

Demeter: Persephone?

[She crosses the stage in a panic searching for her daughter. Calling her name to no avail, the Chorus and Zeus reflecting lost looks as well, unable to help her]

Demeter: Where is my daughter? Give her to me. The inhabitants of earth have betrayed me. They have rejected the gift of grain. I shall let neither seed nor root, nor leaf, nor bud, nor stem, nor flower, nor fruit bear bloom until my daughter is returned. The earth shall be as barren and infertile as my heart. [Tosses down her crown]

[She wanders back and forth, becoming slower, older, and more haggard looking as she does. Eventually covered in black, bent and veiled, she crosses to upper stage left, and crumples to a kneel, crying.]

Justus: For a year, Demeter refused to allow grain to grow, or the land to flourish.

Hannan: Her heart was so broken at the loss of her daughter.

Haldis: Yet none would tell her where her daughter was.

Demeter: I have searched and searched for my daughter to no avail. Will someone's heart not feel compassion for a mother's wound? I must know. Please. Where is my child? I do not know if she is even alive or dead.

[Demeter kneels at the river Styx. Zeus lifts a hand to her and appears as if he would go to her, but before he can Styx rises up to speak to Demeter.]

Styx: Good Demeter, your daughter is alive, and yet she is not. She lives among the dead. She is the bride of Hades. Hades dropped this among my waters as they crossed over into the underworld. [Hands her the girdle]

Demeter: I mourn the loss of her each moment she is away, both day and night. I mourn the absence of her embrace. Sweet Persephone, my daughter, my joy, my love. Let the darkness and grief within my heart reflect upon the land.

[Styx returns to the river.]

[All is silent for a time. Then Hermes enters stage left, regarding Demeter. He crosses to Zeus, and addresses him.]

Hermes: Zeus! Oh Great Ruler of the Universe, the people are cold and hungry. They will soon starve to death. The land is barren, and no crops will grow. Winter has been long and harsh. If you don't do something soon, there will be no one left to worship you.

Zeus: Send a message to Hades. Tell him if he doesn't give back Persephone we are all undone. Demeter is refusing to allow the earth to bring forth food. The people of earth will soon starve. We must appease Demeter.

[Hermes bows as Zeus crosses to Demeter. Zeus helps her to rise. Hermes turns as Hades joins him stage right.]

Hermes: Zeus sends word, my Lord.

Hades: Does he, indeed. Let's have it then.

Hermes: Demeter is enraged over the disappearance of her daughter and has caused the earth to be barren. The people of the earth are suffering and will soon expire. She has learned of the abduction and demands that Zeus force you to return the maiden to Her. You must release the maiden to her Mother.

Hades: Hmmm, tell Zeus we'll be right there.

[Hermes crosses to Demeter and Zeus, but dares not interrupt them, the Chorus kneels as Persephone joins her husband, and she administers to them as Queen of the Underworld. Hades and Persephone speak stage right, while Zeus and Demeter speak stage left]

Demeter: [To Zeus] I plead to you as a mother, of the case of your child, and my own.

Hades: [To Persephone] Your mother misses you.

Persephone: I miss my mother too.

Demeter: [To Zeus] If you disown the mother, then allow the child in her distress to move a father's soul.

Hades: [To Persephone] You seem to be finding your way around in my kingdom.

Persephone: Your people are lost. They have no direction, no hope, no opportunity for growth, happiness, or rebirth.

Hades: They seem to have found hope in you.

Persephone: Yes, they do seem to find happiness in my presence.

Hades: As do we all, my Queen.

Zeus: [To Demeter] She is our daughter, the token of our love and ours to cherish. But we should give the proper name to the facts: She has received the gift of love, unhurt. Nor will he harm us as a son-in-law. And if he has no other merits, then it's no disgrace to marry my own brother. For all he needs is your good will, my dear. His great fault is: he does not hold my place. His lot is to rule over the Underworld.

Persephone: [To Hades] You do not understand. I am my mother's daughter. She will die without me. Everything she does she does for me. I cannot abandon her to your dark kingdom. Even if I wanted to...

Hades: I have offered you everything I have. Do you not find happiness here?

Persephone: I have found purpose.

Demeter: [To Zeus] I can endure the knowing she was raped if he who has her shall return her to me. Surely any child of yours should never take a thief for her true husband.

Zeus: If your will is fixed on her divorce, the girl shall rise to heaven on one condition. That is, if no food touched her lips in Tartarus. For this is law commanded by the Fates.

[Demeter and Zeus embrace]

Hades: [To Persephone] You have yet to eat, and I cannot take you back to your mother without providing you with nourishment. She will think I have mistreated you, and want revenge. I do not want your heart to be heavy, for I do love you. Here, eat, and then I shall take you to your mother.

[Persephone eats a few seeds absent-mindedly as Hades takes her for a stroll among the dead. Hermes enters stage left, crosses and joins Demeter and Zeus stage right, they appear to converse.]

Hades: I have given you my heart, my kingdom, my love, all I have to offer. Never has the face of another moved my heart to love. You have restored hope and happiness to my kingdom. You will be sorely missed. My Queen, look upon the face of your husband. Have you not found love?

Persephone: [With longing and indecision] I... I... I don't know.

Demeter: This is ridiculous! I have waited long enough. Is he coming or not?!?

[Hermes, Zeus and Demeter look at each other as Hermes spreads his hands, unsure.]

Zeus: Hades, Lord of the Underworld, I do summon, stir, and call the forth.

[Hades and Persephone approach Zeus and Demeter. Demeter and Persephone run together and embrace, Demeter fussing over Persephone checking to see if she's unharmed.]

Demeter: Tell me child, did you eat anything?

Persephone: No mother, my heart was so forlorn, I had no appetite.

Hades: Yes, it's true. She refused to dine, or drink. Oh, except for today.

Persephone: [Innocently] Yes, I ate today, after hearing the joyous news that I would be returned.

Demeter: I have been tricked again! I will not return to Olympus. I will not release my hold upon the land. My daughter cannot be returned and I will make every living creature feel my wrath.

Hades: But, I love her. She is my Queen. She has brought my kingdom renewal. She has touched the hearts of the miserable and forlorn. [Gestures to the Chorus] Surely you, gracious Mother of All, understand the sacred power of love. Bless this union, Demeter. Allow your daughter to become the Goddess She is destined to be.

Demeter: I cannot suffer my daughter to be Goddess of the Shades. She was born to shine, like me. She was born Goddess of Spring, to bring renewal and rebirth to the earth and all upon it. How can I stand by and allow her to be doomed to darkness forever?

Persephone: Do I not have any say of my own destiny? You speak of me as if I were a child with no will of my own. Does no one care what I say? I am no longer the Kore, little maiden of spring, but a woman full grown, a Queen and a Goddess. Death has transformed me, and I have found my own renewal. I have found purpose and strength. I have reached within and found love.

Zeus: Very well, Persephone. What say you?

[Persephone looks confused again as she looks back and forth between her mother and husband.]

Persephone: I don't know. I cannot choose. My heart would betray me with either choice. My mother, and the land that I love, brings me such happiness. I rejoice at the blooming flowers and the ripening fruit. The people of earth need me at my mother's side. But in my husband's kingdom, Tartarus, the souls cry out to me. My presence there brings hope, and relieves the misery of those who have passed from this world. I cannot leave them to suffer eternally. The dead need renewal as much as the living.

Zeus: Very well, it is left to me. As Persephone ate six seeds of the sacred pomegranate, her journey shall bring renewal to both worlds. She shall spend the light half of the year with her mother, bringing renewal to the earth and it's many inhabitants. She shall spend the dark half of the year with her husband, as Queen of the Underworld, and shall bring healing and renewal to the souls of Tartarus. And in this, so shall she grace the cycle of death and rebirth. Shall the souls of the living soon reunite with her, and the souls of the dead return with her at spring. So Mote it be!

Demeter: So Mote it be!

Hades: So Mote it be!

[Persephone links hands with her husband and mother while Zeus take Demeter's other hand. The Chorus rises, dancing about them deosil]

Chorus: All Hail Persephone, Queen of the Dead, Goddess of Spring. Hail Persephone, Hail Persephone.

Persephone: May the mysteries of Love and Death bring rebirth to us all.

Ostara Ritual – The Return of Persephone

Seedlings from Imbolc, and/or any other varieties you wish to plant.
12 dyed eggs with runes or other divinatory message
Set up altars with symbols of spring. Clean up all the debris that has collected from winter. Prepare garden temple for spring and summer use.
Have a Goddess statue to move from indoor altar to outdoor altar or temple.
Make an entrance at the east quarter

Cast, Call, Invoke

Each person transplants his or her seedlings from Imbolc around the outside of the circle, placing an egg under each one. Focusing on the intent behind the plant, and the goal that each plant represents.

When you are through planting, begin drumming and circling around the circle. When all have finished planting, and are drumming together, the Summoner cuts a door in the circle. The Priestess leads the procession, as they continue to drum, to the Indoor Altar to retrieve the Goddess statue. The Goddess is carried to the circle, through the eastern portal, and placed on the altar. The participants follow through the circle, symbolizing their rebirth and return from the underworld. Offerings can be made now. Drumming stops after power peaks.

Each person goes and locates the eggs beneath their plants, and interprets the divinatory message for each goal. Eggshells can be given back to the earth, to enrich the soil with calcium, completing the cycle of life.

Cakes and Wine,
Close Quarters,
End Circle.
Feast!

Beltaine – 15° Taurus
On or about May 1

Return of the Light, Height of Spring, Season of Earth
Gives form and structure to new identity
Motivated to ground things in the physical, and create tangible representations of lasting beauty and value
Self – Actualization, merging with partners and communities

Beltaine – Correspondences

Colors – Bright Pastels and Red
Gods – Oak King, Maiden
Direction – South East
May Pole, Great Marriage, Great Rite
Magic – Fertility, Abundance, Connecting, Bonding

Beltaine is the time of year when the God and Goddess marry. It is time to make commitments with partners, to expand your sphere of influence and take your goals into the greater world. You have been focused on your self. Now it is time to begin to shift your focus outward, on the world around you and contribute your part to the growth cycle.

Hormones are rampant at this time in our physical lives, and Aphrodite/Persephone, Goddess of Spring, is flooding the planet with the urgency to connect with others. Spring fever encourages outdoor activities, more sunlight, warmer temperatures, and lighter clothing, which make for a lighter heart. The celebrations of physical delights, beauty, and love are prominent now.

Beltaine is celebrated at 15° Taurus. Taurus is fixed, earth, and ruled by the planet Venus, Goddess of Love. Taurus is concerned with stability, beauty, and sensual pleasures. It desires to create beautiful things with lasting value. It is at this time in our development that we notice the opposite sex, and desire to explore our relationships to others. But, Taurus also desires to acquire and own things. Emotional relationships must be accompanied with promises of commitment, such as marriage.

As we begin to reconnect ourselves with others on the planet, we experience the first sense of reconnecting with the Universe. Our desire for individuality fades away, as we begin to miss the feeling of being a part of something greater than ourselves. We long for family, and friends. We begin to focus our goals on how they benefit the greater good, and work towards becoming a benefit to others in addition to ourselves.

We celebrate this time of year by pledging our love to our chosen mates, with Handfastings. The Oak King has found the Maiden to whom he wishes to devote himself. The Maiden has accepted the Oak Kings advances, and found him a suitable match. The ritual of handfasting satisfies the Taurean desire to make this emotional coupling a lasting bond, a foundation from which things of lasting beauty and value can be created. It should be remembered that those who get handfasted at the Beltaine ritual stand as physical representatives of the Goddess and God.

The May Pole represents the phallus of the Gods. Dancing around the May Pole, weaving in and out of the dancers, represents the consummation of the Great Wedding. It is a simulated Great Rite. Performing a May Pole Dance after a Handfasting is a ritualized consummation of the Handfasting, and insures fertility in the relationship.

Personal rituals could include; renewing vows with your lover or mate, making a Beltaine "bower"[7] in your circle, and 'fertilize' your plants with lovemaking, jumping over your rows of plants, while splashing them with an aphrodisiac to encourage their growth, crafting an item, or any form of artful creativity. Since Beltaine is also known as The Lady's Day, or Mother's Day, rituals honoring our mother and the role she plays in our lives, is also appropriate.

Beltaine Ritual – The Handfasting – Mother's Day

Preparation:

A May Pole should be erected in the center of the circle prior to ritual.
Decorate the circle with spring flowers and other appropriate items
Guests and clergy officials gather inside the circle, to prepare the sacred space.
Bride and Groom wait to be summoned away from the circle in separate places.

Cast, Call, Invoke

Groom is summoned to stand at the gate of the circle. Then the **Bride is summoned** to join him (Bride could incorporate flower girls and the usual entourage accompanied with the Bride's approach to the altar). The Bride and Groom are not to see each other before the Handfasting.

The Summoner joins the couple's hands (Bride on the left, groom on the right), stands with them at the Gate, and alerts the Priestess that they are ready to enter.

HP – (approaches the gate) *"Today you seek to join your lives in sacred Vows. Know now that these vows are being taken within the boundaries between the worlds and will be heard by not only your friends and loved ones, but your Goddess and God. These vows that you speak today will strengthen your unions and bind you to each other for 1 year and 1 day (Or if legal marriage, for the remainder of this lifetime). Do you still seek to enter?"*

---

[7] A small tent decorated with pillows, blankets and aphrodisiacs to function as a miniature Temple of Aphrodite.

Initial Crown Chakra Activation - The Wheel of the Year - Beltaine

Bride and Groom answer. HPS cuts a doorway and Summoner escorts the Couple to stand before the altar."

HPS – *"As it is the truth of all things, everything which is alive, whole and holy, must contain the five sacred elements that create all things. To make your union whole, you must become as one, therefore you must be joined by each element. Priest, please escort them to the east."*

The HP escorts the couple to the East Quarter. HP – *"Guardian of the Eastern Portal, these have come to seek handfasting. If you see the truth of it, bless their union with Earth."*

Eastern Guardian (holding a plate with bread and a green cord on it) – *"I am Earth. I am the element of birth, spring, and renewal. I give you beginnings and foundation, I am the dawn of your togetherness, and I bless you with steadfastness, groundedness, and endurance. I bless you with nurturing, and understanding, fertility, security and prosperity. May the blessings of earth be upon you* (feed them bread). *I join your bodies together in strength and beauty that you may bring forth new life with the power of Earth* (take the green cord and wrap their clasped hands in a loose spiral wrap)."

HP escorts them to the South Quarter. HP – *"Guardian of the Southern Portal, these have come to seek handfasting. If you see their passion, bless their union with Fire."*

Southern Guardian (holding a lit red candle and a vial of oil) – *"I am Fire. I am the element of protection, defense, desire, and instinct. I provide the quickening in your heart that drives you to bond together. I bless you with sheltering contentment that warms your home and drives away ill fates. I bless you with courage, fidelity, trust, and passion. I connect your consciousness in power and compassion that you may always have awareness for the others needs so that you will always be the one to ignite their dreams with the power of fire* (place the candle in their clasped and bound hands and anoint their heads with oil)."

HP escorts them to the West Quarter. HP – *"Guardian of the Western Portal, these have come to seek handfasting. If you see the depth of their feelings for each other, bless their union with Water."*

Western Guardian (holding a chalice filled with wine) – *"I am Water. I am the element of death, rebirth, transformation, and initiation. I test you with fear, so that you may find love. I face you with obstacles so that you may grow. I force you to look at ugliness so that you may find beauty. I give you pain, so that you may know love. Therefore know this, your love will last as long as you are learning and growing together. I bless you with the ability to accept and trust the feelings that threaten to overwhelm you, to allow yourself to float upon the waves of emotion. I give you the ability to welcome the storms that deepen your devotion, and the healing showers that strengthen your love. I join your hearts with honor and humility that you may always recognize how your actions effect the other, and have the ability to overcome pride with forgiveness through the power of water* (give them both a drink and place the cup in the man's free hand)."

HP escorts them to the North Quarter. HP – *"Guardian of the Northern Portal, these have come to seek handfasting. If you see mutual respect and adoration for each other, bless their union with Air."*

Northern Guardian (holding an athame and a sensor or smudge stick) – *"I am Air. I am the element of thought and mental clarity. I breathe understanding and resolution into your darkest conflict through communication. I give you the projective power to achieve your goals and aspirations. I bestow you with ambition, teamwork, diplomacy, compromise, humor, and laughter. I bring the winds of change into your minds and join you together as one breath with joy and reverence that you may always find the answers you are looking for within the boundaries of your selves through the power of air* (places the athame in the woman's free hand and smudges them both)."

HPS – *"Please turn and face each other. The four elements have blessed your union and given you the tools to make your handfasting whole. You must provide the fifth element of spirit with the sacred vows you speak to each other. These vows will create a new reality within which you will spend the coming year and a day (or the rest of your life)."*

Groom (holding up the chalice to the Bride) – *"As I hold up this Chalice I know I am holding you in my hands, soul, heart, and mind. I vow to you before Gods and Goddesses and all who are listening here today that I will: (couple's personal vows inserted here)."*

Bride (holding up the Athame to the Groom) – *"As I hold up this Athame I know I am holding you in my hands, soul, heart, and mind. I vow to you before Gods and Goddesses and all who are listening here today that I will: (couple's personal vows inserted here)."*

Example vows - *always honor, love, respect, and cherish you. I will turn to you when I need help, and help you when you are in need. I will strive to fill your days with joy, beauty, passion, and humor. I will honor you, be faithful to you, care for you, and provide for you. I give myself to you in perfect love and perfect trust. So Mote It Be.*

Then the Couple performs the symbolic Great Rite. HPS and HP stand on either side of the couple building an energy field around the two.

Groom – *"As the Chalice is to the Goddess."*

Bride – *"The Athame is to the God."*

Together – *"Joined together they bring blessedness."*

HP takes the athame and the couple drinks again from the chalice.

HPS – *"It is done."* (the HPS takes the ends of the green cord and ties them in a knot around the couples hands) *"The Handfasting is complete and the couple is as one. You may kiss the bride".* (The HPS draws a circle in the ground around them with the sword saying) *"Let no man come between what the Gods have brought together today."*

(If rings are to be exchanged) **HPS** – *"The exchange of rings is one of the deepest symbols of a union. It is a constant reminder of this sacred union. Today we joined two people as one. This ring symbolizes that wholeness with no beginning and no end."*

(If cups are to be exchanged) - **HPS** – *"The sharing of the chalice represents the blending of our hearts. A couple exchanging cups is equivalent to exchanging your heart. The Chalice should always be recognized as a symbol of our emotions, and a wedding chalice should be revered and treated with as much love and care as you would your lovers heart, for within it is the depth of your love."*

HP raises the chalice in a toast to the couple, and drinks then passes the Chalice around the circle so that each guest may bless the couple.

Then the cake is brought forth, and the top layer removed. **HP** – *"As the cake represents your abundance, let us always remember to save first, when there is plenty, so that we may have a surplus when in need."*

The Groom blesses the cake, and the Couple feed each other. Then cake is passed around to the guests.

A broom is laid before the bride and groom. They jump over it together, symbolizing their transformation into this new phase of their life. Everyone cheers and throws rose petals, birdseed, or whatever the couple has chosen to be showered in.

Then the couple and others who want to join in dance around the **May Pole** so symbolize the consecration of the Goddess and God's marriage.

Close quarters, end circle.

Litha – 1° Cancer
On or about June 21

Peak of Light, Beginning of Summer, Season of Fire
Concerned with creating an emotional and soul identity
Focused on protecting and preserving the family
Discovering how far we have come in our individuality away from our connectedness with the All.
Reaching and overcoming your challenge with this cycle.

Litha – Correspondences

Colors – Red, Yellow Gold
Gods – Oak King, & Holly King, Mother Aspect
Direction – South
Swords, Sun Symbols
Magic – Transformation

If your year were a movie, Litha would be the climax. This is the time where the energy will be at its height and your lessons will be right in front of your face. Litha is celebrated at 1° Cancer. For the crab to grow he must release his hard shell, and be vulnerable for a time. This gives his body a chance to grow before the outer shell hardens again. We experience this vulnerability at Litha, when we must shed our hardened outer shell of ego, which is impeding our spiritual growth, leaving us vulnerable, but also transforming us through our vulnerability.

It is here when we realize that through our individuality, we are incredibly alone, and we seek to take action towards reconnecting ourselves to the All through the creation of the family. Now is the time when we are ready to conceive child, and give birth, thus fulfilling the cycle of life, and reconnecting ourselves to our ancestors and descendants. This conception and birth is symbolically manifested in many different ways, through the yearly cycle. Check your goals at this time. You will have successfully completed many of them, possibly without even realizing it.

The myth that is associated with this ritual is the struggle between the Oak King and Holly King. It tells the story of the internal conflict of man giving up his individual freedom for the commitment to the love of his wife and children. It can be seen in the King giving up his personal gratification to focus on the prosperity and abundance of his people, or in the way we each have to sacrifice an immaturity so that we can reach our goals.

The Oak King is the young, fertile Warrior God. His job is to re-fertilize the earth in spring. You can get a good idea of the Oak King by comparing him to any standard

Initial Crown Chakra Activation - The Wheel of the Year - Litha

18 – 25 year old male, who is desperately looking for Miss Right, while checking out any and all willing participants along the way. Re-fertilizing the whole planet is a big job, and the Oak King is hormonally geared specifically for the task.

The Holly King is the Father God. He offers safety, security, wisdom and commitment. The Holly King can be found reflected in the face of every father, who devotes his energy to the benefit and welfare of his wife and children. His job is to raise a family and make sure there are new Oak Kings and Maidens to fertilize the future. This transfers to each of us individually in the way we relate to what we have worked towards this year. As we give birth to that which we have worked to create, we become responsible for keeping it safe, helping it grow, and ensuring it's success.

At Litha, the sun is at its peak. Fertilization is done. The Oak King has married the Maiden, and they are giving birth to a child. It is the pivotal moment of moving from a couple to a family that brings about the change from Oak King to Holly King, from son to father. Oak Kings love their youthful immortality. They fear and avoid the Holly King's burden of eternal sacrifice of time, money, freedom, and individuality. Holly Kings find blissful joy and a sense of purpose, and are proud of the sacrifices they make for the growth and prosperity of their family.

This moment of transformation from son to father is a very real internal struggle that man faces in each lifetime, and that we each face every year as we transform and mature in our yearly incarnation.

The Yule Log (a tool of fire) is used in the depth of winter to bring balance to the season of air. The traditional sword fight (a tool of air) between Oak and Holly represent bringing balance to summer, the season of fire.

Litha begins the time of Harvest. Finally you are reaping the fruits of your labors. You must transition from a state of growth and expansion, to taking responsibility for that growth, so that you are able to protect the abundance you are about to receive. We take this time to recognize and bless the harvest, and remember that all our blessings flow from the mother, and as Her children we must give back for that which we have received.

This is a dramatic and showy ritual, as befitting the climactic transformation of our inner selves. It is written with an audience in mind, and is included as another example of pagan drama. Once again, it purposefully includes humor to keep the watching participants entertained while the mystery is being revealed.

A personal ritual could consist of reviewing your goals for the year, recognizing the obstacles in your way, and personal resistances that are keeping you from attaining your goals (ex. Some people have a hard time being successful, because they think successful people are evil, or that money is evil.) Now would be the time to search out these types of obstacles, and release them. End the ritual with casting fresh lavendar into a small cauldron fire, while making wishes for how you would like your yearly story to end.

Litha Ritual

PREPARATION

lavender
rose petals
Cauldron prepared with a quick lighting fire.
The Oak King should be dressed in red and gold, the Holly King in black, green and red.
Swords

CHARACTERS

Earth Goddess
Fire Goddess
Water Goddess
Air Goddess
Oak King
Holly King

Cast, Call, Invoke

HPs – "Welcome to Litha. Today's ritual is an external re-enactment of the internal struggles that you are experiencing at this time. You begin this journey as the Oak King. The elementals represent the struggles that you face, as you try to hold on to the freedoms of youth. Yet, your desire to grow, love, and connect is stronger, and you eventually sacrifice your immaturity to become the responsible adult, the Holly King. As we watch the drama unfold, look within and search out the obstacles that are keeping you from connecting with your path, or achieving your goals, and allow the Oak King to carry them away with him when he crosses through the west gate."

Fire - "Today is Midsummer, the longest day and the shortest night of the year. It is a time of fullness, a time of plenty. A time of lazy summer days and sultry summer nights. It is the time when we tell a story - a story of two kings."

Earth -"One of these kings is the Oak King, the eternal son. His task is to breathe new life into the Goddess after the harshness of winter. He is focused on reseeding the land, bringing forth abundance and fertility. He stimulates outer growth."

Initial Crown Chakra Activation - The Wheel of the Year - Litha

Water - "The other is the Holly King, the eternal father. His task is to protect the sacred balance, and care for the harvest. He ensures the longevity of his People and brings about inner growth."

Air - "As our story begins, the Oak King is in power. He began his rule long ago when the world was cold and dark, and he has brought light, warmth and abundance to the world and to his people. Life is good."

OAK KING - "Yeah, it's good to be king. (struts around acting kingly) Yep - life is good. There's plenty of food, there's plenty of warmth, everyone's happy. We should celebrate!

Fire Quarter – "Great King, your kingdom is so invigorating. Leo expresses gratitude to so mighty a monarch for all that you have created. The people are so talented and motivated. They are so full of drive, and PASSION. However, their passion has lead to conflict. Their self-involvement has given rise to fighting against each other. Please share with me your plans on bringing order to the kingdom?"

Oak King – "Government? Why would you bother me with issues of government? I don't want my people to have to follow a bunch of silly rules. Let them be free to do as they will, explore, conquer. Conquest, anyone?"

Fire turns away, with a look of disapproval, as the Holly King moves to the north quarter and listens.

Earth – "Great King, your kingdom is so abundant. Virgo offers thanks for all your hard work. The crops are growing strong, as are my sons. However, there are those who need medical attention. You're body is strong, but there are those in your kingdom who are weak. What will you do to ensure their health?"

Oak King – "Health care? Are you kidding me? I am the Oak King, mighty and strong. There is no room in my kingdom for health concerns. I am the eternal sun. I am immortal. Medical care. I scoff at Medical care. Are there any more maidens who need to be fertilized?"

Earth quarter turns away disappointed.

Air Quarter – "Your Highness?"

Oak King – "What? What!! Oh, thank goodness. At least I know you will have something sensible to say."

Air Quarter – "Well, Yes, my lord. Of course, I do."

Oak King – "Well, thank God for that. Oh, That's right I'm God. Thank ME for that."

Air Quarter – "Oh quite right, my lord. Libra sends words of praise and gratitude for the many gifts you have given to enrich the Kingdom. Fresh new minds with new ideas flutter through our mighty realm. We are so excited about the possibility, which awaits within the seeds you have planted. We see these seeds coming to fruition, and ask that universities, and institutions of learning be prepared to enrich their lives, to forge great thinkers and a great civilization."

Oak King – "Schools? You want me to build schools. Of course you do. Are you out of your mind? Education robs us of our individuality. It makes us conform. It puts all kinds of crazy thoughts into our heads, that make us, I, I… No! No schools. I hate school." (Shooing Air away, Air returns to her quarter.)

Water Quarter – "Most Noble and Gracious King. Scorpio shares heartfelt appreciation for the many acts of love and kindness that you have bestowed upon our kingdom. You have single-handedly reawakened the kingdom from its dark sleep, and refertilized our fields, livestock and women. Rebirth has transformed our mighty land, and it is you we honor. And yet, we are soon to cross a new threshold. Change is ever upon us. Who is there to give us meaning to the changes we face? Who comforts us when we struggle to understand the obstacles that challenge us? How do we understand the spiritual significance of what we do? How do we honor the rituals of our existence?"

Oak King – "Ministers? Clergy? You want me to waste my time on churches? Oh, let's worry about the afterlife. Yeah, that's what I want to do today. I am the giver of life. I know nothing of death. I cannot be bothered with spiritual transformation. (looking at fire) Maybe I should make a law that no one dies. You did hear me tell her I am immortal, right? What's gotten into you? You just haven't had enough attention from me. That must be it. Huh?"

Water scowls fiercely and turns her back coldly.

Oak King – (speaking to all) "I don't know what's gotten into you. Winter was here, and everyone was scared, hungry, and begging for help. Great Oak King, bring us the sun. Great Oak King, refertilize the earth. Great Oak King, help us. I did all that, and very successfully, thank you for noticing. But, now you have all these new ideas; government, doctors, teachers, priestesses? Come on. We're having so much fun here. Every thing is growing. It's warm. Things are great. Admit it, things are great."

Quarters offer half-hearted agreement.

Oak King – "See there. Now, I'm off to fertilize more maidens. There has to be at least one or two left."

Earth – "No, my lord. I think there all fertile."

Oak King – "Are you sure? Let's double check. I'm sure there is bound to be more maidens in my kingdom in need of my attention."

HOLLY KING - "THAT'S ENOUGH!"

OAK KING – "Holy Me, you scared me to death."

HOLLY KING – "Looks like you're having another party."

OAK KING – "Well, we're trying to?"

HOLLY KING – "I see you've been hard at work."

OAK KING – "Yeah, work. I guess you can call it that. I prefer to think of it as spreading the love."

HOLLY KING – "Yes, I'm sure you do. Do you know what day today it?"

OAK KING - "Memorial Day?"

HOLLY KING – "No."

OAK KING – "Flag Day?"

HOLLY KING – "No."

OAK KING – "I know… the day you crashed my party?"

HOLLY KING – "It's Midsummer, my lord. It's time for the birth of all that you have created. All your work comes to fruition now. You must care for that, which you have created, or all that you have done will be laid to waste."

OAK KING – "Oh, no, nothing will lay waste to my Kingdom. I will fight all would be attackers. They are no match for me. I am the conqueror. As you well know. Or maybe your forget Yule, Old Man."

HOLLY KING – "No, I have not forgotten, but unlike you I am willing to give up my power for the good of my people. You, young one, lack the wisdom to do the same."

Oak King – "How dare you insult me. Traitor. I'll show you wisdom… You know, you're right. I have done good work, and I will continue to do more. Look around you! We've all done such good work! There's long days, plenty to eat. These people are happy! They've worked hard. They deserve to celebrate! So, let us not keep you any longer. Thanks for visiting, sorry you can't stay."

Holly – "Yes, things are coming along quite nicely. You should be proud. You have served your people well. You provided for them exactly what they needed, but, what about their needs now? The crops that you have raised must be protected as they bear fruit. If you continue to grow in power you will scorch the earth and destroy all the great work you have done. It's time for you to step down. Do it for the good of your people."

OAK KING – "I won't let you bring cold and darkness back upon my people. I'll defend them to the death."

HOLLY KING – "You are mismatched son. You're fire and passion may defeat me when the earth is cold and barren and needs your mighty lance to bring about rebirth. But, now it is hot, and the earth is full with your seed. Wisdom and skill is what is needed to restore the balance. Don't allow your arrogance and self-involvement bring about your own death."

Oak – "How many times am I going to have to tell you people that I am IMMORTAL?"

Swords are drawn.

HOLLY KING – "I'm thinking that's probably the last time."

FIGHT SEQUENCE – Oak King and Holly King fight with swords, words, jokes or some other battle of wits. Oak King is defeated in the end.

OAK KING dies. - <bent over looking up at Holly King, who takes crown from Oak and places it on Holly's head> "Oh Me, I mean YOU."

Holly King – "I send you to the west, where you can rest, and renew."

West opens, embraces him, and allows him to pass. Oak King moves to north outside of view

Holly - (as an eulogy) "We will need you again, bright King. When darkness and cold grips the land, it is your fire and power we will turn to. Rest in Peace, my son."

Holly - "Loved ones, tonight we gather in celebration. We are standing at the pinnacle of our current incarnation. We have labored, unyielding, and now is the time to honor those deeds well done. It is time to rejoice in anticipation of the abundant harvest ahead. You've worked hard to nurture the seeds you have planted and make them flourish. Soon you will harvest them, and reap the rewards of your labor."

(Each quarter comes forward and blesses the cakes.)

Earth – "Mother Demeter, Mighty Goddess of grain, Bestower of fertility, Mother of us all, Bless the fields that they may come to fruition. As we are eternally connected may the Harvest be bountiful for all the lands. May the abundance flow into the homes and businesses of the earth. Creating plenty, and prosperity for all. May we never hunger. So Mote it Be."

Fire – "Dionysis, God of the Vine, bring the fruit to ripeness. Celebrate with us at this time of abundance and joy. Entice the Goddess to her fullness. Bring forth the Sacred Gift of Abundance and Fertility, and imbue those gifts with the marriage of alchemy. Allow the intoxicating spirit of motivation ignite our passions, and send us forth to rapture through the achievement of our deepest desires. So Mote it Be."

Water – "Persephone, Queen of all Witches, Goddess of death and rebirth. Bless us with your healing, love and compassion. Help us see beyond the murky illusion of this world. Let us recognize the pain and struggles we encounter as obstacles within our own selves. Embrace us with your love, so that we may gracefully make the transition without fear. Let us feel you in our hearts, and know you are guiding our path, so that we can confidently abandon the shallow pools of ego and dive deep into the healing fountain that leads to your realms. May we ever remember that we are all connected. May we Never Thirst. So Mote it Be."

Air – "Hecate, Goddess of the Crossroads, Keeper of the Mysteries. Blow your gentle winds upon our minds that we may awaken to the sacred knowledge that dwells within us all. Allow us to see the results of the choices we must make, so that we can walk with reverence and joy together as a community. Lift us above our daily struggles, and bless us with vision, that we may see how our actions today will effect the many generations of tomorrow. Sweep away our troubles and conflicts. Help us cast aside our judgments. Inspire us to work together to build our community, to enrich our future and the future of our children. Bring forth a new pagan civilization to rise from the ashes of the old that once again connects the people to the Gods and the Gods to the People."

HOLLY KING – "Let us honor the sacrifice of the Oak King with feasting and merry making."

Bread is passed

HP and HPs bless wine

Wine is passed

Fire is lit in cauldron.

HPs blesses lavendar – "As we move onto the next phase of our incarnation, we leave behind the aggressive, conquesting Oak King, and the flirty, carefree Maiden, as we accept the responsibilities of reaping what we have sewn. It is tradition at Midsummer for the pagan folk to honor this sacred transition by making wishes upon lavendar and casting them into the fire. Midsummer rites of old were celebrated with sweet Lavendar. Make wish upon the lavendar and throw your wishes into the Midsummer fires. May the benevolent Gods smile upon us this bounteous night. May all your wishes be granted."

Everyone makes their wishes, throws lavender into the fire, dances, and plays drums.

All circle as people continue to cast wishes. Encourage people to go time and again until wishes become silly and atmosphere has become giggly.

When baskets of lavendar are empty, quarters stand by fire. Each quarter empties basket into fire, says line and turns to face quarter.

Earth – Just as our fathers have done before…so we do today…

Fire – Prepare to receive the blessings of Harvest.

Water – Believe in your dreams. Nourish them to grow…

Air – Remember and care for all those dearest to you…

Holly – And the love will sustain you always.

Release Quarters and Close Circle

Feast!

Initial Crown Chakra Activation - The Wheel of the Year - Lammas

Lammas – 15° Leo
On or about August 1

Waning Light, Height of Summer, Season of Fire
Focused on exploring our relationship to collective consciousness or group
Seeks to win the approval of the group by being special
Reaping the rewards of your efforts, goals reached
Recognizing and Honoring Sacrifices made to achieve goals

Lammas – Correspondences

Colors – Red, Gold, Yellow, Orange
Gods – Priest King, Mother Aspect
Direction – South West
Corn, Hay, Gourds, and Harvest Items
Magic – Offering Thanks for the sacrifices made by others on our behalf, honoring our fathers, healing the wounds of childhood

Lammas is a celebration of the First Harvest. It is time that we begin reaping the rewards of all the hard work we have done in our yearly incarnation. We desire to reconnect, and the first step in that is recognizing that we did not achieve our goals alone. There were many helping us along the way. It is time to express gratitude to those who have nurtured, supported and encouraged us on our path. We offer thanks and share our bounty with those who shared our burden.

Celebrated at 15° Leo, Lammas celebrates the Priest King, the forces of resistance, government and civil order, health and healing disciplines, education and systems of learning, and death. Leo is fixed fire, the King of the zodiac. It is generous, creative, and giving. Yet its generosity is not unconditional. Leo demands appreciation, and acknowledgment, as well as results for it's endeavors. It desires to lavish the worthy with gifts and praise, but only after having proved their worth. Leo sees its' offspring as an extension of itself and takes failure of it's kingdom or progeny personally. Leo's generosity stems from this deep seeded desire to succeed, and does all it can to ensure the success of its' lineage.

The Priest King is the disciplinarian in our lives. He forces us to grow into responsible adults. He offers the resistance that necessitates new growth, new ideas, and new inventions. Thus ensuring our spiritual evolution. We often resent this force of resistance in our lives. But, now is the time to recognize that without this resistance, we would not embrace growth, or develop the techniques required to embrace adulthood, nor willingly accept the power and responsibility that comes with it.

It is basically the Wiccan equivalent of Fathers Day. We honor the God for his sacrifice, and recognize that the sacrifices made by the men in our lives are many. We do not recognize all the sacrifices that our fathers make for us. They leave early in the morning, and come home late, and we have no idea what goes on in their lives while they are gone. But, they leave behind their hearts, and they bring home what is necessary to keep us warm, safe, and happy.

Now that many mothers are working too, we have shared burdens and the sacrifice of our fathers goes even less noticed. It is important to recognize that men express their love differently from women, and value them for their contribution. Just as women want to be valued for their contribution to the family, men need to be honored and valued as well.

Those of us, who have been hurt by neglectful fathers and husbands, should recognize that it is possible that they were neglectful because they were never allowed to embrace their father status by sharing in the powerful moment of our births. Maybe they couldn't make the sacred transformation required because they haven't been taught their own sacredness in the circle of life. Today new generations of fathers are welcomed into the birthing room. But, previous generations of fathers were kept from this sacred moment, separating them from their most pivotal right of passage, alienating them from their children and maybe their wives too.

As women struggle to reach our own sense of self-worth and sacredness, we should realize that men have lost the connection with their sacredness as well. Only through healing both sexes will we find wholeness. If you have lessons to learn here, finding some way to express gratitude to the men who have made you who you are today is a very healing ritual, and a big step towards balance and wholeness.

I grew up with a disdain towards men. By my teen years, I had concluded that they were to be blamed for everything that was wrong with my world. For many years, I resented my father, even though he was always there when I really needed him. He was not perfect, compared to my ideal of the perfect father. But he was there, doing what he could to ensure my growth, making me rely on my own strength when possible, picking me up when I failed, and doing for me what I couldn't do alone. He was the perfect father for me. When I showed up one August with gifts of appreciation and a letter expressing my thanks, he was touched and it changed the nature of our relationship.

In ancient times, our myths and legends tell us that Kings were wed to the land, and sometimes sacrificed to the land to bring forth it's bounty. Today, we can recognize and honor the sacrifices of our own fathers, and ritualize their gifts to us so that we may raise our awareness of what they bring to our lives.

At Lammas we give thanks and honor the God for all that he provides, and for all the bounty that we enjoy. We also honor our fathers, recognizing the sacrifices they make to provide for our safety and well-being. A personal ritual could consist of making corn chowder and taking a card to your father, writing a letter and mailing it, or even expressing your pain towards your father in writing and releasing it by burning it. A more positive ritual could include rewriting your memories of your father from a different point of view, taking into consideration that he sacrificed many aspects of his relationship with you to ensure your growth and development as a responsible adult.

By focusing on what your father did right, you can change the way you remember your past, and therefore change what you received from your childhood. There is much magic that can be done here.

Lammas is also the time of recognizing our personal contribution to the whole of society. We explore what each of us individually has done with the time we were given, and take notice by what deeds we will be remembered. A personal ritual to honor these thoughts and actions is to sit with friends and discuss what each of you have accomplished over the year, and what we remember about each other and the adventures we have shared together. This can be done ceremoniously in toasts and boasts over a Chalice, or casually around the kitchen table.

Now is the time to harvest the plants you have been growing all year. Collect any seeds, appropriately label them and store them for the coming year. Hang bundles of fresh herbs up to dry.

Lammas Ritual – Father's Day

This is a very simple ritual, but it brings forth a lot of memories, and a real sense of connectedness.

Preparation:

- ✓ Build an effigy of the God out of sticks.
- ✓ Make bundles out of hay that can be tied on to the effigy.
- ✓ Harvest seeds from the plants that you have been growing, or purchase new ones to plant at Imbolc next year.

Cast circle and call quarters and invoke as usual.

The effigy is dedicated to serve as a symbol of the God. Valerian Nightshade wrote the following invocation for this purpose.

Great Sun God, Lord of the grain, You who are known by many names;
Lugh, Tammuz, Adonis, Dionysus, Balder- it is time!
The summer has been very long.
Lay thy shadows on the sundials and on the meadows, let the winds go loose!
Command the last fruits that they shall be full,
Press them on to fulfillment and drive the last sweetness into the heavy wine.
We thank thee for thy sacrifice, for the bounty of the harvest
For the grain that sustains our body, for the divine spark that ignites our souls,
For the love that nourishes our hearts.

So Mote it Be.

The HPS states the purpose of the ritual is to express gratitude to the God. Three times a charm, so once to HP, once to God, and once to your own father.

Each covener picks up a hay bundle, approaches the effigy and expresses gratitude while affixing the hay bundle to the stick figure.

After everyone has said his or her piece the Priests light the effigy and all hold hands and watch it burn.

Seed Blessing:

The chalice is placed on the pentagram plate that is covered in seeds that you have gathered from the plants that you grew, or new seeds can be purchased. If various types of seeds are used, they may be kept in separate envelopes so they may be easily identified at planting time.

HPS (to HP) – "Come unto me once again so that we may plant a seed that will emerge in the new year. (holding up the Chalice) As the Chalice is to the woman."

HP – "The Athame is to the Man." (Placing Athame in Chalice)

HP/S – "Joined together they bring blessedness."

HPS – "I bless these seeds as they contain the power of rebirth within them. They will be kept in a sacred place, and wait for Imbolc when they can return to the soil to sprout and grow. We sow seeds of prosperity as we harvest the fruits of our labor." Allow each participant to bless the seeds.

Cakes and Wine

Release Quarters and Close Circle

Feast!

Mabon – 1° Libra
On or about September 21

Light and Dark in Balance, Beginning of Fall, Season of Water

Recognizes others as individuals with same feelings, drives, wants, and needs as ourselves.

Libra seeks to reconnect to the group, which is a source of balance and harmony

Concerned with expressing our mental and social identity

Accepting life lessons, and integrating them through rest and reflection

Mabon – Correspondences

Colors – Red, Orange, Black
Gods – Priest King & Crone
Direction – West
Black Shrouds
A give away gift, something that you wish to release and/or pass on to others
Magic – Reaping, Resting, Re-connecting

Mabon is the second Harvest. It is the time of our yearly incarnation that we pass away from the trials of the year, reap our rewards and embrace rest. We reflect on the year's lessons, and try to gain clarity as we integrate with the whole. We ritualize the myth of Persephone's abduction and descent into the Underworld, and follow her on her journey into the dark. We recognize that we are leaving behind our individuality, and embracing the connectedness with spirit with which we have longed to reunite.

Mabon is celebrated at 1° Libra, the time when we physically give up our body, or ego, and embrace the collective whole of humanity through death. Libra recognizes others as the same as itself, and seeks to embrace partnership, and serve the Universe through releasing the ego, and embracing its' purpose. The rape of Persephone symbolizes the ripping away of the ego that comes through merging with your purpose.

Demeter and Persephone love each other, and share the true joy of each other's company. As Goddess of spring, Persephone explores her individuality, and brings rebirth and renewal to earth. However, Persephone also has the love she shares with her husband.

The joy she shares with her husband, Hades, is in connectedness as Lord and Lady of Tartarus, King and Queen of the Underworld. By comparing her strengths to Hades weaknesses, and vice versa, she has found her specialness and can contribute her individual talents to bring harmony and balance to the union of the couple, and also to the greater realm of the Underworld as a whole. Persephone knows her duty to this connection and finds a true sense of purpose as a piece of the greater whole.

Through this mystery, we also find our true purpose as a piece in a greater whole, for until you compare your individuality with another, you cannot know your unique assets, or how you fit into the greater scheme of things. All of us are unique and have a single purpose to fulfill. But unless you know that other people can't do what you do, you take your own gifts for granted.

Persephone was not happy in the Underworld until she saw that she could ease suffering and pain of the inhabitants there. She found that by using the powers of regeneration as Goddess of Spring, She could complete the cycle of birth and death with rebirth.

Mabon is a funeral. It is the passing into the dark half of the year. It is the death of our current yearly incarnation. But it is a birth into your understanding the transformation of death, and how your unique talents not only contribute to the evolutionary process, but also transform it into something greater than it was before. The relationship between man and God, individual and whole is symbiotic. Without the individual there would be no whole, without the whole there would be no individual. Without mankind there would be no God, without God there would be no mankind.

A personal ritual could include finding items within your home that you no longer need or want, clean them up, and store them away as presents to give to loved ones at Yule. It is time for the final harvest of the plants you have been nurturing all season. Nothing can be taken from the garden after Samhain, so do all your final reaping now. Prepare your garden for winter.

Mabon Ritual – The Descent of Persephone

Participants:

- ✓ Demeter
- ✓ Hecate
- ✓ Persephone
- ✓ Hades
- ✓ Zeus

Preparation:

- ✓ A gate of Death for everyone to pass through
- ✓ Gift to give away
- ✓ Fire placed in the center of the circle
- ✓ A flower for Demeter

Cast, Call, Invoke

Hecate, Demeter, Persephone, Hades, Zeus, step into the middle and draw down.

Hecate – "Hecate, teacher of Witches, I call unto thee, descend into the body of this thy priestess."

Demeter (with flower)- "Demeter, goddess of grain, I call unto thee, descend into the body of this thy priestess."

Persephone – "Persephone. Queen of the Underworld, I call unto thee, descend into the body of this thy priestess."

Hades – "Hades, Lord of the Underworld, I call unto thee, descend into the body of this thy priest."

Zeus – "Zeus, Ruler of the Universe, I call unto thee, descend into the body of this thy priest."

Demeter and Persephone move together, holding hands or in a casual embrace dancing around the circle exclaiming their love and sharing the joy and happiness of being together.

Hecate – "Now is the time for Persephone to return to the Underworld to once again be united with her beloved husband Hades. For six months she is to be with her husband, and for six months she is to remain with her mother, Demeter, Goddess of Grain, within the realm of the living. This is the cycle of balance. This is the wheel of death and rebirth."

Zeus – (said to Persephone) "Persephone, it is time."

Demeter – (gaining Zeus' attention) "The agony of parting tears at the very core of me, for I love my daughter so, that I cannot possibly continue to bear fruit (emphasize the flower in hand) while she is away. I am incapable of such acts within this state of grief. I mourn the loss of her each moment she is away, both day and night. I mourn the absence of her embrace. Sweet Persephone, my daughter, my joy, my love…"

Zeus – (moves a hand to Demeter's shoulder or another comforting gesture) "She cannot remain among the living any longer. Life and light has reigned high and the balance needs to be set right, or the land shall grow stagnant."

Hecate – "We cannot truly rejoice in our abundance without knowing the absence of it as well. To know life, we must know death."

Demeter - [Crumple the flower in your hand, turn away] "Let the darkness and grief within my heart reflect upon the land, so that all will miss and wish for the return of my beloved daughter,(fading energy now) Persephone,…Goddess of Spring." (Demeter, and Persephone embrace for last time, then break)

(The gate of death emerges from the west. Hades comes through it to greet Persephone.)

Hades – "Persephone, my love. I have come to escort you to my domain. I have missed you greatly. I cannot bear to be without you any longer. Return to me at long last and take your place by my side as my radiant queen." (Hades then is handed the veil, which he applies to Persephone)

Persephone – "Farewell, dear mother. I will miss you. Do not grieve so, and cause the land to suffer. When I return in six months we shall rejoice. But now, I must return to my lovers embrace and resume my duties as Queen of the Underworld. I will inspire divination, and magic, and grant knowledge to those who seek to know the mysteries of death. Be proud of me mother, as I go and fulfill my destiny."

Demeter starts the chant:

"Seed and Grain, Seed and Grain,
All that falls will rise again,
Hoof and Horn, Hoof and Horn,
All that dies will be reborn."

[Persephone goes to the center of the circle, and places that which she needs to release upon the table. She tells what it represents and why this is what she has chosen to give away. She then walks through the gates of death and begins walking widdershins outside the circle of participants.]

[Then in turn all of the people in the circle take the thing that they have decided that they want to give up (this is symbolic the item should represent a part of yourself that no longer works for you that you would like to transform), throw it into the fire and follow Persephone through the gate.]

[Persephone will usher everyone to circle Widdershins. As more and more people go through the gate and begin circling, start clasping hands until it's a widdershins rune. But don't go too fast, because remember, this is a funeral, we have passed into the underworld.]

[Demeter and Hecate will be the last to go through the gates. When we are all circling widdershins together and chanting and the power peeks, the Priestess will shout "NOW" at which time all will stop send the energy up and shout "Rebirth"!!!!]

Cakes and Wine

Release Quarters and Close Circle

Feast!

Samhain – 15° Scorpio
On or about October 31

Return of Dark, Height of Fall, Season of Water

Seeks to experience union once more, to lose all sense of individuality, to die and be reborn again.

Death, rebirth and transformation

Confronting our demons and acknowledging them

Pierce the veil of illusions

Mending fences, honoring your teachers, and ancestors

Samhain – Correspondences

Colors – Black and Orange

Gods – Priest King and Crone

Direction – North West

Standard Halloween Decorations, Pomegranates

Magic – Honoring Ancestors, Teachers, and Adversaries

Samhain is the time of year when the veil is thinnest, and our holiest celebration of the year. At Samhain we honor our ancestors and those who have made an impact on our existence. At Mabon we crossed into the Underworld. Samhain is our reunion with all those who have crossed over. We dress up like the dead, or in our finest robes, and make special foods for those ancestors that we want to honor.

Celebrated at 15° Scorpio, the sign of fixed water, Samhain (pronounced sow (as in cow) –en) is a celebration of Scorpio's desire to completely merge with another individual to the annihilation of the self, or death of the ego. Scorpio confronts the inner demons, pierces the veil of illusion and bares its' soul, so that it can deeply connect with the soul of another. At Samhain, we are dead, and reconnected with the collective unconscious of the All. It is a very celebratory time, as we have made the long journey around the wheel, and there is nothing to do but enjoy this time of reunion and catch up with loved ones. All conflicts are put aside, and all come together in love and harmony to celebrate the connectedness, and the love of family.

Pomegranates are the food of the dead, and what Persephone ate in the underworld that bound her to Hades. Sharing pomegranates with each other is a Wiccan cultural tradition. It is customary to share the seeds of the pomegranate accompanied with a kiss.

In times past, people would put out food and candy to appease the dead, and dress up like ghosts, so that the ghosts wouldn't try to scare them. Trick or treating is a modern interpretation of partaking of these offerings and sharing in the community spirit of reunion and celebration with our ancestors.

Because the veil is so thin, Samhain is the best night of the year to do divinations, prophecy, and communication with the dead. Wiccan traditions include celebrating Samhain with a Feast to honor our ancestors, setting them a place at the table, and then each participant filling the plate with food they prepared for their loved ones. A personal ritual could include making a special meal that reminds you of a passed loved one, setting a place for them at the table, putting a picture of them where you can see them while you are eating, and having a conversation with them.

If you have had a particularly difficult year, and have a lot of bitterness to process, now is a very good time to make special efforts to find the good in the lessons that you were given, and to honor those who stood as your adversary and became a catalyst for your growth.

Most seasoned Priestesses modify their circle cast to included added protective measures to contain the many souls who will cross through the west when invited.

*Note – This ritual is a séance. While this is not a dangerous ritual for those adept at dealing with the deceased, it can be a real energy zapper for even the most seasoned Priestesses. Invoking the dead is not the same as invoking Deity. Deity has your best and highest good at heart. The dead don't always have such high aspirations. Not only that, but the dead have a much heavier vibration than Gods, or Ascended Masters. Make sure that if you invite the dead across the veil, and into your realm, that you can contain them inside your circle and send them back when you are ready for them to go. You never know what can creep out of that west quarter when you are unaware. This is not a ritual that you can just get lost in. Be sure that you or someone you trust is in control of the energies within the circle at all times. Forewarned is forearmed.

Samhain Ritual

Preparation:
- ✓ Banquet tables are set up in the circle.
- ✓ Special Foods and Memorabilia of Ancestors and Loved ones who have crossed over
- ✓ Divination items (tarot cards, crystal balls, mirrors, whatever)
- ✓ A special place setting for the dead is set up with the memorabilia and pictures of the Ancestors placed around it like an altar for the dead.

Cast, Call, Invoke

HPS – Opens the doorway of the West quarter and invites the relatives and Loves Ones of those present to attend the feast.

Members make various offerings to their loved ones, by placing food on the empty place setting and offering any words or messages of love. Other members present are to monitor the energy and give any readings or messages from the other side, as warranted.

Each member takes their turn honoring the dead. When all have finished the Lord of Misrule takes over. The Lord of Misrule's job is to send the ancestors back across the veil, and take the energy back up to a happy place. Sometimes the energy can get very serious, bringing up feelings of grief and sadness. A little comic relief is necessary to reinstate the celebratory atmosphere.

A fun way to get the energy back is to hold an awards ceremony, where you honor your friends and loved ones for their deeds over the year. In the true spirit of Samhain, this could be a spoof, including silly, made up, or homemade awards. Other ideas for fun are bobbing for apples, having a pumpkin carving contest, a costume contest, or other activities that are usually accompanied with Halloween parties.

Cakes and Wine aren't included in this ritual, because the whole ritual is a feast, and there is much eating and drinking through out. You should leave the plate that you make the offerings on outside in the yard in a secluded place.

Release Quarters and Close Circle

Feast!

Yule – 1° Capricorn
On or about December 21

Depth of dark, beginning of winter, Season of Air
Fundamentally concerned with identity
Analyzing past accomplishments and projecting future desires
Setting aside all pains, judgments, and hurts
Re-assessing the now
Honoring family, friends, and allies.

Yule – Correspondences

Colors – Red, Green, Gold, Silver
Gods – Holly King, Crone Aspect
Direction – North
Herbs – Holly, Mistletoe, Cinnamon, Apple, Cranberry, Bayberry
Magic – Prosperity, Success, Peace, Joy, Happiness, Family, Friends

Yule is when we are in the depth of dark. We are fundamentally focused on what the past year has brought us and how the new year will come into being. We are reaping the rewards of our successes and failures, and analyzing things that we need to do differently in the year to come. Celebrated at 1° Capricorn, we are faced with the task of accepting the responsibilities of our actions, weighing those actions against our intentions and purpose, and considering how those actions and behaviors served the whole of humanity.

We do not have to look into a mysterious past for the answers to this season. Santa Clause is a perfect representation of the Holly King, the Father God that is joyously rewarding us with the fruits of our labors from the previous year. Myths about how Santa Clause rewards good children, and brings bad children a bag of switches, or a lump of coal, are referring to you reaping the consequences of your actions. Even if you deserve nothing, the Holly King will bring you a little something to burn on the fire to keep you warm on the longest night of the year.

The Holly King/Santa Clause is the wise father, the doting generous grandfather. He is clothed in Red, Black, and White, the colors of Maiden, Mother and Crone. He is often shown with Holly leaves and berries, representing his role as Holly King. He is the old father who is giving way to the new young Oak King.

The God's purpose is to manifest, or make material, the gifts the Goddess has for us on the physical plane. Santa Clause delivers gifts. Santa Clause is the Holly King, a pagan spiritual mystery, shrouded in commercialism. Other special pagan symbols are the star, the Christmas balls, which represent eternity, the evergreen tree, which represents the Goddess in her immortality, and the Yule Log, which helps us release our judgments.

The Pagan symbolism in Christmas abounds. It's actually harder to find something that isn't Pagan than to find something that is. Even Christmas carols have the meaning of the Winter Solstice in them.

The birth of Jesus is a retelling of the birth of the Oak King. It is customary for Pagans to hold vigil all night at the Winter Solstice to await the rise of the new sun/son, and bless the birth of the Oak King. Christmas being celebrated several days after Yule, is a wonderful time to remember the Oak King, and shouldn't be a source of stress with your Christian family members at all. Once you can see past what you have been told Christmas means to Christians, and begin to see the pagan roots of it, you will be able to embrace Yule with all your usual family traditions, but see the pagan meaning behind them.

Your ritual for Yule could include a decorated evergreen tree to represent the Goddess, a Santa Clause or Holly King representative, and a gift to represent the fruits of your labor from the previous year, and a Yule Log.

A chalice ceremony is an excellent way to toast and honor each other at this time of family. Express what you are grateful for from the previous year, and what you intend to accomplish in the coming year. Open your gifts as recognition of the completion of the cycle from the previous year. Lastly, utilize the Yule Log to unburden yourself of any pains and attachments from any difficult trials that you may have encountered from the past year, and allow them to be burned away in the fire. This helps to release any negative karma, so that you may prepare for the New Year unencumbered with the burdens of the past.

Recycled gifts are a new tradition that allows us to embrace the spirit of giving without going into massive debt every year. At Mabon you choose an item to give away. This gift should be passed on to someone else at Yule, who will love and cherish it as you once did. As you walk through your home, you are sure to find many such treasures gathering dust, and no longer serving their purpose. Clean these gifts up, and pass them on as well, so that they may be reincarnated and serve a new purpose in the coming year. It is also a good idea to explain this tradition to your relatives and loved ones receiving the gifts, so that they may appreciate the gift in the sacred spirit in which it was intended.

Yule 2001 Ritual

Preparation:

Yule Log – to prepare a Yule log of Oak, soak it in Everclear, or another quick-lighting accelerant that will not soil your hands. Decorate it with holly, mistletoe, and other burnable expressions of the season

Yule gifts – the gifts you set aside at Mabon, or gifts you would normally exchange, or symbolic gifts, such as a sprig of mistletoe, a pentacle carved into a wooden disk, etc.

Holly glitter

Fire in hearth, or center of circle

Cast, Call, Invoke

Raise Power – a somber cone of power around the HP and HPS performing the great rite.

Group chants – *"Lugh, Pan, Belin, Herne, Cernunnos"*

HPS –(Performing the great rite, Holds up chalice and speaks)

> *"In the beginning there was the Void.*
> *The Black emptiness of the Goddess.*
> *The simple creative essence.*
> *She was the womb of space, where nothing,*
> *Suddenly is a spark and becomes something*
> *Without thought or form,*
> *She was the expanse of the Universe."*

HP – (Inserts Athame into Chalice and speaks)

> *"Until ... within her came the spark of thought,*
> *Which grew into desire.*
> *To grow, to create, to evolve.*
> *That desire grew within the void of the Goddess Mother,*
> *Until it became whole, and burst forth from the void, as light."* Quarters throw holly glitter. The HPS returns to the altar with the chalice.

HP – Stepping into the circle wearing all red – *"I am the Holly King, I am all that I am. I am God. I am the fire that breathes warmth upon her skin that she may burst forth with the fruits of her abundance. I am the spark that manifests her desires into your physical realm. I bring to you the sacred gifts from your mother. These are a symbol of her love."* - Passes out Yule Gifts. Group can take time to open their gifts if appropriate.

Initial Crown Chakra Activation - The Wheel of the Year – Yule

- **HP Leads Chalice Ceremony** –First round to express gratitude for gifts received, and gives thanks for the lessons of the previous year. Second round to express hopes and wishes for coming year.

- **HPS tells story of Demeter/Isis' time of mourning** on earth, and reveals how the mystery of immortality lies within releasing the pain and judgments you have collected over the year. Pain and judgment cause you to harden and age. Forgiveness restores flexibility and youth.

- **The Yule Log is blessed** and passed to each person, who unburdens themselves by giving that, which has caused them pain and sorrow from the previous year, to the Yule log to be released. Then the Yule log is placed into the fire.

Food is blessed

Quarters are closed.

Circle is ended.

Feast Begins.

You have now completed your yearly cycle, and are ready to begin again at Imbolc, clean, renewed and ready to tackle a new incarnation. Make every year count.

Certification Requirements

Plant seeds at Imbolc, follow seeds through the wheel of the year to harvest. Document your experience. Relate how the magically charged plants interconnect with your goals.

Write and perform, or attend each sabbat celebration for one year. Write your personal experience about each one, and what you have learned from it.

Awakening Spirit – Freshman Course – www.WISESeminary.com

8

Initial Transpersonal Point Activation
The Trials of the Goddess

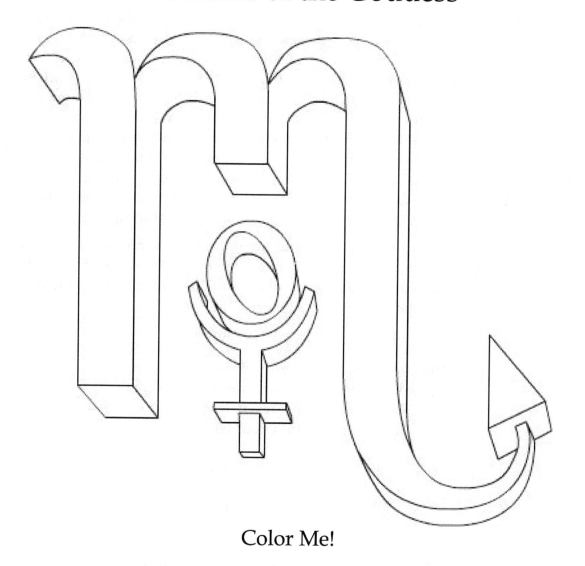

Color Me!

The moon dances a spiral all of Her own. She shows us a different face every night, and sometimes none at all. She travels quickly through the sky and even quicker through the zodiac, visiting the entire universe in slightly under 28 days. She's a tough act to follow, and quick to change Her mind. As soon as you think you've got Her figured out, She's changed again.

The moon is reflective, forcing us to look inside. She is a mirror of the sun's light. She shines Her mirror into your world, reflecting back the images of your truth, for you to reconsider and weigh their value under different circumstances.

True to man's nature, Sun festivals are about external influences, the gifts of the gods, and what is happening in and around your environment. Moon festivals, more fluid, and womanly, are about what is going on inside you. They are emotional, restful, reflective, and touch deep parts of your psyche.

The moon teaches us balance. She makes Her way through the zodiac every month, challenging us with the lesson of balance. As the new moon conjuncts with the sun, She presents you with a new lesson and a new opportunity. As the moon waxes, you are captivated by Her pulsing energy, enticed by Her charm, drawn deeply into Her spell. You experience Her lesson as a reward or blessing for the hard work of the past. At full moon, She has enchanted you out into waters you didn't realize you were treading. Tensions build and conflict manifests as you are drawn into opposing viewpoints. You are challenged to side with either the moon or the sun, as they sit on opposite sides of our planet. As She begins to withdraw her energy into the waning phase, hopefully you have found a way to give equal respect to both sides of the equation, bringing an agreeable resolution to the issue, and restoring balance.

Her lessons can seem abstract and random to those who aren't following the zodiac. Many may not even realize She's the one causing the drama. But She is stirring up your feelings, causing you to react to stimuli. Peeling away the dead layers that bind your soul, so that you can be free to fly with Her.

The Lesson of the Moon

Directing Her energy is for the brave at heart.
For She has been known to tear mountains apart.
She enchants the tides of the ocean,
And runs wild with your emotions.

She can trap and enrage you,
Leaving you howling in despair.
While teaching you to let go,
And be free from your snare.

The lessons in balance are challenging tests.
Until you succeed you will find no rest.
So, if you're willing to accept the Moon is happy to oblige.
But be warned, in Her world there is no place to hide.

And if you dare dance with Her,

> Remember this one clue.
> When the choice is either/or,
> The answer lies with two.

The Moon begins Its journey at New Moon through a zodiac sign in conjunct with the Sun. The lesson that sings to your soul will be personal, but related to the influence of that sign. The lesson will not look like a lesson at all, but more like an opportunity, or blessing. As She leaves the Sun behind and travels through the solar system, She intensifies the opportunity and matures it through Her journeys. By the time She reaches full, She is in opposition to the Sun. She has changed Her influence on the seed thought that was planted at the new moon, and has you, or someone around you, focused on the opposing force. If you say details, She says big picture. If you say right, She says left.

What she is trying to teach you is that whenever you are on an opposing side of an issue, you are not applying the principle of balance. It's not either your way, or the other way, it is both. You must find compromise to bring resolution. This is a very difficult principle to master, especially if you are used to trying to prove yourself right. But, it's spiritually sound, as we are all connected. Opposing viewpoints have validity and must be considered into the equation for harmony and balance to exist.

Compromise doesn't exist when one gets their way and the other agrees to have his way the next time. Nor does it exist when both decide to withdraw, and neither goal is accomplished. Compromise is realized when both sides accomplish their goals and all needs are met.

Wiccans are charged with keeping the balance. The Moon teaches you the lessons needed to learn how to keep the balance. Here are some examples of these lessons. These are only a few examples. There are many different interpretations of these energies.

- ✓ ♈ Providing for your needs without imposing your will on others, or precluding the needs of others.
- ✓ ♉ Balancing your values and what brings you fulfillment with what you pursue.
- ✓ ♊ Establishing a network of friends and loved ones who are beneficial to your growth without using people.
- ✓ ♋ Recognizing and coping with your emotions and subconscious motivations without retreating from reality.
- ✓ ♌ Expressing our unique and special talents without destroying, criticizing or undermining the goals or needs of the group, family, or community.
- ✓ ♍ Perfecting the details without losing sight of the goal.

- ✓ ♎ Connecting and harmonizing with others without losing your self.
- ✓ ♏ Experiencing Transformation without needless destruction.
- ✓ ♐ Achieving your goals without manipulating others or losing focus.
- ✓ ♑ Protecting and honoring tradition and rules while honoring the spirit of the law.
- ✓ ♒ Promoting compassion and freedom for the whole, without detaching from individual needs.
- ✓ ♓ Healing and transmuting negativity without placing judgment.

Planning your moons around embracing and understanding this energy will be most beneficial. If you circle with others, they will be experiencing the same undercurrent, possibly creating actual opposition with you or other members of your circle, as you each are challenged to learn this lesson together.

There are many other ways to celebrate the Moon. The Sabbats lend their energy to the celebration of the Sun and the God aspects. True to the balance, Moons are more closely associated with the energy of Goddess. There are Goddesses associated with each Zodiac sign that can be honored and worshipped as a focus of your moon celebrations.

But, the Moon doesn't easily lend Her energy to rules, or a fixed path. She will resist your desire to map Her out, or pigeon Her into any hole. There are many books available on the market that will give you an idea for each moon celebration in the year. All of these traditions are interesting to explore, each focus is different, and contains many valuable lessons. Yet, the lesson of balance continues to call, and your true balance will never be easily packaged or discovered within the pages of a book.

The Moon will continue to throw you curve balls, upsetting your reality, and forcing you to re-evaluate, adapt, and adjust until you can swim in Her waters without maps or signposts. She wants you to use your intuition. Go with the flow. Dance with her through the wild night.

She would rather you resourcefully plan a meal from ingredients scrounged up out of your yard, than follow a recipe you do not understand, even if it's the recipe of a gourmet chef. The Moon isn't about looking good, following the rules, magnificent feats of memorization or gymnastics in organization. The Moon is about reaching within, expressing your love, receiving Her love, and realizing your connectedness, while fulfilling your purpose.

She's your mother. She will make sure She provides the exact right environment necessary to help you succeed in fulfilling your purpose. If this means tripping you up on the rug, or stealing your dog-eared copy of "13 E-Z Moon Rituals for Witches", then so be it. You can't live your life out of a cookbook. Magic happens within you every day. Your Moon celebrations should reflect that. If this means; sitting on your porch with your Chalice and your Journal, enjoying Her beauty and writing about your thoughts and feelings, She will be honored by your honest expression of love.

So when you're planning your moons, imagine what it would be like if you were blind, and no one would see anything. Focus on what you feel, and deal with that. Ritualize your emotions and seek balance. Plan Moon rituals that are true to who you are, that really mean something to you. If you don't know how to plan a Moon ritual, then that is true to your nature at this time, and your nature is appropriate to Her. Go outside and offer Her a toast, take a moonlit walk in the woods, spend time appreciating Her beauty and energy. That is all it takes.

Loving your Mother is not rocket science. Don't over think it, just do it.

Awakening Spirit – Freshman Course – www.WISESeminary.com

Lineage & Service

Color Me!

Lineage

Groups have a consciousness, whether they are families, couples, religious groups, educational groups, government bodies, nations, or planets. Being a part of that group makes you a part of that consciousness, like one cell in the body of the Goddess.

Initial Transpersonal Chakra Activation – Lineage & Service

A life of awareness would require one to look beyond the needs of the self, and recognize the needs of the greater whole. This is a self-less act, and the stuff of which heroes are made. Desiring to belong to a group, to connect with something larger than ourselves, is a spiritual longing. When we are in spirit, we are part of the whole, and it is comforting. Yet, to the physical being we are so obviously physically separate individuals. We want to feel like we belong, but we can think of so many reasons why we don't.

Reaching that level of connectedness with another makes you feel safe, and loved. It's a precious feeling that is to be protected, and nurtured. But, to receive that connectedness you must let go of that which makes you separate. This is a very difficult thing for the human ego to do. All our lives we have been trying to prove that we are special and have a purpose. It's difficult to let go of that uniqueness for any group, even if it's your family of birth. However, a support group validates uniqueness. Among others you realize your uniqueness and find your purpose. It is through witnessing the talents and uniqueness of others, that your special qualities are noticed as well. If you don't know that others can't draw, it doesn't seem special to you.

You are born into this universe with a special set of instructions and a purpose. The fates oversee your life, and ensure that the appropriate events happen to set your feet on the path that will lead you to accomplish that which you are here to do. Your parents are instrumental in that role, as are your teachers, ministers, doctors, and government representatives. You may not yet understand all the lessons you've been taught. You may feel some were harsh, or counter-productive. But they did happen for a reason. Hopefully you can find something positive to take from the experience in which to help yourself and others grow.

You are the combination of many things. There are a complex variety of factors, circles within circles, which make you who you are. One of these is lineage. You are literally a reincarnation of your parents. Their combined DNA brought you into existence. You are a natural clone of them. This clone, that is your body, is pre-programmed with your parents' dharma, their purpose, the divine truth of their existence, as well as some of their karma, the karma that relates to the family's dharma/purpose. Each family has a purpose, just as each person has a purpose. It is through careful observation, meditation and prayer that this purpose is revealed to you.

As your spirit incarnates into this cloned version of your parents, your chosen physical vehicle, your first breath sets in motion the wheels of fate. You carry with you your personal karma and dharma, as well as that of your parent's, family's, religion's, clan's, community's, race, species and any other groups with whom you are interconnected. You chose these responsibilities and rewards as part of your experience, planning challenges that will help you and your chosen groups progress towards your individual and collective pre-destined goals.

As a member of your family, you are an heir to your family's rewards and responsibilities. The Catholics refer to this as "the sins of the father", and claim that infant baptism relieves that burden. I don't know, maybe it does. But, for the rest of us, we are affected by the choices of our ancestors eight generations back. Your children and progeny will be affected by your choices for eight generations to follow you. You may want to disown your family, as they are a constant source of growth, which often feels like resistance and conflict. But, through working with your family you can discover your own dharma, or purpose.

Children of policemen often become policemen. Children of doctors often become doctors. The apple doesn't fall far from the tree because our lives are intertwined. You are a combination of your parents. Of course you would make similar choices. Naturally your life will develop similarly to theirs. This is another cycle of the wheel. Look at families and notice the trends. What are the trends in your family?

I have chosen the life of a minister. I look through my family, and I find many who have devoted themselves to the same life. They have found many different religions to explore, few of which are mainstream. My mother was baptized into a new religion at the age of 22. I was initiated into Wicca at the age of 22. She spent the subsequent years of her life in devotion to God, with daily prayer and study. Even though she's a very busy woman with eight young grandchildren, and a business to run, she devotes time in her schedule to temple work. She teaches Sunday school, and takes her callings in her church very seriously. I've been actively talking to God as far back as 5 years old.

My father is an entrepreneur. He can't work for someone else. He's tried. He just can't justify making someone else money when he could be making it for himself. I can relate to that concept. I have been self-employed most of my life. I'm sure if I were a man, I would have learned brick masonry, like my father, and my grandfather, and several fathers before that. I want my son to learn this sacred art from my father, as building structure is part of who we are.

Thank goodness that my family's health has always been good. With the exception of high blood pressure, we are a pretty hearty bunch. We all have very strong opinions, and have to put forth an effort to get along with each other because of our different views. But, that has also strengthened us, and made us find ways to grow as we have a deep love for each other, and place value on family.

You have traditions and truths within your family as well, ideas, contracts, vows, burdens, and inheritances. Some of these you are aware of, and some you aren't. They say a witch isn't made. She is born. The first time I heard that I thought, "Well, there's

Initial Transpersonal Chakra Activation – Lineage & Service

no way I'm a witch then, because my parents are definitely not witches." And in truth, they are not. But my parents are magical beings, with a deep connection to God. They have a strong faith in the power of spirit to work miracles in their lives, and I see them manifest their reality differently, but no less powerfully than I. Their beliefs are very important to them, and a central part of the focus in their lives, just like mine. They may not call themselves pagan, or cast circles to the moon, but they strive to better themselves and they are expressing their truth in the highest way they know it. I'm sure if you search for the meaning behind how your parents live their life, you will find that in similar ways you are finding the same values, but expressing them in different ways.

Honoring your Father and Mother is one of the Christian Top Ten. What does that mean exactly? Honor was always one of those nebulous terms that I never could pin down as a kid. I always thought it meant to do what they said, and sometimes I just couldn't agree to do that. "The heck with the Ten Commandments anyway, I'm not Christian." my impudence would scream. But, Christianity, like all religions, holds spiritual truths, and many lessons can be found here.

Now that I'm older, and can look at my childhood experiences with less attachment, I have come to a different understanding. One should honor his lineage by improving it, being loyal to it, caring for it, and strengthening it. It means being an asset, a positive link in the chain, a stepping stone, upon which generations of children will be able to continue to improve, evolve, and have a more profound, meaningful, and joyful existence.

It means going to PTA, and helping with homework, learning how to balance meal plans, and treat the sick. It means remembering birthdays, throwing showers and celebrating holidays. It means thinking about something other than yourself, and being a devoted participant in something greater than yourself. It means listening to the advice of a pair of people whom you are almost identical to, and understanding that they are you ~20 years down the path. Their path may look differently on the surface, but it is basically the same path you are walking. You have a chance to relive it knowing now what they know ~20 years into your future. Listen to them. Utilize their wisdom and experience. Learn from their mistakes and their successes. Who else is more invested in your success than your parents? Appreciate the fact that they are the closest link you have to 8 generations of ancestors, all of whose personal programming is a part of you.

You are going to have to deal with all the struggles and trials that they have unknowingly passed down to you, and the most direct way to do that is through healing your relationship with them. Your parents are external manifestations of yourself. They are your anima and animus (male and female halves) manifested in physical form, right in front of your eyes. The way they interact with each other is how you interact internally. How you get along with each of them is a reflection of the conflict within yourself.

If you know your parents, working on loving, uplifting interaction with them is the best way to access this level of healing. If you have several sets of parents, or are lacking parents, then that is symbolic of your internal relationships as well. You may have other people who fulfill these roles for you, or you may avoid dealing with these issues. Explore these relationships, or lack thereof, and try to heal them. Write letters to those who have passed, or with whom you are no longer able to communicate.

Do all that you can to find meaning and happiness within these relationships. You will struggle with being proud of who you are, if you are not proud of where you came from. These people created you, if you're special, then so are they. You are inseparably connected. You cannot be that much different from them, you came from them.

Focus on the positive and revision your relationship with them into one that reflects a parentage in which you can find love. What mistakes did they make that you can improve upon? What lessons did they teach you that made you stronger, wiser, or more capable? What terrible misunderstandings need to be straightened out? What pains need to be healed? This may take years. And you may not actually be able to do it with your parents. But that doesn't matter; you have to do it inside first anyway. You will have someone in your life, who is willing to help you learn these valuable lessons. But, it all starts with you.

Spiritual lineage is similar to maternal lineage. Wicca is an initiatory religion. Meaning that clerics are initiated into the Priesthood, and birthed into a spiritual family that has certain goals, truths, philosophies and traditions. If you look deep enough you will find that the concept of spiritual lineage runs basically the same as blood kin.

Spiritual families, however defined, have missions and goals. This is their dharma. Each Priestess that starts a coven was called to do so, to serve a purpose ordained by Goddess. This purpose sometimes harmonizes with the seeker. Sometimes it doesn't. Some covens are called into existence for short-term goals, others for long-term goals. One isn't more important than the other, as each serves a purpose.

The initiate is adopted as a spiritual child of this teacher. The initiate inherits many of the teacher's positive attributes as well as many of the negative ones. You will also inherit talents and gifts from Goddess as you join this special family, so that you too can take up the dharma of the group, and work to fulfill its purpose.

Do your personal goals harmonize with those of the groups with which you participate? Do you understand the role you play in your family, and how it connects to

Initial Transpersonal Chakra Activation – Lineage & Service

the family's dharma? How are you recreating dramas and issues that your parents lived in their past? Do you love and respect your parents for their positive attributes or are you stuck in a negative pattern that you will eventually recreate with your own children? Have you identified their contribution to the universe, and found that reflected in your own life? Are you putting up with a spiritual teacher that you don't respect, to avoid being without a teacher at all? Does this reflect the same challenges that your birth parents presented to you? These are important connections that one needs to take into consideration, while walking a spiritual path towards enlightenment.

As a human you experience life as an individual, free to do what you want, disconnected from all others. But, as a spirit, you experience life as a being connected to every one and every thing. The human illusion of loneliness is a painful experience for the spirit, as we long for the interaction of our brothers and sisters, whether they are blood kin, or heart kin. The people in our lives were put in here to teach us lessons. Your conflict is real, but it is generated within you. Change your focus and shift your perspective to searching for the positive, and you will transform these very important relationships to ones that will serve for your highest good. Everyone has flaws and everyone has positive attributes. It is your choice to make each person in your life an ally or an adversary. It's your choice to rise above the pitfalls of human existence, and transform the negative experience into positive lessons from which you can grow.

Service

Ministering is about service. Clerics serve the community, within which they live. This is not my opinion. It is part of the job.

Participating in community events is not just some other way to entertain yourself during your off time. It's a sacred duty. Community builds unity and unity empowers us. Power shared is power gained. If we all work together, we can accomplish amazing things. Teamwork is about getting more done as a group than one person could do on his/her own.

One man did not build the pyramids of Egypt, nor did slaves build them. Free men worked tirelessly for years in the Egyptian desert to build those sacred monuments. They believed in something together, and together they created something that no single man could.

By reaching out and being of service to the community, you actively begin to make the world a better place. By combining your efforts with others, you can build schools, churches, governments, and health institutions. Your direct efforts can and will make the world a better place, if you care about people, and work to uplift others.

Service to Goddess is about service to Her children. Whereever you see a need that you can fill is where you are called to serve. If you don't see a need, find one. Sometimes this means healing a sick friend. Sometimes it means writing a moon ritual. Sometimes it means liming toilets at a campsite, or cooking breakfast for 250 of your closest friends. It can mean going to a prison and talking to prisoners, or visiting a senior's center. You don't even have to tell anyone that you're ministering. Just help others, and give of your positive energy to people who need it. The children of Goddess have various needs. It takes every member to make community happen.

Don't discount your value because you're new to service. Serving selflessly and with a joyous heart makes you a valuable member of community, whether new to the path or eldered. Elders are called upon to do different things than neophytes, but elders can't do their job without neophytes for whom to do it. Likewise, no one will enjoy a drum circle without someone having chopped wood (or purchased it) for the fire. Everyone has to eat and it doesn't take a degree in theology to fix a lovely meal.

Clerics are ministers, and public servants. They are not rock stars, politicians, or sports heroes. It may look glamorous to watch an HPs put on a ritual for 500 people, but you weren't there the 15 to 30 hours that it took to prepare, write, memorize lines, and organize all the different factors that go into a ritual. Nor did you see the scrambling it took to replace someone, who didn't show up last minute. It takes a lot of work, and personal responsibility to generate a spiritual experience for many people. She didn't suddenly luck up on that position. She got there after years of public service, and study.

So get over your excuses. Go out and be a part of things. Be helpful. Be an asset everywhere you go. Look for what needs to be done, and jump in there to do it. Ministering is about service. Clerics serve the community, within which they live. This is not opinion. It is part of the job.

Initial Transpersonal Chakra Activation – Spells and Magic

Spells and Magic

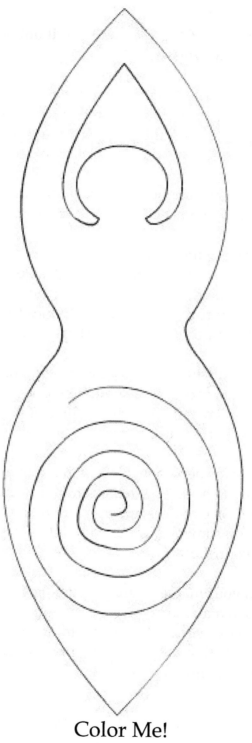

Color Me!

These are a few simple but practical spells that come in handy on a day-to-day basis.

When doing spells, remember:

- ✓ Have Faith in your magic – Once it's done, put it out of your mind. Don't keep wondering if it's going to work or not.

- ✓ Trust that you are loved, and Goddess wants you to have what you need. – Don't strain trying to put energy into it. Relax and enjoy the spell. Communicate your needs with the intent that everything is going to go according to your wishes. Visualize that you already have that for which you are asking. Then let it go.

- ✓ Explore the ripples – Think about the consequences of your actions. Act in ways that are for the best and highest good of all concerned.

- ✓ Think ahead – don't wait until you are in a crisis to do a spell. Think about what you will need in the future and plan accordingly. Don't do spells when you are in a desperate state of mind. You only manifest more fear that way. Try to plan your spells based on appropriate astrological times (phases of the moon, etc) to avoid doing impulsive, spur of the moment spells that are not well thought out.

- ✓ Write them down – you will forget what you have done over time. If something works, you may want to repeat it. If something doesn't work, you may want to research why. You can't do either of these things if you don't have them recorded in your Book of Shadows.

- ✓ Don't use your magic for personal gain – Don't bother Goddess with lottery numbers, a new pair of shoes, or a fancy car. If you have a need, then work to fulfill that need, and ask Goddess to help you find a way to fill that need. But, don't try to conjure up someone to show up with a bag of money so that you can sit around and not contribute.

- ✓ Be responsible with your magic. – Use your magic for the growth and healing of yourself and others to make the world a better place. By demonstrating responsibility, and only using your powers for the good of all (not just your good) will demonstrate that you are ready for more power and responsibility and will keep your path moving forward.

Grounding

Grounding is used whenever you feel off center. When you get angry, or scared, if you will remember to ground and breathe you will instantly transform your situation.

Glitter

Glitter is one of those easy spells. Glitter makes you instantly feel better. Throwing or blowing glitter on anything scary makes it less scary. It also finds its way into the strangest places, and clings to almost everything it touches, giving you a constant reminder that your magic is still working for you. Children respond well to glitter. If they are scared, glitter makes it less scary.

Place glitter in your palm. Hold your intent in your palm and in your breath. Blow glitter on or at intended object. For example, if someone is real stressed out, and needs to relax. You can hold the intention of them relaxing, and charge the glitter in your hand with your intent. As you blow think "Relax" while sending relaxing energy with the glitter.

Flying Ointment

Flying Ointment helps you astral project. Astral projection is a deep form of journeying, but is usually so blown out of proportion in the aspirants mind that they have much difficulty doing it.

Usually, one's first experience with astral projection doesn't feel like you've left your body at all. It's hard not to focus on the feeling of leaving your body, which in turn keeps you in your body. This causes frustration, which keeps you from journeying. Resulting in striking the whole experience down as another failure.

You must be patient with yourself to do magic. You will never be able to do it, if you get mad at yourself every time you don't live up to your own expectations. Relax, and have faith that with practice you will be able to do all of it.

To astral project *you have to focus **all** your energy on the journey*. Any thought about your body will cause you to jump right back in it. If you want to see what it "feels" like to leave your body, you will never get out, because you're asking to notice a physical sensation. You need a body to have a physical sensation. This is a conflicting goal. Another conflicting goals is: wanting to walk around and look at your body or other people. You don't walk when you astral project. You don't feel the same. Sometimes you're not even in the same dimension as your body. Release your expectations, and just let whatever part of your consciousness that journeys, experience the journey.

Broom Polish
Used for astral projection and for polishing and charging your broom.

1 cup Olive Oil
1/2 tsp clove oil
1 tsp soot from fireplace
1 T dried cinquefoil
½ tsp dried mandrake powder
1 T dried mugwort
1 T dried poplar, or 1 fresh poplar leaf
1 T dried thistle
1 tsp dried vervain
2 tsp. benzoin tincture

In a glass or ceramic pot or small cast iron cauldron slowly heat all ingredients over a low flame, stir together deosil. Simmer for ten to fifteen minutes. Strain and remove herbs. Store in an amber, indigo, or green glass bottle in a cool dark place (refrigerator is best).

Anoint your chakras, hands, wrists, ankles and feet. If you feel you need even more help, you can rub it all over your body. Lie down in a warm place. Cover up if you need to, your body will get cold while you're gone. Breathe deeply and relax. Imagine your consciousness rising up out of your body and taking a journey. It may help to hold onto to a broom, and imagine yourself riding it. Don't discount your experience. Don't think about your body, and DON'T wonder if it's happening or not. Just do it. Let your imagination do the traveling. The more you focus on what your imagining the deeper you will go into trance. Your consciousness will catch up.

Getting back. All you have to do is try to move, or think about your body. Your entire consciousness never leaves your body, and space and time are an illusion anyway. So just try to feel your body and you will be in it. You may feel extremely heavy, or your teeth may feel like wood, or foreign objects in your mouth you want to spit out. But this only happens the first couple of times. It's a brief experience, and it's more like a validation than an inconvenience.

Be sure to record your experiences. Happy Travels.

House Clearing

It is appropriate to clear a house after you move out and before you move in. There are several nice incenses for this purpose that we have discussed. I usually use frankincense and myrrh for this particular purpose, but I'm sure others would work too. Begin at the front door, leave it open so any negativity can escape and move deosil throughout the house. Take care to circle deosil in every room, making sure to get in closets, under beds, and inside cabinets. Once you begin, do not stop until you are back at the front

Initial Transpersonal Chakra Activation – Spells and Magic

door. House monsters don't like to be evicted and will go to many lengths to stop you from finishing.

To layer your intent, you may want to sprinkle salt or powdered mandrake on the floor. Spray lavendar in the air, and light a candle in each room. You can also chant something like "Love, Joy, Prosperity, Health" or something else to bless the house with positive energy.

Shielding with Kanji

Kanji are Japanese characters. These characters operate as sacred symbols and can be drawn in the air to invoke the power they represent. For instance, if you want to ground, the Earth Kanji can be drawn to invoke the energy of grounding. The Water Kanji can help you deal with emotions. The Fire Kanji can help energize you. The Air Kanji can help you access hidden information, or remember information that you may have forgotten.

A powerful shield can be erected when you face each direction and use your athame or pointed fingers to draw the appropriate Kanji for that element. This shield is excellent for stopping psychic attack, bad dreams, or for extra protection from any threat. There is no need to banish this shield, as it will naturally respond to your needs based on your intent and focus.

Breathing is important when using the Kanji, as is the order in which the lines are drawn. See diagram.

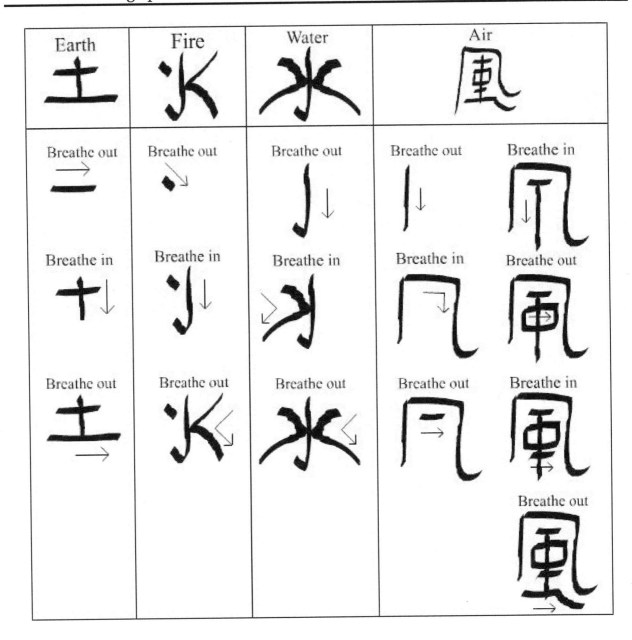

Smudging

Wafting incense around an object alters its vibration according to the incense. Smell is connected to the heart and emotions, which gives incense the power to control moods, invoke gods, and send messages through the veil. Light incense while focusing on or speaking your intent.

Onion to absorb sickness

For viral or bacterial infections, including colds or flu, cut an onion in half and place it under the bed where the sick person will be sleeping. When he goes to sleep his spirit will astral project away from his body during his normal sleep pattern, leaving the virus or bacteria behind as a sort of astral mucus. This is absorbed into the onion. When the spirit returns the body has been cleansed, and health is restored. If there is much sickness you can repeat this every night. It does not harm the body or spirit. Remember to remove the onion the next morning.

Candle Spell

For a simple candle spell, just light a candle with your intent (or prayer) in mind, and leave it to burn down completely. Keep this in mind when choosing the size of your candle. A big pillar candle will burn for several days. Votives burn for a few hours.

To layer your intent, you could choose an appropriate color, or anoint the candle with an oil that lends the appropriate vibration to your spell. You may want to carve a pentagram or other symbols into the candle, or carve words stating your intent, as you focus your energy on visualizing yourself already having what you wish.

Basil for anger

Basil quickly dispels anger and negativity. If someone is mad or venting, get him or her to smell some basil. The mood will immediately begin to improve.

Clearing Psychic attack with athame & wand

When someone is under psychic attack, it will feel like flu symptoms, headaches, or other aches and pains. To clear someone of possible psychic attack, cut along the outside of their body with your athame or your wand, with the intent of removing any external unwanted attachments or any psychic drains on the energy field. To clear psychic attack in your own field, holding your athame should be all the protection you need.

Rescue Remedy

Bach's Flower Essences work on emotions. Whenever you or someone around you has experienced emotional trauma, three drops of Rescue Remedy is a sure bet for instant relief. It won't make the trauma go away, but it will make it easier to deal with.

Banishing Pentagram

A Banishing Pentagram banishes negative energy. If something is causing you discomfort, a banishing pentagram is an effective means to remove that energy from your presence. Draw the pentagram in the air, encircle it into a ball and throw it at the offending energy. You may wish to practice your accuracy by shooting baskets. Use your energy to make the ball hit the basket.

Certification Requirements

Write and perform, or attend each moon celebration for one year. Write your personal experience about each one, and what you have learned from it.

Perform the 12 spells included in Chapter 8. Record your results.

9

Second Root Chakra Activation
Creating Your Personal Temple
Red

Color Me Red!

Every Priest and Priestess benefits from connecting with his or her spiritual self each day. It is an opportunity for you to remember who you are, refocus on your goals, your dreams, your hopes, and what you need to do to achieve them. It is also a time for you to express your gratitude, and ask for guidance through your daily trials.

When you think of the word Temple, what kind of place comes to mind? Is it a simple, natural, clearing in the woods, or a beautifully, and elaborately decorated stone monument? Do you see the Parthenon, the pyramids, a secret cave behind a waterfall or a hidden grove deep within a medieval forest?

Committed sacred space allows you to quickly make a shift into a spiritual mindset, and step away from the daily grind into a place of peace and harmony. It should be a place that spiritually speaks to you, and nurtures your soul. It should be a place where you can go and just be, without any cares, demands or worries.

Choosing the Space

Your personal temple could be a table by your bedside, the top of your dresser, a place in your garden, or a spare room in your home. It is important to consider if you would like privacy, or if you would prefer a place that you pass often during the day. A foyer is a very good place for a family altar, as everyone passes by it coming and going from the home, and can take a moment to remember that they are entering or leaving sacred space.

Any temple should take into consideration the direction of North. If you know where north is you can then make conscious choices about altar placement. If your space is limited and you have one choice of where to put an altar, then that's the place. Direction is not a factor, because it's there or nowhere, and the Gods will accept your intent. But, it would be a good idea to know what factors might affect your altar.

Standard Wiccan text will encourage an altar in the North. However, this may not be the best place depending on your needs. If you are already a very intellectually minded person and need a little intuition to balance out your analytical nature, an altar in the west may be a good idea.

If you are trying to conceive a child, building an altar in the east would help increase the fertility of the female partner, while one in the south would enhance fertility in the male partner.

If you lack motivation, an altar in the south would increase passion and enthusiasm. There are many variables. The rules are bendable based on your intent. The

Second Root Chakra Activation – Creating Your Personal Temple

important thing is to consciously make decisions, and be aware of the energies you are calling to you.

For years I rigidly insisted on having my altar in the North, because "that's the way I was taught". I now enjoy my altar in the east because it helps me connect with the abundance of the mother, the power of birth, and it feels more Goddess centered than my north altar. I still appreciate the north altar. I am just not so rigid about positioning it now.

Items to place on the Altar

Choose a sturdy foundation. Rickety tables are not suggested. I like an old desk, or chest of drawers, because the drawers come in handy for storing items you don't want on display. Altar cloths can vary. You may have one in particular that you want to use all the time. I like to change mine to reflect the current sabbat.

Your altar should move energy deosil. To create this movement, place a Purple or Black (or Silver) candle to represent the Goddess on the Left, and a White (or Gold) candle to represent the God on the Right. Black represents the Goddess because she is receptive, and black absorbs light. White reflects light and represents the projective male energy.

You will want to include your standard tools, chalice, wand, athame, and pentacle. But you could also add an incense burner, a bell, a vase of flowers, a musical instrument, special crystals, divination tools, anointing oil, magical jewelry, or any item that is sacred to you, or that you use in ceremony. For example, a disposable lighter is not really considered a sacred tool, but you need one on the altar to light candles and incense.

To complete your temple, place appropriate colored quarter candles in each direction, along the circumference of the space where you will cast circle.

(Picture of Lammas Altar)

The WISE Temple

When space allows, it is a good practice to build up the quarters by having an altar in each direction. Your main altar can still remain in the North, but a table at each quarter allows for you to build an earth altar, fire altar, water altar and air altar in addition to having your main altar. This would include spreading out your tools amongst the different altars, and adding any additional items you feel appropriate.

A fire altar would include such items as a red quarter candle, your wand, brooms, staffs, rattles, sistrums, extra red candles, and maybe a cauldron or brazier.

A water altar would include, in addition to the Chalice and blue quarter candle, other magical liquid containers, such as pitchers and pottery, divination tools, crystal balls, a fountain, a harp or other string instruments, pictures of your ancestors, or items that remind you of them.

An air altar would have a yellow quarter candle, incense, your athame and sword if you have one, feathers, glitter, fans, bells, wind chimes, horns, masks, Book of Shadows, and writing instruments.

An earth altar would include your altar pentacle, a green quarter candle, grain, salt or seeds, drums, shields, crystals, and totem images.

Second Root Chakra Activation – Clearing Negative Energy

Clearing Negative Energy

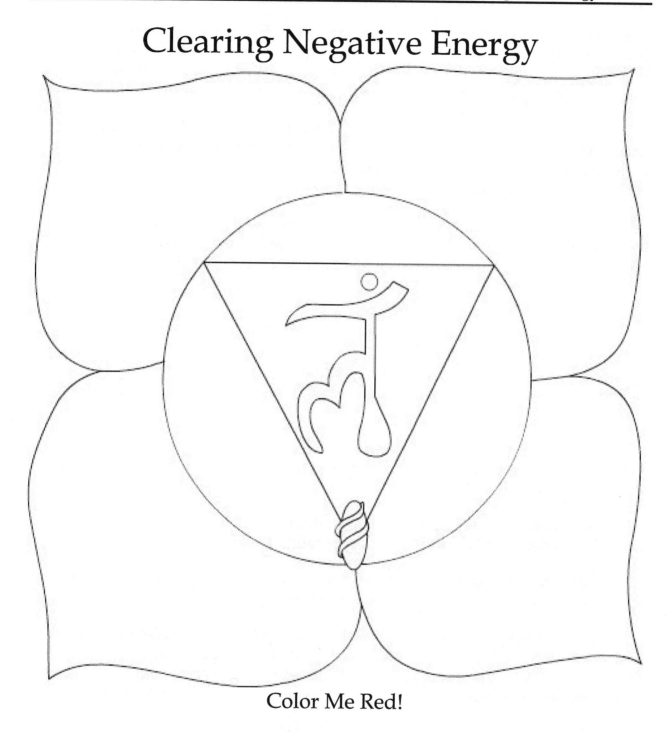

Color Me Red!

As above, so below; recognize the power of the physical action of cleansing. Every time you take a shower you are cleansing yourself of negative energy. When you wash something you are cleansing it physically as well as spiritually. We have a tendency to overcomplicate things. We like to separate spiritual from mundane, but you can't affect one without affecting the other. If you are physically cleaning something, there is spiritual cleansing that is taking place as well.

In relation to setting up a temple, you want to clean any place where a temple will be erected. Sweep, wash, dust, paint, vacuum, mop, clear out the cobwebs, and get rid of everything that doesn't belong, before bringing in your magical things. Clean and cleanse everything before you bring it into your sacred space.

Any element can cleanse. You cleanse a tool by removing the negative energies attached to it. Just like anything else this can be as simple as running water over it under the faucet, or as elaborate as you can dream up. The important part of cleansing is that you feel it has been cleansed.

If you are cleansing something that you know was purposefully desecrated by blood sacrifice for who knows how long, that tool needs a more elaborate ritual than a rock you just picked up out of the yard. Every magical action should be appropriate to the situation.

To cleanse with Earth

The most extreme earth cleansing would be to bury the object for a determined time: a turn of the moon (~ 4 weeks), a turn of the wheel (~ 6 weeks), or a full turn of the wheel (year).

You can coordinate this effort with astrological correspondences and numerological influences, and add mandrake and sandalwood, crystals, or salt in with the buried object.

A more simple, yet still effective method is to place the object in a dish and cover it in salt, or a cleansing herb like mandrake or sandalwood.

Another earth cleansing would be to place drawing crystals, like smoky quartz, apache tear, or garnet to remove negative energies.

Be mindful when using salt. Salt is like spiritual Clorox. Consider the item, and how it is going to be affected by the salt. You would not want to pack certain items in salt, as it may damage the item. Certain crystals can get degenerated by being packed in salt. Therefore, use salt only for the things that have a really bad case of the ickies.

To cleanse with Fire

When you cleanse with fire you have to make sure you do not burn or melt what you are cleansing. Most things that benefit by cleansing with fire are metal tools such as pentacles, swords, athames, talismans, etc. You cleanse with fire by running the object through the flame, or by thrusting it into the coals.

Second Root Chakra Activation – Clearing Negative Energy

You can also cleanse with fire by rubbing the object with anointing oil, sweeping it with a broom, or by using the drawing end of a wand to pull out the negative energies. Shaking a rattle or sistrum over or at an item will also clear it of negative energy. Rattles and sistrums are fire tools.

To cleanse with Water

Remember that water is death, rebirth, transformation and initiation, and is the quickest, easiest, most complete, and most preferred method of cleansing. The easiest way is to run water from the faucet over the object. This simple, mundane task is often overlooked as a very spiritual process.

Taking a shower or a bath is a cleansing ritual. A ritual bath is nothing more than a bath with a spiritual intent. If you recognize that a shower is a cleansing ritual, then every shower is a ritual bath. If you incorporate soaps, shampoos, oils, powders, and lotions that are made with magical herbs you add a layer of depth to your purpose. But, not using those things does not change the fact that you stepped into the water and cleansed your physical self, as well as all the other selves that make up you.

One thing to avoid is submerging an object in water and leaving it for a long period of time. The stagnant water takes on the negative vibrations of the object, and cleansing may not be fully effective. Running water is the best choice. Another way you can cleanse with water is to make a potion of cleansing herbs, and use that to wash the object. Again, you can add depth by utilizing astrological and numerological influences. You can add salt to the water, or place the object in a flowing river, or in the ocean.

To cleanse with Air

Cleansing with air affects the spiritual vibration but does not have a prolonged affect on the physical form. A common use of air is smudging. Smudging is to blow or waft incense smoke on the object with a feather, fan or your hand. The incense changes the vibration attached to the person or item thereby cleansing it of negativity and resetting it to your intent. Cleansing incenses can vary; frankincense and sage are two commonly used smudges. This method will work with a variety of herbs, and involves personal preference and situation specifics. Feathers and fans can be used to cleanse, with or without accompanying incense.

Tibetan Bells and spiritual gongs are a great quick easy way to clear anything.

Swords and athames are used to clear a space by ritual cutting around the object, and/or by drawing a banishing pentagram towards the object.

Making Incense

It is a good practice to anoint and smudge yourself and those you are working with at the beginning of ritual. This utilizes the masculine elements to remove any negativity from us as we enter sacred space. We should always enter circle in a state of perfect love and perfect trust. This process activates our subconscious, reminding us of who we are, and what we are about to do.

Smudge first to clear yourself of negative thoughts, stress, psychic attack, etc. Then anoint yourself to seal your defenses, allowing yourself to be safe and protected, as you open yourself to the bridge between the worlds.

To smudge, get an incense that you harmonize with. If you would like to make your own magical incense there are a couple of ways to blend herbs, resins and oils to make a well-balanced energy to lend 'power unto your spell'. Choose as specific a concept as your can, then blend a balance of this concept with an herb, resin, or oil from each of the four elements.

Resins create a long burning smoke, which carries the vibration in the air for longer periods of time. In incense, resins carry the base note. There are a limited number of resins to choose from. My favorites are benzoin, frankincense, myrrh, dragon's blood, and copal.

Herbs provide balance and bulk, and allow the incense to breathe. They help fine-tune the intent, as well as give the oils a carrier to keep the oils from burning up too quickly. There are a large variety of herbs, each with its own magical note that connects with your soul, should you sit close and listen. Growing your own herbs is a magical prayer unto itself. Planting an herbs means planting that intent into your life. Sacred Gardens provide a collection of prayers, and offerings to the Goddess. Scott Cunningham's *Encyclopedia of Magical Herbs* is an excellent reference.

Essential Oils help blend the ingredients together, and prevent them from separating. Only use essential oils for magical or spiritual workings. Fragrance oils are synthetic and do not carry the energy of the herb or plant. Essential Oils coat the resins and herbs, which keep the oils from burning up too quickly, allowing their fragrance and energy to linger.

Remember to record your experiments, as you may want to recreate your incenses later.

The trinity of resins, herbs, and oils, together with the four elements, creates a fully balanced thought form for your incense. Using this basic model, you can create the right incense for any need you may have. I've included the list of herbs I use in a couple of my favorites for you to practice with. Add a little of each ingredient and adjust the amounts to your liking. Burn these incenses on a self-lighting charcoal disk, which can be purchased in stores that sell loose incense.

When you are making magical incense, smell is a secondary concern. Focus on the right magical blend. If you are in harmony with the energy that you are invoking and you blended the right magical properties, the smell will be perfect.

Elemental Smudge
Can be used as a potion, an anointing oil*, a packing material, or a smudge. It is for cleansing and consecrating.

Mix equal parts of the loose herbs
- ✓ Rosemary (fire),
- ✓ Mugwort (earth),
- ✓ Lavender (air),
- ✓ Chamomile (water)

Add a few drops of Rosemary and/or Lavender oil to make sure that it blends well, and does not separate. (Notice that I did not include a resin in this smudge, because it's specifically used to cleanse, and not for prolonged burning, like an incense.)

*To make the anointing oil, mix equal parts of each essential oil in an olive oil base.

Horned God Incense
To Invoke the Horned God

Mix variations of the following herbs, oils, and resins to your liking:
- ✓ Clove
- ✓ Patchouli
- ✓ Cinnamon
- ✓ Bay
- ✓ Sandlewood
- ✓ Myrrh
- ✓ Vervain

Venus
To Invoke the Goddess of Love and the properties of the planet Venus

Mix variations of the following herbs, oils, and resins to your liking:
- ✓ Dragon's Blood
- ✓ Clove
- ✓ Cardamon
- ✓ Rose
- ✓ Lavendar
- ✓ Rosemary
- ✓ Orange Powder
- ✓ Thyme
- ✓ Ylang Ylang

Invoking
To invite the presence of deity

Mix variations of the following herbs, oils, and resins to your liking:
- ✓ Sandlewood
- ✓ Lavendar
- ✓ Benzoin
- ✓ Lemon Grass

Divination & Prophetic Dreams
To call for and help interpret messages from spirit

Mix variations of the following herbs, oils, and resins to your liking:
- ✓ Benzoin
- ✓ Mugwort
- ✓ Bay
- ✓ Cinquefoil
- ✓ Jasmine

Second Root Chakra Activation – Mars – Oak King/Warriors

Mars – Oak King/Warriors

Color Me Red!

The infant babe pushes forth from its mother's womb, instinctually. Kicking against the contracting uterus, fighting it's way through the tight, and restrictive birth canal, until it bursts forth into freedom.

His birth cry is a declaration of his newly claimed independence. He draws his life-giving first breath and immediately begins searching to suckle at his mother's breast. The next seven years of his life will be spent in self-absorbed discovery, as he ventures into a world ripe with possibility.

The vitality of new life surges within his veins. Nothing in his universe is more important than him, and his needs. He is showered with unconditional love and abundance. All his needs are magically manifested in this realm, in which he is King. The entire world exists to sustain and entertain him, and he quickly adapts to fully partake of his wonder-filled environment.

He delights in the eternal admiration and ever-watchful attentiveness of his nurturing mother. He never tires of expressing his affection. He entertains her with gifts of his inventions, and discoveries, and demonstrations of his power, and greatness.

His displeasure is expressed in explosive and passionate cries. His joy is exclaimed in squeals of delight. He is filled with the inexhaustible quest for discovery. The titillation of his existence bursts forth from him in laughter, as his only concern is for the adventure of the moment. His ability to learn and adapt are at their height. His imagination and senses are tingling with input. He drinks in the wonder of his universe with zeal and passion.

He is the Warrior!
He is the Oak King!
He is Mars!

He must be closely supervised and reminded of his direction, or he will easily find his blind courage landing him in situations that will threaten his very survival. He exudes immortality, and pays no heed to the dangers that seem all to real to his doting mother, who is quick to kiss away any misery that dares detour him from his quest.

He is power. He is passion. He is conquest. He is new life, full of promise. He will not reason. He will not be stopped. He is relentless in his pursuit, and fully confident of his right to pursue. He will fight with you or against you, your choice. But, beware; he will win, for even if you defeat him today, he will be back to fight tomorrow, and the next day, until victory is his.

He has a mission, a will to survive, a drive to conquer, a yearning to experience, and a commitment to discovery. You are either an obstacle on his path, or a comrade in arms, and he welcomes the challenge, either way.

Feel his power. Drink deeply of his existence. Join him and let him take you on the most amazing journey you will ever know…. the fantastic, magical, amazing and wonder-filled journey of self.

You will find him in Egypt, as the young Falcon God, Horus, avenging the wrongful death of his father, Osiris. His is the power of the great Roman army, boldly consuming the continent of Europe and it's surrounding lands. He is the Ares, the bloodstained warrior, who delights in battle for it's own sake.

By any name you call him, he is the divine newborn son of spring: aggressive, temperamental, warlike, and hot-tempered. He is the force of death being brought to birth. He is protective, courageous, and brave; a force to be reckoned with in any situation.

Certification Requirements

Create an Altar. Explain the symbolism of everything on your altar. Note the history behind each magical tool, and explain why you chose to include it on your altar. Include Pictures.

Create your own incense. Explain the magical intent of the incense and why you chose each specific herb. Include Recipe.

Journal

How do you feel about your new altar? Where did you choose to put it and why? Is there anything specific to you that you would want to place on an altar that may not be initially considered a magical tool? What other creative ways have you found to make altars throughout your home?

10
Second Sacral Chakra Activation
Sacred Tools
Orange

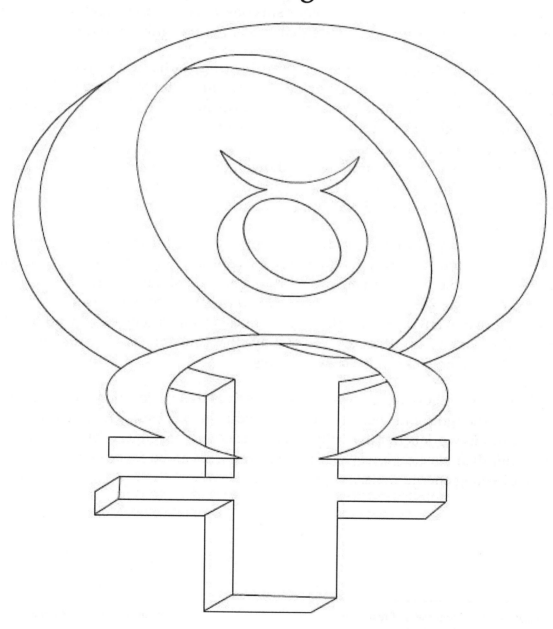

Color Me Orange!

When learning to work magic it is important for you to be able to make the intangible tangible. Putting an energetic idea or concept into an object that you can see or touch makes it easier to grasp the idea or concept. It engages your conscious and your subconscious mind and encourages connections that affect many different levels of your awareness at once.

Tools are symbolic, archetypal, universal, and tangible. They speak to you through the tarot, in your dreams, in sacred texts, in the mysteries, in sacred space, and in mundane reality. Tools have gained the power of the ages. They have entered into the causal mind[8] speaking volumes to your subconscious at a single glance. They have become universal icons of everyday use that you either recognize or overlook.

When you sit down to dinner, you probably don't notice the sacred bonding ritual that you are performing. Do you recognize the importance of sharing food and drink with your loved ones as a special time of nurturing and emotional support? Do you notice the sacred tools that are involved in mealtime? Or do you dash through a fast food restaurant, eat alone, and hurry on through your day, missing the sacred moments of the Now? Do you jump in the shower, throw on your clothes and hurry off to work, all in an effort to beat the clock, or do you allow your morning to be a time of conscious renewal, and directed beginnings?

Every breath you take is a sacred moment. Magic is not something that exists outside you. It permeates everything you touch. Your intent colors everything in your world. You do not need to learn how to work magic. You already do it. What you desire is to raise your awareness of the magic you already possess, so that you may consciously use it in a way that creates and manifests what you want, instead of randomly throwing your energy around in ways that cause chaos, destruction, sorrow, and pain. This can be done with the use of tools.

Tools are symbols and extensions of our selves that project our conscious and subconscious thoughts and energies. Anything you deem appropriate can be a magical tool. Some things work better than others, such as copper facilitates the movement of energy better than plastic. However, a big plastic globe can be an excellent tool to visualize directing energy towards world peace.

---

[8] The Causal Mind is a dimension of reality, which each species shares that determines instincts, and inherited traits, as well as subconscious knowledge and information.

Earth Tools

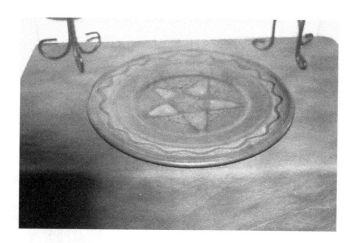

Earth is the element of birth, foundation, new beginnings, security, and prosperity. Its dominant gender is feminine, and has receptive energy. It is represented by a shallow dish, pentacle or shield. Shields are essentially the same shape as a plate, and I always find it interesting how food protects you as equally as a shield. Food is used to nourish and strengthen our physical form. A shield will strengthen a warrior, by making it harder to land a blow. Magical shields actually receive the blow, by drawing projective energy to them, and grounding it.

My earth tool, or altar pentacle, is a green ceramic plate with a big pentagram drawn on the inside to represent the earth element (see picture). Among other things, the plate is used to hold, bless and consecrate our cakes at rituals. Recognizing the tool as a plate that holds the abundance of the Goddess Mother is very helpful in spell work. Whenever you are trying to manifest physical needs, you want to visualize that need being manifested on your earth pentacle.

Sit with the plate, ground, then pull the energy towards you through the plate with your hands. Visualize and form the energy into the thing that you are manifesting. If you want money, visualize money flowing up through the pentacle and spilling over the sides as the abundance continues to flow. If you need clothes, food, a car, whatever you need, visualize the energy taking that form.

Remember it is the portal of birth; everything that manifests on the earth plane into physical form must enter through the earth quarter. Using this tool in this way opens up that quarter and brings the necessary energy through it. Provide the other elements for the energy to find physical cohesion, and you have just manifested your needs. All you have to do is wait for them to physically materialize.

Examples of Earth tools

- ✓ Pentacle, Pentagram, or Plate
- ✓ Shields and Masks
- ✓ Talismans
- ✓ Salt, Grains, Seeds, Bread, Cakes, Cookies
- ✓ Food of any kind
- ✓ Money
- ✓ Crystals
- ✓ Drums

Fire Tools

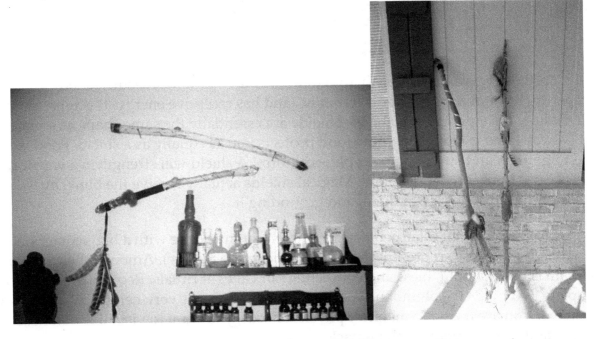

Fire is the element of action, protection and defense, creation, conscious awareness, instinct, beliefs, passion, desire, and heat. Its dominant gender is masculine. Its tools are the wand, staff, or broom. Wands are essentially the same shape as a phallus, and have fertilizing, projective energy.

Wands direct creative energy. When trying to create something material, use the wand in conjunction with the earth pentacle. Pull the energy through the pentacle, and form it with the wand. Use it when trying to receive inspiration, decide on right action, defending from psychic attack, or for healing. A wand or staff is used to move energy into a receptive force (earth or water). It will deflect projective energy. However, it is not very effective in projecting energy towards a non-receptive force (fire or air). In other words, don't take a stick to a knife fight.

Second Sacral Chakra Activation – Sacred Tools

Wands are excellent tools to teach grounding and defense. Fire is instinctual, making wands excellent tools for helping the beginner reconnect with and become aware of the instinctual energetics they are already utilizing. Wands are able to move energy for someone who does not know how to move it for him or herself. They are excellent tools for beginners, who have not yet learned how to discipline their energy (i.e., looses temper easily, has trouble maintaining focus, etc.). Safety devices can be installed, such as a protective stone like garnet, to avoid negativity from being projected towards others or into the universe.

Wands can be programmed to work a certain way, requiring little to no expertise by the holder. I encourage all new witches to start out with a wand and buy a blade as your *last* tool. Sacred space can be safely cast with wands.

The Wand is a tool of the Oak King, who acts instinctively. As with the boldness of youth, fire is a very powerful, yet undisciplined element. With a little skill and direction, it can be transformed from reckless abandon and destruction into a limitless force of creation.

Fire has a mission that it can neither ignore nor deny. It is driven toward its goal, often unfocused on the consequences of the victims that get in its way. Therefore, fire works best when it is slowly fueled, and well contained in a circle of earth. Envision the campfire surrounded by rocks. It is a happy fire, where you can warm yourself, and roast marshmallows. But remove the rocks, and the fire will escape and consume everything it can reach, it will grow out of control, and destroy everything with which it comes in contact.

Goddess is to God, as Earth is to Fire, as Priestess is to Priest. Earth channels her energy through the Fire, feeding it, containing it, and producing either positive or negative results through Her own wisdom. If Earth abuses Fire it will destroy Her. Just as well as if a Priestess abuses the power of her Priest, he will turn his power against her. Of course fire cannot create alone, as no element can stand alone to create wholeness.

Fire energy is generated at the quarter; it doesn't move through it, like the earth or water quarter. Fire is a sentry along the pathway from birth to death, providing the spark of creation that allows birth to take place, and destruction that allows death to take place. Death and birth are two sides of the same coin.

Examples of Fire Tools

- ✓ Wands, Staffs and Brooms
- ✓ Candles and Wax

- ✓ Oils, and Perfumes
- ✓ Accelerants
- ✓ Make up, Woad[9], and War Paint
- ✓ Alcohol
- ✓ Runes
- ✓ Rattles, and Sistrums

Water Tools

Water is the element of death and initiation, which is rebirth and transformation. It is also the element of emotions, from love to fear. Its dominant gender is feminine, and it has receptive energy. A deep dish, such as a Chalice, cup, or bowl, represents water. The masculine tool would be the Trident.

The Trident sends out a spray of transformational energy, different from the wand, which pulses with quick bursts, and Athame, which sends a direct beam. It is interesting to note that the Christian God, Satan is often depicted holding a Trident, relating to him as God of Eternal Death as opposed to the Christian Father, God of Eternal Life. Most Christians fear death, as they do not appreciate its transformational properties. Their God of Death is considered evil, making death and transformation a

---

[9] Woad is the blue paint that Celtic warriors wear. You may remember it worn by Mel Gibson in the movie "Braveheart".

negative action to avoid, fear, and dread.

Change can be painful, scary and very difficult. But it isn't the change that scares you; it is the unknown that you fear. You do not know what is going to happen tomorrow, but when tomorrow gets here you cannot escape it. You can walk right off a plate, but try climbing out of a chalice. You can more easily dodge a laser beam than a wide angled spray. When it's your turn to be reborn, there is no escape.

Every change has an uncertain outcome. But, that doesn't make it evil. If you are aware of the laws of karma, and send out only good energy, then you can trust and have faith that only good things will come to you. Every action can generate a feeling of love or fear, it is your choice how to receive and perceive the energy coming to you.

Rebirth can be a transformation to a better state. Falling in love is a rebirth, as you gain a completely new perspective on life by merging your world with another's. Any drastic life transforming experience is intensely scary, but at the same time invigorating. Embracing the change and accepting it helps you transcend the fear. It is helpful to remember at the bottom of the Chalice is the other side of the circle, which is East, Earth, birth. Turn a chalice over, and you will be looking at a smaller version of a very familiar tool.

The Chalice is used to communicate with the Gods. Anything said over a Chalice is said directly to the ear of Goddess. Toasts, boasts, prayers, and promises are spoken over the Chalice to deepen the connection to spirit and each other. Sharing a Chalice, toasting with wine, and drinking together are common traditional, unifying experiences. Expressing our emotions while our tongues are loosened by alcohol is a custom that transcends most societies. Deepening our emotional attachments to others is a transformational experience as it deepens our connectedness to each other and therefore to divinity.

Experiencing our feelings together bonds us and allows us to move closer to love, it helps us find a common ground, and pulls us into an awakening that is enlightening and conscious raising. This puts our fears to rest, and initiates us into an awareness that is closer to Goddess.

The Chalice is also a tool to see through the veil, as the Western Portal is the gate to the Underworld. Scrying into your chalice, a cauldron, or a bowl filled with water puts you in touch with spirits, who have passed over. The gifts of intuition, psychic powers, and the mysteries of the universe are discovered here.

Use your Chalice to charge potions for emotional healing, and intuitive discovery. Pour the potion into your chalice. Hold it in your hands, swirl the potion deosil, and chant your intent. It doesn't have to be fancy. I will put juice in a glass for my daughter to get rid of the hiccups. We will put our hands on the glass together, swirl the liquid deosil and chant "Hocus-Pocus, Hiccus-Piccus, get rid of Tatiana's hiccups". She laughs, drinks the juice, and just like magic her hiccups are gone.

Examples of Water Tools

- ✓ Chalice, pitchers, urns, and other similar vessels.
- ✓ Potions, Drinks, Teas, and Water.
- ✓ Scrying Tools, and Mirrors.
- ✓ Trident.
- ✓ Glass, Pearls, Coral, and Sand.
- ✓ Sea Shells, Sharks Teeth, and other sea fossils.

Air Tools

Air is the element of offense, direction, and invocation. It is the realm of the mind, conscious thought, communication, diplomacy, organization, strategy, government, conflict, and cold. Its dominant gender is masculine. It is represented by the sword, athame, or blade. Swords are phallic in shape, and have projective energy.

Swords are used when you are commanding energies, or elementals. When you hold your Athame or Sword, you are in command of your space. Swords are extremely good for clearing an area, or stopping a foe. When someone is actively attacking you, your athame will stop the attack from reaching you. A sword is used to move energy into a non-receptive force, and it will stop projective energy.

Second Sacral Chakra Activation – Sacred Tools

Swords are excellent tools to work with when you are trying to convey ideas, win an argument, control a situation, learn a new skill, pass a test, make a winning impression, invoke power, cast, or direct your will. All you need to do is carry a small athame in your pocket to benefit from it. No one needs to know it's there. This is probably why so many older men carry pocketknives. You use swords to bless and consecrate. The use of swords requires education, skill, forethought, patience, and responsibility.

No safety devices are available with a blade, and they can easily be used to project negative energy. You cannot undo what has been done, so you must make sure you know what you are doing, and take care to do it correctly. The sword should be the last tool you attempt to master.

Swords are the tool of the Holly King, who acts with wisdom and responsibility to provide for and protect his home and family. With the experience of age, air is self-sacrificing, in pursuit of what is sensible and logical. It is very strategic, cold, and calculating. Air is logical, and rational, a persuasive and manipulative element. It is used to manifest your reality and realign your world to suit your will. Used carelessly the sword can cut your own head off, causing unseen wounds that cannot easily be repaired.

Spells are usually the first thing students want to learn, yet often they find their spell backlashes on them, because they did not consider the consequences. Air demands that you consider all possibilities, and then still proceed with caution. The sword has patience, but when used its effectiveness leaves no room for error. Therefore it is best used in conjunction with the written word.

Writing out your spell gives you time to consider your thoughts. Seeing it written on paper gives you a second chance to review. Repeating the spell after you have written it, gives you yet a third opportunity to pass over the same idea, making sure you have explored all the possible outcomes.

The expression "The pen is mightier than the sword," outlines a magical truth. Words are a tool of air and can influence many people at a time. The written word, symbols, and hieroglyphs are all physical manifestations of your thoughts. Just like a sword, words cut deeply, and cause painful wounds, which take time to heal. Unlike a physical cut, wounds made with words are harder to see, harder to acknowledge, and therefore harder to heal. But they also stand the test of time, and can be an eternal expression of truth.

One of the interesting associations with the air element is a feather, which historically has been used as a writing instrument. Incense is an air tool, and carries our words to the Gods. Smoking is recognized by the American Indians as a means to communicate your prayers to the Gods.

The tools of air are often associated with other elements as well. Incense is created by fire and earth. You burn (fire) herbs (earth) to create incense. But, the smoke is the desired result of your focus. Swords are made by heating (fire) metal (mined from the earth), then cooling it with water, yet the skill of the craftsman tempering a blade requires education and mastery, or the blade will not stay sharp and will easily break under pressure. Pens have liquid ink (water), and write on paper, which comes from wood (fire), but you are writing down thoughts. Such is the way of Air. It is elusive, confusing, everywhere and nowhere. It can be hard to pin down.

Thoughts are constantly changing with new information. Air is intangible, always moving, blowing back and forth. Likewise it is very easy to misunderstand the information you are receiving because it is colored by the filters you have created with the other elements. It must pass through your belief systems (fire), emotional reactions (water), and current needs (earth). The words you generate come from your belief systems, emotional reactions, and current needs. Seldom are your words received exactly as they were sent out. Seldom are tools of air, actually made out of air.

Examples of Air tools:

- ✓ Sword, Athame, Blades of any kind
- ✓ Writing Instruments
- ✓ Book of Shadows, and sacred literature
- ✓ Incense and Censer
- ✓ Glitter, and Magic Powders
- ✓ Feathers, and Fans
- ✓ Pipe, and Smoking Items
- ✓ Bells, Horns, and Wind Chimes

Blessing and Consecrating

Color Me Orange!

Blessing and Consecrating involves imbuing the essence of the elements into a person, place or thing, in order to make it holy or sacred. *After calling quarters, the circle is blessed and consecrated with the four elements by walking the circumference of the circle with each element.*

I consecrate with earth by sprinkling a representative of earth. Traditionally this would be salt, but I prefer cornmeal. Salt is damaging to the flowers and grass. But also cornmeal is a staple in the southern United States, where I am from. Corn vibrates to the planet Venus, which represents love, harmony, and order. It is of the earth element, feminine in nature, and provides the powers of protection and fertility. Corn has long been used in magical practices to bless and has been called the "Giver of Life", "Sacred Mother" and the "Seed of Seeds".[10] For all these reasons, I feel that Corn is a more appropriate vibration for the work I do than salt would be.

To consecrate the circle with earth, pick up the bowl or plate filled with cornmeal (or whatever you choose to represent earth), charge it with earth energy and begin sprinkling it on the ground or floor as you walk the perimeter of the circle to the south quarter. Then holding the bowl up to the south quarter say, "I bless and consecrate this circle with the element of earth". Follow the circle around to each quarter, sprinkling the cornmeal as you go. Stop to repeat the incantation at each quarter. The consecrating is complete when you have come full circle and repeated the incantation at the earth element.

To consecrate with fire, carry a candle, or torch around the circle moving from the south quarter to the west. At the west stop, hold the candle up to the west quarter and say, "I bless and consecrate this circle with the element of Fire." Continue to each element, being careful not to walk so fast that the flame is extinguished. Stop at each quarter, repeat the incantation, and end in the south.

To consecrate with water, sprinkle water from the chalice or a bowl around the perimeter of the circle, stopping at each quarter saying, "I bless and consecrate this circle with the element of Water".

To consecrate with air, carry the incense around the circle in the same method as the other elements, repeating, "I bless and consecrate this circle with the element of Air".

To bless and consecrate a magical tool, you basically use the same concept; only you are creating a thoughtform that you want to program with specific intent. You may want to refer to your consecration ritual at a later date. I suggest writing the consecration ritual down, reading through it a couple of times, and having it to follow while you are doing the ritual.

The following is an example consecration of an athame. You should adapt the wording appropriately for whatever you are blessing and consecrating.

---

[10] Cunningham, Scott: Encyclopedia of Magical Herbs, Llewellyn Publications, 1985 p. 82-83

Second Sacral Chakra Activation – Blessing & Consecrating

Consecrating an Athame

★ Place the athame on your altar pentacle. (If you do not have one, you can make a one by drawing a pentagram on a piece of paper.)

★ Beginning with earth, sprinkle the cornmeal, or your chosen earth representative, on the athame. Visualize forming an energetic, green field around the athame and say, *"I bless and consecrate this athame with the element of earth, that it may serve to give structure and foundation to my ideas, that they may more easily manifest on the physical plane."*

★ Next do fire; wave the athame in the candle flame. Visualize layering a red energy field on the athame and say, *"I bless and consecrate this athame with the element of fire, that it may inspire my will with creativity and motivate my thoughts into action."* Place the athame back on the pentacle.

★ Move to water; sprinkle it with water. Visualize layering a blue energy field on the athame and say, *"I bless and consecrate this athame with the element of water, that my thoughts will always take into consideration the effects of my will on others, that I may direct my thoughts with honor, humility, love and kindness."*

★ Finish with air; wave the athame through the incense smoke. Visualize layering a yellow energy field, and say, *"I bless and consecrate this athame with the element of air, that my will may be educated of purpose, clear in focus, and pure in intent."*

★ Finally, give life to your tool. Take the athame into your hands, inhale deeply, and then blow the breath out over the athame. Breathe life into the thoughtform that you have just created, saying, *"I breathe life into you and name you _____, that you will serve as a symbol of my will, and aid me in directing my will, thoughts, and ideas in service of the Goddess, to the best and highest good of all concerned. So Mote It Be!"*

You should tailor your words to each tool. Such as for a chalice you would want earth to give stability and strength to your emotions. Fire would give passion and compassion. Water would lend depth and fulfillment. Air could add mirth, and joyfulness.

Each element adds a layer of depth to your intent. Make sure you program your tool with the appropriate details and vibrations that you desire. The combinations are limitless. After blessing and consecrating each tool, be sure to use it. Drink out of it. Eat off it. Cast a circle with it, etc.

Second Sacral Chakra Activation – Venus – Maidens

Venus – Maidens

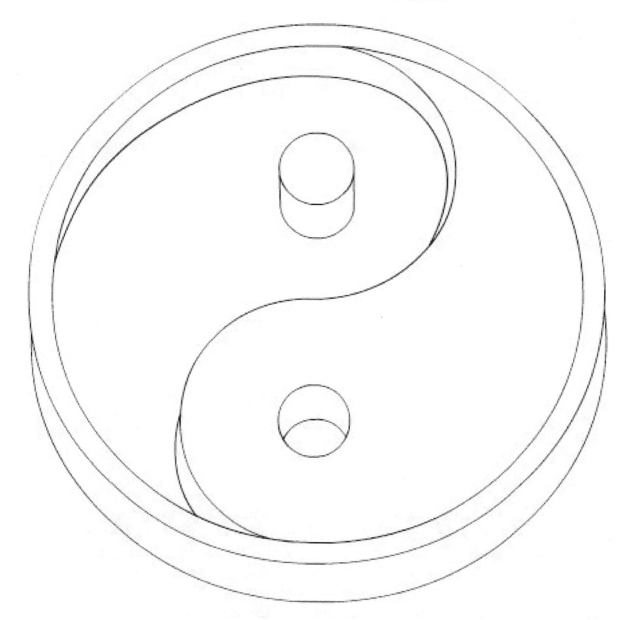

Color Me Orange!

In the child's seventh year, many changes take place. Through the many adventures of the Oak King/Warrior, he has discovered and conquered many wonderful things. But, one mystery eludes him. He has slowly become aware that the other people in his world are not solely there for his amusement. They seem to have interests of their own. They do not seem to be impressed with his bravery and courage, and aren't nearly as doting as is his dear mother.

Everything suddenly changes as he is reformed into a world of society, beauty, music, and art. Sometimes suddenly, sometimes gradually, Mars moves to the back seat and Venus takes the wheel. From age 7 to 14, Venus will be the driving force that develops and shapes her world.

She desires to connect with these newfound friends. Compassion emerges as interactions with others become more and more desirable. Relationships and social status take the place of conquest.

Her appearance, her actions, the way others receive her, and how they treat her in return becomes far more important than the discoveries of the past. As she searches for ways to find acceptance in this new world she develops an interest in the fashions, fads, and trends of her generation.

As the projective male energy of the infant, gives way to the receptive energy of Venus, Goddess of Love, the opposite sex suddenly causes a very distinctive reaction in the life of the budding Maiden. She is both curiously repulsed, and oddly attracted to the mysterious differences of her polar opposite. She becomes acutely aware of her place in society. She wishes to accept, and to be accepted, to love and to be loved, to appreciate and to be appreciated, to admire and to be admired.

Her personal appearance is a preoccupation. The mirror takes on a very new role that quickly develops into a trusted friend and hated enemy at the same time. Self-grooming is very important, as she realizes that mother is not hip to all the newest looks and cool trends. She is enamored of her appearance, but also finds there are imperfections and areas that are changing, becoming awkward, and not at all suiting her balanced vision of perfection.

Possessing popularity takes center stage, as she places her self-worth on how many friends she has, how many social engagements she is invited to, and how many talents and expressions of beauty she has to decorate her world. Learning the Top-40, and the current lingo, is way more important than anything in English class. She is growing up and wants to look and act the part. But at the same time she curses all the weird changes in her body, her teeth fall out, her face breaks out, her hair gets oily. Just when she needs the perfection of her youthful beauty, hormones kick in.

She begins exploring music, dance, and enjoys all types of artistic beauty and pleasurable expression. She desires to connect with peers, and spends hours discussing with her circle of friends, the various relationships that are more important to her than any of her childish adventures of the past.

She finds satisfaction in owning beautiful things, and delights in filling her private space with items that reflect "her generation".

Second Sacral Chakra Activation – Venus – Maidens

Venus emerges and begins the slow, almost unnoticed, separation from the mother that was so important to Mars. She must be with those who understand her, like the things she likes, place value on what she values, and yearn for the same deep connections for which she yearns. Venus is obsessed with discovering her relationship to her world. She is willing to compromise to fit in, to risk danger to be accepted, and to face the demons of hell for love.

She is not about sex. She is about creating, pleasure, fun, beauty, relationships, connecting, and possessions. She is the eternal romantic, fun, joyous, and endearing. She bubbles forth with spontaneous laughter as she sprinkles our world with her delightful indulgences. She is our best friend, our creativity, and our desire. She makes the world a beautiful, happy place filled with wonderful variety, and whimsical smiles.

She can be found in the face of Aphrodite, rising from the emotional sea, beautiful beyond beauty, desired by all the Gods. She is like her doves, a symbol of purity, grace, peace, and beauty. Her story is told in the obsessed Venus' infatuation for the mortal Adonis, and Her broken-hearted grief over his death.

We know her in the music and poetry of Sarasvati, riding on her white swan giving birth to civilization with education and spiritual enlightenment for humankind. We feel her tender, and protective embrace in the arms of the benevolent cow-Goddess, Hathor, as she showers us with milk and honey, symbols of her fertility, abundance, and devotion.

Awakening Spirit – Freshman Course – www.WISESeminary.com

Certification Requirements

Collect your tools and consecrate each one. Write your consecration ritual down, including necessary details. After performing the consecration, meditate with each tool, work with its energy, and ask it to speak to you. Write about your experience during the rituals.

Prepare a record of magical tools to keep within your Book of Shadows, a tool log. Include every magical tool you posses. Document with pictures, a short description of item, where or whom you obtained it from, the date you received it, any history behind it, and the rituals you performed to consecrate it. Other pertinent items to include may be the receipt or gift card, a tag, instructions, etc.

Tool Log

Tool	Date Aquired	Previous Owner	Cost	Other

Journal Entries

As you work with your tools this week, record the different impressions you get from them. Notice how the energy moves. Spend time meditating with your tools. Record the results in your journal.

11
Second Will Chakra Activation
The Power of the Circle

Color Me Yellow!

The circle represents wholeness, wellness, completeness, balance, and harmony. The circle is used in many different ways, to represent many different things in our universe. Many sacred symbols are drawn inside circles to represent that the sum of the parts inside brings wholeness.

In Wicca we worship inside a cast circle. The cast circle represents so many different levels of reality from the smallest atom to the entire expanse of space. It is a tool that connects the incomprehensible expanse of the All into a simplified workstation that we can relate to at whatever stage of magical development we are in at any given time.

We cast circle to create a microcosmic replica of the universe from which we can work. The circle represents wholeness. Within it's boundaries we are able to do the sacred work of the Gods. We can worship, create, learn, and grow. It is a blank slate between the worlds that connects us to the cosmic void, and provides all the tools that we need to do our work (whatever that may be). It is "between the worlds" and therefore provides a link to both physical and astral reality.

Through relating situations on both small and large scales to the circle, we can see a very clear spiral pathway that explains and guides us through the wandering cycles of our life, the evolution of mankind, and the universe as a whole.

The circle teaches us, gives birth to us, motivates us, and transforms us into greater and greater levels of awareness. It is the cosmic womb, the expanse of space, the single cell, and infinity, all at the same time.

It is the most versatile and personal tool of any magical person. Being that it is so versatile, a circle can be cast in any number of ways. The particular incantation that you use is much less important than the energy you put into it. You can cast a circle as fast as you can think it into being or, you can draw it out and take hours to construct it. It doesn't matter which way you do it, as long as the astral barrier is there to protect and contain your work until you are ready to release it.

But, also being that it is so personal, a circle cast should speak to you, personally. You should understand the symbolic and real meanings and references of all the words that you speak into being. If you do not know what the words mean, don't use them. It is irresponsible to speak magically in a language that you don't understand, or use references that you are not familiar with, as you cannot know what it is that you are conjuring into being.

I feel that it's important for the seeker of the Wiccan path to first learn to cast circle with the traditional Gardenarian incantations. I think it's important to any group's work that all are able to be in tune and work in harmony. Repetition gives an incantation more power, and creates a stronger bond between the participants, and the Gods and elementals.

Second Will Chakra Activation – The Power of the Circle

Standing in circle you should know your incantations and speak them from memory. Reading a circle cast while you are trying to cast circle impedes the ability to do both the energy work and say the words at the same time. When you are speaking and moving energy at the same time you are engaging both sides of your brain, as well as your conscious and subconscious.

Reading your circle cast is disruptive to the power flow, and reinforces that you aren't really sure what you are doing. When casting a circle you should speak loudly enough for all participants to clearly hear you, and with confidence. You need to concentrate and focus on moving the energy and creating the barrier. The words should *add* power to your working, not *be* the power. If you are going to use an incantation to cast circle, memorize it!

There are those who write a new circle cast for each ritual they write. They use it as a tool to detail the work that they are doing. I can't argue with their right to do this, nor would I try. Although I would suggest they memorize it, and not try to read it from a script.

I have found casting circle with song or dance a fun change for certain workings. It's important to experiment with different things, if for no other reason than just to keep an open mind and validate that you still prefer your chosen method. I support each Priest and Priestess in finding what works best for them.

Incantations

I teach a particular standard set of incantations and ask that they be committed to memory. I use them because they are the oldest, traditional incantations that I have found, and because when picked apart they make sense. Just as in the charge of the Goddess, each incantation I use have mysteries hidden within them. They have been used over and over by brothers and sisters of the craft, and therefore they have gained a power unto themselves.

The newest aspirant can feel the energetic response of the elementals and the Gods, and can connect to those energies by the spoken incantation alone. That in its self is good enough reason to use them. But, when coupled with the energetic dynamics of a trained Priest or Priestess, the strength of the cast is assured.

Awakening Spirit – Freshman Course – www.WISESeminary.com

Casting the Circle

Color Me Yellow!

To form a circle you should utilize a cord, 9 ft. in length. Tie one end around the hilt of your athame, and plunge your athame into the ground in the center of where you wish to cast circle. Tie the other end of the cord around your wand or staff. Now you have a compass to help you form the standard 18' diameter circle. Use the wand or staff to draw the circle in the ground.

It is customary to put something around the outside of the circle to show you the barrier, that way you won't accidentally step outside the boundaries, and it will be easier to visualize the circle. If you don't want to designate this area as a permanent space, you could use flour or cornmeal to draw a white line on the ground that will

Second Will Chakra Activation – Casting the Circle

disappear quickly after you are through with your working. I don't recommend salt for this, as it will not be as easily seen and it will sterilize the dirt, leaving a barren strip of ground identifying your circle for all to see.

The circle incantation that I ask you to learn is this one:

"I conjure thee, O Circle of Power, that thou beest a meeting-place of love and joy and truth; a shield against all wickedness and evil; a boundary between the world of men and the realms of the Mighty Ones; a rampart and protection that shall preserve and contain the power that we shall raise within thee. Wherefore I do bless and consecrate thee, in the names of Diana and Pan."[11]

I like this cast for many reasons. But the most important reason is because it teaches you how and why you cast circle within the incantation itself. I think that it has a timeless quality passed down from the ancients, and I honor the sacred magic of any incantation that will do that. I will go through and explain each part and how it applies to the casting of the circle.

We begin in the North at the Main Altar. You pick up your Athame or Sword and charge it. There are many ways to charge a blade. The energetic involves drawing the etheric power into your blade and directing the power to form your circle. Envision your blade charged with an electric-blue light, and as you point your blade at the circumference of the circle, the blue light shoots forth out of your blade tip, striking the ground and creating a three dimensional sphere that arcs all the way to the center of the circle both below and above the ground.

To Charge my blade I say the following:

> *I call earth to bind my spell,* (touch the earth with the blade)
> *Air to speed its travel well,* (wave it in the air)
> *Bright as fire shall it glow,* (wave it through candle flame)
> *Deep as tidal waters flow.* (touch it to chalice)
> *Count the elements four fold,* (hold it up to the sky)
> *In the fifth the spell shall hold.*[12]

You do not have to say anything to charge your blade. It is my personal preference to use it. Speaking aloud helps to keep the focus, and makes the ritual more powerful, active, dramatic and interesting. Also, this prelude to the circle cast gives

---

[11] The incantations I reference were taught to me by my initiating High Priest, and other teachers along the way. However, they have been documented as originally passed down from Gerald Gardner by Janet and Stewart Farrar in *The Witches Way* and other publications. I checked to be sure I was passing on correct wording in *Eight Sabbats for Witches,* Janet and Stewart Farrar, Phoenix Publishing, Inc., 1981
[12] *Witchcraft for Tomorrow,* Doreen Valiente, Robert Hale, 1978

everyone a chance to get in the mindset to focus with you.

After charging your blade point it at the circumference of the circle at the center of the North Quarter (main altar) and begin speaking the incantation, as you walk deosil, tracing the circumference of the circle with your blade. Be sure to visualize the energy creating the sphere as you say the words.

I conjure thee, O Circle of Power, that thou beest a meeting-place of love and joy and truth;

Notice that the North Quarter is the element of Air, and this is where you begin. Conjuring is an action of air. It is taking the active stance. It is offense as opposed to defense. You are telling the forces that be, what you want them to do. This is why you cast with a blade, because you are commanding the elements to create "a circle of power, a place of love, joy, and truth".

a shield against all wickedness and evil;

By this time, if your circle is 18 ft in diameter (9 ft radius), you will be standing right in front of the earth quarter. The earth quarter tool is a shallow dish or a shield. We want to "shield" any negative presences that may happen upon our circle from being able to enter our circle and prevent them from affecting our work.

a boundary between the world of men and the realms of the Mighty Ones;

By this time you will be standing in front or close to the fire quarter. The tool of fire is the staff, wand, or broom. These tools are used to defend. "A boundary" is a defensive tactic. It is important to create this boundary between the worlds, as it clears our workstation to be an open void, a womb of the mother, into which we are free to interject the spark of creation, which will direct our intent, and manifest it into reality.

a rampart and protection that shall preserve and contain the power that we shall raise within thee.

Now you have moved around to the water quarter. The Chalice is a deep dish, bowl, or cup. It is made to hold liquid or energy. "Containing the power" within the circle is important, because it would be as ineffective to build energy within an uncontained area, as it would be to hold water in our hands.

Wherefore I do bless and consecrate thee, in the names of Diana and Pan.

You have at this time returned full circle to the North, air quarter, and the main altar. "Blessing and consecrating" the circle is also an action of air, and dedicating the circle to the Gods and Goddesses is an action of diplomacy and worship, to honor them,

Second Will Chakra Activation – Casting the Circle

their presence, and their effects on our lives.

We want the Gods to be present and to assist us in accomplishing our tasks. We want our actions to be in accordance with their will and desire. If you have another God or Goddess that you are calling upon, you may change the names of deity as you see fit.

A formal circle cast is appropriate when you are doing formal rituals. But there are other times that you would want to cast a circle that do not require the formal cast.

If you were in immediate danger, taking time to cast circle would not be appropriate. You would not have time to pull out your Athame and say the incantation. You need to be able to just think "Shield", and immediately generate safe space.

If you are blessing a potion, or doing a healing, a quick circle cast around you and the things you are working on would be appropriate. But it may not be necessary to go through the whole ritual; just walking the circumference with your athame may be good enough.

It's important to gain mastery of circle casting so that you can erect an appropriate safe space whenever necessary, and to what degree necessary. This comes with practice and use. I encourage you to work with the full circle cast until you feel you have it correct, and then start experimenting with different degrees of casting, if you feel so motivated.

Psychic Attack

Most Psychic Attacks are not intended. People get angry and don't recognize that the powerful energy they are feeling is being directed in a negative way towards the person they are angry with. Learning to control your temper, and appropriately direct those energies can be a very daunting task. Magical people, who have become adept at directing energy, and sensitive to receiving it, can find themselves under psychic attack or the projector of a psychic attack.

Psychic attack feels like a head cold, or an achy feeling in your back, neck, or shoulders. You may feel unnecessarily burdened, or unexplainably upset, angry or crying without reason. I often wonder how many cases of depression are caused from prolonged psychic attacks. People hold in their anger, and silently seethe for years sometimes. It is irresponsible to do this, but in our culture, we are often not given the appropriate tools to process our emotions.

Anyone dealing with energetics must find a way to appropriately process his or her emotions. Simple, honest communication is very effective. Journaling is also very therapeutic. Projecting your anger at a punching bag, while visualizing the face of your intended victim is negative magic, and intended psychic attack. It sounds like a really good way to release your anger, without hurting anyone. But, it can be very damaging to yourself and others. If you need to physically express yourself, try to focus on grounding the negative energy into the earth, while you are punching a bag, instead of focusing on beating up the person you are upset with.

If you are under psychic attack, you do not want to receive the attack, nor do you want your energy to go out to that person either. If you are angry with someone, it is irresponsible to allow your anger to randomly and negatively impact the world around you, so you should shield and ground. Remember that anything projected inside a cast circle is multiplied, so be careful to ground your negative energy when shielding. Otherwise, you may temporarily intensify the experience.

The easiest and most powerful way to deal with negative energies, either coming from you, or at you, is to carry a Black Tourmaline and a Pyrite. They are both easy stones to purchase, and they will instantly deal with the energy until you have become competent enough to handle it yourself.

The obvious cure for psychic attack is to talk to the person with whom you have conflict. Most conflicts are misunderstandings, and can easily be solved with simple, honest communication. Of course, this takes courage. It truly does. But, it is also the spiritually mature thing to do. Walking the path takes courage. Hiding behind anger or perceived hurt is not a courageous act. Work out your differences. Don't harbor hate, hurt or ill will for someone, and don't let others be upset with you without you trying to work it out. You cannot be a force of negativity against your brothers and sisters, and still serve the highest good.

Sun - Oak Kings

Color Me Yellow!

At sometime during her 13th year, Venus will come into her full being within the young, budding teenager. She has learned to connect, and how to be a part of things. She has made friends, and established peer groups. She has even helped her mother understand the hip new ways of her generation. She has discovered a fascination with her sexuality and an undeniable attraction for the opposite sex. She has connected to and become a product of her generation.

She is the oldest of the children. She has their respect, and admiration. But, she has not yet found her place in the world of adults. They do not include her, share with her, or connect with her. They still consider her a child, who is fun and entertaining, but not to be taken seriously.

She suddenly becomes aware of a world previously beyond her notice. This new terrain is a world free from the rules and restriction of parents. It is a world where one is at liberty to partake of all the luscious, decadent pleasures they desire. It is a world without limits, where anything is possible, and she is enamored by it. She desires to experience it.

This desire burns within her to become an obsession. The thing for which she desires is just slightly out of her reach, teasing her, frustrating her. She knows she need not toil alone. She is used to enlisting the help of others. She understands the value of teamwork. She needs a champion to aid her in her pursuit, a hero to secure her treasure.

As her obsession grows, the passion inside her explodes into a bright, hot, fiery, all-consuming force of will, and by her 14th birthday the Sun is born.

He is unaware that his reign will only last seven years. In his reality, there was nothing before him, and there will be nothing after him. He is the immortal Messiah, come to save us from certain death. God save the King!

The Sun God cuts his teeth on the crown of his glory. He was sent here with a mission, and he is singularly focused on completing that task. He must save the world from the callous destruction of the old guard. Reseed it with hope, truth, justice, wisdom, and love. It is time for change. It's his world now, and he is here to make a difference.

He knows no restriction. He governs all he surveys. His will is stronger. His force is mightier. He cannot be conquered, for he is the maker of rules. He is the new crowned King, and before he is complete, all in his world will bow to his greatness or be exiled from his grand and glorious kingdom. Mars and Venus sit back, look at each other, buckle up and smile.

The Sun looks back at you through the eyes of a sixteen-year old, and you know that nothing you can say in disagreement will mean anything to him. He is sure of his power, convinced of his invincibility, and may indeed die proving his immortality.

He has no fear, as he defiantly laughs in the face of rules and restrictions. It is his world, and while Venus in the back seat may be able to convince him that a condom is a good idea, the cautions of society never will. He is either unaware or uncaring of the consequences of his actions. His future is now; he is bullet proof, unbreakable, and immortal.

The Sun/Oak King has his power in his hands and he knows it. He is master of the world and the world is a better place because of his presence in it. Defy him and feel the power of his wrath. He will see to it that Mars gets to conquer this new world of adults, and Venus gets to explore every pleasure available in his realm.

He sees himself as a glorious wonder of creation, and marvels at his own perfection. He is the hero that will right the wrongs of the previous generation. He will vanquish the wicked and champion the meek. He has a mission to fulfill and is focused on the task. He must sow the seeds of righteousness, reawaken our sense of purpose, and help us understand the error of our ways.

The Sun has no sense of how others see him. He is so intent on self-expression, that he is completely oblivious that his grandness may eclipse yours. He wouldn't dream of being inconsiderate, but lacks the perspective to notice.

Be direct, he won't take a hint. He evaluates everything at face value. He is not adaptable or flexible. The world bends to his will, not the other way around. He will not be wrong, corrected, or restricted.

He is easily manipulated by flattery. He is convinced you mean every word, as he would never stoop to misrepresenting the truth, or manipulating your feelings for his gain. He offers loyalty and honor and expects that in return. He is truly broken-hearted at the frailties of human character, and seeks to cast out all evil from his realm.

He must be allowed to be who he is. Parents should take note that Venus is the receptive social creature, willing to follow the rules and courtesies of society, and take advantage of teaching her well, for she is the only council the Sun will listen to once he succeeds the throne.

In truth he is glorious. He is power incarnate. He is sexual virility at its peak. He is beautiful beyond compare, the inspiration of music and poetry. He is the voice of prophecy. He is bright optimism, pure energy. He is the hope for tomorrow, and the creation of today.

He is excitement, lust, and adventure. We long to be like him, to possess him, to experience the world from his lofty domain. His word is truth. His heart is pure. His presence is noticed by all.

No need to teach him. He already knows everything. He sees our mistakes and feels called to bear the burden of making it right. He does not intend defiance. He's just so brilliant; he can't help but point out our weaknesses. It is beneath his character to continue to let you flounder around in your ignorance, when he could easily show you an easier path.

What?!? You're offended? Don't be. He doesn't intend to offend. He doesn't have a malicious bone in his perfect body. He assumes you want his help. He knows how to make you better, more like him. Why would you not want that? He doesn't blame you for being weak. But, surely you don't want to stay that way. He has been tested, and sees no honor in cowering in the face of battle. All he knows is victory, and he is sure he can show you how to be a winner too.

We find him in Greece in the face of Apollo, young, beautiful and pure, the creator of Medicine, and celestial musician. He is the great and powerful Ra in Egypt, creator of mankind. Rising each day, like the phoenix, newly born. He is the Christian, Jesus Christ, embracing the meek, uplifting the poor, healing the sick, sowing the seeds of eternal life, and rescuing man from sin, ignorance, and evil.

By whatever name you call him, the Sun brings life, abundance, and order to our universe. Too much or to little of him can threaten our very survival. But, when he is in balance, our world is a paradise, blessed with riches, pleasures, adventures, and wonders to fulfill our every desire.

Long Live the King!

Second Will Chakra Activation – Certification Requirements

Practice

Memorize your circle incantation this week.

Practice casting with energy first, and then with the incantation. Notice the difference.

Remember to banish the circle when you are through practicing, by walking the circle widdershins and drawing the energy back into your blade. When you are finished picking up the circle, stand still, ground, and release the excess energy into the ground.

"I conjure thee, O Circle of Power, that thou beest a meeting-place of love and joy and truth; a shield against all wickedness and evil; a boundary between the world of men and the realms of the Mighty Ones; a rampart and protection that shall preserve and contain the power that we shall raise within thee. Wherefore I do bless and consecrate thee, in the names of Persephone and Hades."

Certification Requirements

Record your experience with casting circle.

Journal Entries

How does it feel to cast circle? How does it feel to shield? Have you used shielding in a mundane setting? What were the results?

12
Second Heart Chakra Activation
The Four Elements

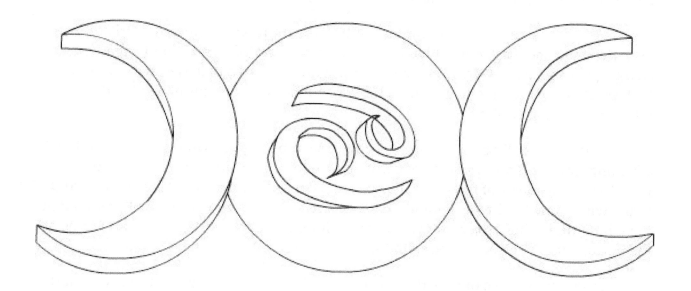

Color Me Green!

Everything that is manifest in physical form has a combination of the four elements within. The more equally balanced the four elements are within a living thing, the more balanced and healthy it becomes. When everything maintains balance, the living thing can ascend to higher levels of understanding, and therefore seek new and more advanced levels of balance.

By connecting with and understanding the elements and polarity, you start to see your world in cycles of growth and expansion, followed by withdrawal and reflection. You can see if you need more fire or if you need more earth energy to balance a situation. Every discomfort stems from imbalance, too much fire, too little fire, too much water, or not enough earth. Everything can be resolved or healed if the balance is restored. Balance is the key to wholeness, and health.

By observing nature, cycles, seasons and the sacred sciences, Goddess shows us the patterns that tell us where the elements fall. Arguments about which element goes where have often been the topic of philosophical debate, but there are undeniable clues that make it very simple.

Astrology is a Sacred Science. If you look, the heavens clearly tell us which elements go where. Water is opposite earth, and fire is opposite air, all the way around the wheel of the zodiac.

If you compare the High Sabbats to the Zodiac Wheel, you will see that Spring is Earth, Summer is Fire, Fall is Water, and Winter is Air.

Also, a fundamental magical theory, and the mundane study of electricity, tells us to generate energy you must have a continuous circuit of positive and negative charges. In other words, you must be +, -, +, -. If you put two batteries in a toy with both positive charges in one direction, the toy will not work because the circuit was interrupted or incomplete.

Wind is a cooling force. It is projective, meaning it affects things around it. Fire is a heating force. It is also projective. Earth and Water can be hot or cold, they are receptive to the forces of fire or air. Earth is in balance in spring and autumn. It is cold in the winter and hot in the summer. Earth is a receptive, feminine element. It is cold in the winter due to the projective force of air. Winter is associated with the cold winds of the north. Summer is associated with the hot climates of the south.

Another example of how this works is earth is dry, fire is hot, water is wet, and air is cold. If you follow that spiral around the wheel, you can have combinations of hot and dry, or cold and dry, but not wet and dry at the same time. You can have cold and wet or hot and wet, but not cold and hot together.

There are many theories of how this has become conflicted over the course of history. We know for a fact that we do not have all the answers, and that many mysteries have been deeply hidden to protect the information from the uninitiated. Ancient masters hid the mysteries in stories, myths, and holy texts.

Initiates, who can interpret the language of symbolism, can decipher the mysteries. So this has proven to be an effective method of preserving the sacred knowledge. We know of the art of "Ritual Tampering", which is a method of purposefully leading those who are not of pure intent to a powerless place where they can do no harm.

Published books of the occult have often had major imbalances that can easily be deciphered by those who understand the mysteries. But human trickery aside, there is no mistaking the cold, analytical, studious nature of winter and air, as opposed to the abundant, spring, fertility of the earth mother.

Second Heart Chakra Activation – The Four Elements

For this and many other reasons, the WISE Tradition puts air in the north, earth in the east, fire in the south, and water in the west. Mike Nichols has a wonderful article on this topic entitled "Rethinking the Watchtowers" that can be viewed in the World Wide Web at: www.geocities.com/mike_nichols.geo/rethink.html.

It has often been discussed by critics of the Wiccan community, that Wicca lacks scholarship. Wiccan Critics are also quick to point out the many sexual scandals that arise from our community. Wiccan and pagans on a whole have a reputation (true or not) for not living stable lives, not being willing to work and not having monetary reserves. At the same time, Wiccans observe that the Christian cross reflects an unbalanced wheel, giving the Christians too much fire, and not enough air, earth, or water. This results in zealotry, a lack of scholarship and a noted absence of the Divine Feminine. Could the reversed elements of earth and air reflect this lesson back to us, making us, as a whole, appear to be more focused on sexual issues, always broke, and somewhat "air-headed" and not to be taken seriously on our faith? Since these are the chief issues that undermine our acceptance to and respect in the community of World Religions, I think this is a matter that deserves serious reflection.

While I do not disagree with others right to place the elements where they find it means the most to them. I have found that when working with the elements in this way, new doorways are opened, and great mysteries are revealed. The power of the circle gains depth that transcends beyond the understanding of it when earth is placed in the cold, infertile north.

Earth

- Elemental Realm/King: Gnomes/Ghob
- Animals: mammals
- Season/Sabbats: Spring/Ostara & Beltaine
- Color: Green
- Direction: East
- Time of Day: Dawn/6:00 am
- Gender: Feminine/Receptive
- Tool: Pentacle & Shield
- Energy: Waxing Moon
- Archangel: Auriel

Earth provides Foundation and form. Earth is the birth, the beginning. Earth is the Maiden, ripe with fertility. It is the Mother pushing out the newborn child. It is eternal abundance, the ever-flowing, unconditional, horn of plenty. The earth awakens with the dawn, and day begins at 6:00 am when all is in balance. The Earth begins with goals and ideas, but is receptive to the outcome.

Earth is the Beauty of Aphrodite, returning from the depths of the Underworld, arising on the waves and stepping forth onto land to hearken the birth of spring. She is the beautiful temptress, who captures the love, and adoration of the passionate Oak King. She is the abundant mother, Demeter, ripe with the fruit of the land, giving birth to abundance and prosperity. She is the earth mother Gaia, overflowing with bounty.

Ostara is the season of earth, and we celebrate new beginnings, births, and awakenings with colored eggs, and the very fertile hare.

Things that represent earth must be stable, and made of earth: stones, crystals, dirt, mulch, compost, & minerals. Many people like to see a tree as a representative of Earth. But any living thing is a whole representation of all the elements working together, and therefore cannot be truly classified into one (i.e., roots-earth, trunk-fire, sap-water, leaves-air). While trees do help you connect with the Earth as a whole entity, it is not a true representation of the isolated earth element.

Fire

- ✓ Elemental Realm/King: Salamander/Djinn
- ✓ Animal: Reptiles
- ✓ Season/Sabbats: Summer/ Litha & Lammas
- ✓ Color: Red
- ✓ Direction: South
- ✓ Time of Day: Noon
- ✓ Gender: Masculine/Projective
- ✓ Tool: Wands, Staffs, & Brooms
- ✓ Energy: Full Moon
- ✓ Archangel: Michael

Fire provides creation, instinctual knowledge, talents, and consciousness. Fire is action, motivation, gut reaction, and the spark of inspiration. Fire is that which tells the seed to grow, the baby to suckle, and the lovers to kiss. Fire is lust, passion, and fury. It is the destroyer that burns away the old and useless leaving room for the newness to be transformed.

Fire is the passion of the Oak King as he seeks the conquest. The Oak Kings' job is to refertilize the entire earth. He is a busy man, hyper-focused on the job at hand. Look into the eyes of any 18-year-old son, and you will see the lusty agenda of the Oak King is to cast his seed into the Maiden.

He is the Green Man, full of laughter, joy, and spontaneity. He is the passionate Pan, playing his flute, and chasing nymphs in the forest. He is the beautiful, youthful

Second Heart Chakra Activation – The Four Elements

Adonis, such masculine perfection that won the heart of both Persephone and Aphrodite.

Fire is the hot season of Litha, when the Sun is full in the sky. It is the time that the Oak King is transformed into the Holly King by witnessing the fruition of his creative activities, the miracle of birth. In this we understand that it is through the results of our own actions that transformation takes place.

Things that represent fire are those things, which are combustible and can be used for fuel: wood, coal, oil, alcoholic spirits (as in wine, beer, and liquor, not to be confused with drunk ghosts), natural gas, and wax. Metal is not of fire because it is not a fuel. Fire cannot survive on metal. Fire tempers metal, but it is the skill of the forge that creates the blade. Wands and staffs represent fire because, among other things, wood is a fuel, wood supports and gives life to fire.

Water

- ✓ Elemental Realm/King: Undines/Niksa
- ✓ Animals: Amphibians
- ✓ Season/Sabbat: Fall/Mabon & Samhain
- ✓ Color: Blue
- ✓ Direction: West
- ✓ Time of Day: Dusk/6:00 pm
- ✓ Gender: Feminine/Receptive
- ✓ Tool: Chalice/Trident
- ✓ Energy: Waning Moon
- ✓ Archangel: Gabriel

Water provides faith and emotion. It is the element of transformation and initiation, according to the traditional incantations. It is the passageway of death. It faces us with our greatest fears, and our most fulfilling bliss. Water teaches us honor, trust, and love. Water transforms us through the grief of loss. Water is the intuitive Mother Moon, and the taskmaster Saturn, the Crone. We know her as Hecate, Isis, Hathor, Inanna, Persephone, Cerridwen & by many other names.

Water sees past the surface, and delves deep into the emotional, subconscious realms. Water knows what scares you, what makes you tick, and why you do what you do. Water reflects your life back to you, so that you can learn, grow and transform.

Death is a transition from one state to another. We die a small death every time we go to sleep. We arise and find ourselves renewed and ready to begin again. We recreate the cycle of death and rebirth continuously throughout our lives. Water is patiently waiting for us to look in the mirror, and find the connections. Water is karma, illusion, dreams, prophecy, visions, and inner knowing.

Water is the season of Mabon, and Samhain. It is the time of letting go, releasing attachment to outcome, receiving your just rewards, celebrating relationships, and reconnecting with friends and family.

Air

- ✓ Elemental Realm/King: Sylphs/Paralda
- ✓ Animals: Birds
- ✓ Season/Sabbats: Winter/Yule & Imbolc
- ✓ Color: Yellow
- ✓ Direction: North
- ✓ Time of Day: Midnight
- ✓ Gender: Masculine/Projective
- ✓ Tool: Sword & Athame
- ✓ Energy: Dark Moon
- ✓ Archangel: Raphael

Air provides wisdom and intelligence. It is your ability to think and process information. Air is communication, interpretation, mental connections, associations, networking, and evolution. Air is government, diplomacy, tact, planning ahead, and forethought. It is presenting new ideas and resolving conflicts.

Air is the wise Holly King, who protects and provides for the family. His job is to make sure that his children have all that they need to survive, and complete their mission. He is the projective force of the father, guiding you with wisdom that only age and experience can provide.

Air is the giver of gifts, protocol, contemplation, thinking before speaking, and education. Air is skill, strategy, weights and measures, and organization.

We know him as Santa Claus, the one who watches and knows and rewards you justly. We call him The Horned God, Zeus & Odin. He is God the Father, protector, provider, and wise counselor.

Calling the Quarters

Color Me Green!

After casting the circle, quarters are called. This means that each element, and its elemental guardian, is called to the circle to lend its power to your working. As Priest or Priestess of the circle, you represent and speak for the God or Goddess. The elements will do as you command.

You can see how this information can be dangerous in the wrong hands. However, as we discussed before, you cannot act outside the will of Goddess. Forcing the elements to act against Divine Will creates chaos. Human activated chaos energy is destructive and acts like a cancer in the body of the Universe.[13] Those who command in circle take on a big responsibility. They are acting in the name of God and Goddess. This means they must appropriately reflect the will of God/dess, or reap the consequences of their actions.

Generating chaos and negativity removes you from the flow of divine life, and begins spiraling you widdershins away from power and towards death. I have often sat helplessly by, and watched a friend or loved one's life completely unravel due to their choice to inappropriately use manipulative magic.

There is a price to pay for everything, and each time you revisit a lesson the price gets higher. If your life isn't working for you, take responsibility for it, and change it. But, do it honorably, and in accordance with divine will. Remember, you cannot see what blessings are in store for you, what you think you want may sadly pale in comparison to what great gifts Goddess has in store for you.

You will reap what you sow. If you use your power to control the forces of the universe for selfish gain, you are creating pain, loss, and suffering for yourself. If you use your powers in selfless service of the God/dess you are creating balance, harmony, joy, and prosperity for yourself.

When called, the elements:

- ✓ Witness the rights,
- ✓ Guard the circle,
- ✓ And lend power unto your working.

Once they are called they must also be released. Never call the quarters to stand watch on a circle and forget to dismiss them. They are not Gods, which would be above malevolence. They are less evolved than human souls. They cannot leave without permission, so they would react pretty much the same as you would if you were invited to go somewhere, and then left stranded there for an indefinite period of time.

Earth Element Meditation
(All four elemental meditations can be found on accompanying CD)

Close your eyes and focus on your breathing. Breathe in to the count of 8, hold for the count of 8, and release to the count of 8.

---

[13] Chaos energy within itself is the inherent energy of the void, and the foundation of Goddess. Divine chaos is not a malevolent force. I am referring to human generated chaos, invoked with ignorance, or mal-intent.

Second Heart Chakra Activation – Calling the Quarters

You are sitting on the ground facing east, in an astral temple. It is springtime. The world is in balance, and the earth is awakened with new life. You see green meadows, gardens of flowers, and expressions of the newness of spring everywhere around you. It is morning, and the potential of the day awakening fills your senses.

The energy of the earth is quickening and you can feel the excitement, and joy that new life brings to the earth mother. There are baby animals and their mothers everywhere, and some of them approach you in curious innocence.

As the baby animals nuzzle you and nip at your hair and clothes, you feel they are pulling at you, as if they are asking you to go with them. Arise and walk with the baby animals. Breathe deeply, and feel the beauty of the earth in spring. You come to the mouth of a cave. It is dark. As you enter the cave your eyes adjust to the darkness and you can hear the sound of metal clinking in the distance. There is a flickering light ahead and the sound of muffled voices.

As you move deep into the cave you can feel yourself descending down into the depths of the earth. The rock walls have carvings and paintings on them, and they speak to you of the ancient wisdom, cycles of birth and death, new beginnings, and the stirring awakenings that are happening within you now. You see pictures of children playing, and beautiful Maidens being chased by handsome young Gods, symbols of fertility rites.

As you move closer to the sounds coming deep from within the cave, the light gets brighter and you begin to notice gems and crystals embedded in the dirt and rock walls of the cave. You descend down deep into the earth of the mother. You feel energy emanating from the crystals, and know that these are power centers, like batteries charged with spiritual vibrations. You feel the energy affecting you, opening your being to new possibilities, heightened sensitivity, and increased awareness.

The cave opens up to a large room, and within you find the scurrying activity of the Gnomes. They are hard working, small, stocky, little people. With pick axes, shovels, and all manners of earth moving tools. They are digging tunnels, mining gems, and shaping stones. They notice you and surround you. They are excited to see you, and welcome you into their world. They motion you to follow them, and they take you through a big, circular, stone opening.

Inside this new passageway you can tell the floor, walls and ceilings are not the same rough, natural passageway of the cave. This is a palace. There is marble, and glittering gems everywhere. The passageway opens to a throne room, and you suddenly realize the Gnomes are taking you to meet their King, Ghob.

Ghob is seated on a huge throne, surrounded by piles of gold coins, finely cut

253

gems, and tables covered with huge platters of food. He is clothed in the finery of the richest Kings and you can see that his wealth is equal to the great bounty of the limitless abundance of the earth's resources.

You are brought before the throne of Ghob, and he greets you respectfully. The Gnomes bring out offerings to you. Beautiful materials of finest silk, large trays of food, trunks of gold and gems, surround you in opulence, abundance and wealth. But before taking any of these treasures, you must introduce yourself and state your intentions of how you will use these treasures.

Think for a minute of how you wish to introduce yourself to this great power. He can be a great ally if treated appropriately and with respect. He can offer you stability, foundation, resources, beauty, and strength. Think carefully, and then introduce yourself to him. Tell him of your needs, and goals. Tell him of your intentions as a representative of the God and Goddess, and how you will channel the resources of the earth element. Promise that you will use his resources wisely, never wastefully, and that you will always channel the energy of his realm with respect and to the best and highest good of all concerned.

When you are finished Ghob rises, and approaches you. He takes two large crystals in his hands and holds them on each side of your head. You hear a high-pitched tone, and know that he is attuning your body to work with his energy. Accept the energetic changes that these crystals are activating in you at this time. Breathe deep and relax.

When he is finished all goes to blackness and you find yourself back in your astral temple. The gift or gifts that Ghob offered you are sitting neatly beside you. Take your time to look at the offerings that the earth element made to you, and take a moment to send a gentle thank you to the east.

When you are ready to come back to your body, take a deep breath, wiggle your toes, and open your eyes. Be sure to stretch and take the time to write down what happened in the space below, right now while it is fresh in your mind, before going on to the next element.

Calling Earth

Stand facing east, in front of the earth altar, think of Ghob and the alliance that you have made with him. Think of the green earth in spring, the strong, powerful foundation, and the rich, overflowing, limitless abundance of earth.

Draw a green invoking pentagram, calling this image forth as you do so, repeating the following incantation: *"Ye Lords of the Watchtowers of the East, Ye Lords of*

Second Heart Chakra Activation – Calling the Quarters

Earth, I do Summon, Stir, and Call thee Forth to witness these rites and to guard this circle."[14]

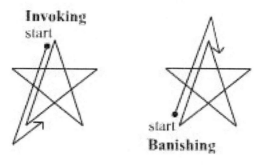

Banishing Earth

After you get through practicing, draw a banishing pentagram, and say *"Ye Lords of the Watchtowers of the East, Ye Lords of Earth, I do thank thee for attending these rites, and ere you depart for your pleasant and lovely realms, I bid thee, Hail and Farewell."*

Fire Element Meditation

Close your eyes and focus on your breathing. Breathe in to the count of 8, hold for the count of 8, and release to the count of 8.

You are sitting on the ground facing south, in an astral temple. It is summer. The sun is at its zenith in the noon sky. It is hot and you can feel beads of sweat begin to prickle the surface of your skin. The earth is laden with bounty. Fruit weights down the branches of every tree.

You recognize that this is the result of the powerful, creative energy of the Oak King, bringing the maiden to maturity, and inspiring her instinctual nature to bring forth the passionate, creative power of the Great Mother.

You hear drums and a rhythmic beat develops. Dancers dressed in red come to you, dancing sensually, spiraling around you, enticing your senses, and arousing your passions. They feed you chocolates, strawberries, and sensual foods that awaken the sense of pleasure within you. As they come closer to you, you smell exotic perfumes, and are intoxicated with their welcoming, alluring beauty.

You sway to the rhythm of the drums as one perfect dancer catches your attention. The dancer has a beautiful tattoo of a very large dragon. The dragon seems to move on the skin of the dancer, as if it moves with, but separate from her. You focus on

---

[14] The incantations in this chapter are the ones passed down to me from my initiating High Priest. However, they can be referenced in Janet and Stewart Farrar's book, *Eight Sabbats for Witches*, Phoenix Publishing, Inc. 1981

the dragon, watching it's rhythmic movement, back and forth, swaying to the erotic beat. The head of the dragon rises and falls with the music, circling it's body around the dancer, as it becomes separate, an entity unto itself, a partner in the creation of this erotic seduction of your senses.

The dragon slithers around the dancer, and then turns towards you. It is fearsome, but gentle as it approaches you. There is no escaping this powerful creature. It wraps itself around you, caressing your skin with soft, hot, leathery scales. You feel a burning sensation inside your body, and you know you are being prepared for your encounter with the Elemental King of the Salamanders.

You look up and see a red pentagram glowing brightly in mid-air. It is burning hot, and flames are licking at the radiant lines that have created a doorway into the realm of the Salamanders. Lizards, snakes and all manner of reptilian creatures are emerging through the portal.

The Dragon's embrace holds you tightly and carries you with it, as it crosses the fiery threshold and transports you into the dominion of Djinn.

You can feel that the heat would be unbearable without the protection of your guardian dragon. But, you feel safe, protected, and free to explore this exciting amusement park of pleasurable delights. Everywhere you look people are laughing, making music, enjoying themselves, engaged in creating great works of art, expressing their passions, and instantly manifesting their every desire. There is a playfulness in here, and you feel it bubbling up inside you.

Djinn approaches you. He is powerful, magnificent, and handsome. He holds the power of creation, and destruction in balance. He is welcoming and menacing, dangerously attractive. He greets you with an intensity that bares your soul, and you feel the motivating passion of fire burning in your veins.

Think for a minute of how you wish to introduce yourself to this great power. He can be a great ally if treated appropriately and with respect. He can offer you drive, motivation, inspiration, fertilization, passion, enjoyment, pleasure, and desire. Think carefully, and then introduce yourself, to him. Tell him of your desires and aspirations. Tell him of your intentions as a representative of the God and Goddess, and how you will balance the explosive nature of the fire element. Promise that you will use his powers wisely, to give life to your creations, and that you will always direct the energy of his domain with respect and to the best and highest good of all concerned.

When you are finished Djinn comes close to you. He picks up his staff and points it at your gut. You feel the burning power of fire entering your body and burning away any dead, counter-productive forces within yourself. You are purified by the fire. All

Second Heart Chakra Activation – Calling the Quarters

the fear, anger, hatred, and negativity are burned away, and a sacredness comes over you that you never felt before. You feel pure joy exploding inside yourself and you begin to ripple with uncontrollable waves of laughter.

Close your eyes and accept this powerful gift. Allow yourself to release the energetic, passionate joy of Djinn in whatever way you feel is appropriate. As you give into the unexplainable pleasure that has encompassed your being, you find yourself back in your astral temple. Still reeling from experiencing the playful, passionate nature of Djinn, take a moment to send a gentle thank you to the south.

When you are ready to come back to your body, take a deep breath, wiggle your toes, and open your eyes. Be sure to stretch and take the time to write down what happened in the space below, right now while it is fresh in your mind, before going on to the next element.

Calling Fire

Stand facing south, in front of the fire altar, think of Djinn and the alliance that you have made with him. Think of the hot, creative power of fire and how it brings the mother to fruition in summer. Feel the instinctual nature, the motivated, active, passionate, impulsiveness, and fertilizing creativity of fire.

Draw a red invoking pentagram, calling this image forth as you do so, repeating the following incantation: *"Ye Lords of the Watchtowers of the South, Ye Lords of Fire, I do Summon, Stir, and Call thee Forth to witness these rites and to guard this circle."*

Banishing Fire

After you get through practicing, draw a banishing pentagram, and say *"Ye Lords of the Watchtowers of the South, Ye Lords of Fire, I do thank thee for attending these rites, and ere you depart for your pleasant and lovely realms, I bid thee, Hail and Farewell."*

Water Element Meditation

Close your eyes and focus on your breathing. Breathe in to the count of 8, hold for the count of 8, and release to the count of 8.

You are sitting on the ground facing west, watching the sunset over a beautiful, blue body of water. It is autumn. The world is in balance, and the earth is satisfied with the success of harvest. The relaxation and release of time well spent fills your senses, and you completely let go in the drifting sound of the gentle lapping of the waves.

The energy of the earth is restful. You feel the relief, and comfort of appreciating the rewards and hard work of the past. You see a school of fish, feeding on the surface of the water, and in the gathering dusk, you stretch out to rest and reflect.

Images from your past come to mind. Loved ones, family members, and emotional connections that bring both joy and pain. Lessons of the past swim through your heart, like a ghost haunting the passageway of your emotions. You remember a lost love, a misunderstood moment of pain, a conflict never resolved, or a regret that never found closure.

A splash in the water draws your attention, and you see someone swimming in the darkening, blue water, floating, and relaxing, just like you. It looks like someone from your past, someone you love deeply, but lost contact with due to a misunderstanding that hurt you both.

You wave and call out, but the person is lost in deep thought, drifting in the water, resting, relaxed, and washing away the sorrows of yesterday. Not to miss an opportunity to reconnect with this person, who was once such a large part of your heart, you dive into the waiting, receptive water.

The black depths engulf your body, and drag you down. You can see the surface and your loved one floating above you, but the more you struggle the farther down you sink. The water seems to be clutching at you, holding you back, wrapping around you, and weighing you down.

You look around you to see what is keeping you from the surface. You see the blue Undines, the water creatures, pushing against you, forcing you away from the surface, away from the air, and down into the dark, murky depths of this deadly terrain. Every one of the Undines holds a different emotion. You feel love, joy, fear, pain, grief, happiness, and sorrow all at once. Just as blackness is about to overwhelm you, an eerie, blue light comes into your field of vision. You realize you can breathe and any fear that you felt suddenly leaves, as you realize you are about to journey to the land of the Undines, and the Kingdom of Niksa.

The blue light seems to be coming from just beyond your field of vision and as you swim over a large cavern a beautiful world comes into view. There are mermaids, dolphins, sea horses, all manners of colorful fish, and sea creatures. The castle of Niksa is in the center of the cavern and you can't wait to see what awaits you inside.

The castle is ornately adorned with shells and treasures of the sea. The doorway is open and you effortlessly float right through. You are in a long hallway lined with mirrors. You look in one of the mirrors and see yourself from another time, a time in your past, a time when something important happened that changed you, transformed

Second Heart Chakra Activation – Calling the Quarters

you, rebirthed you. Each mirror reveals a different you, past lives that you have experienced, both from your current incarnation and previous ones. You move curiously from mirror to mirror looking into the depths of your past with unusual clarity.

You begin to realize the mirrors are reflecting the lessons you have learned that have made you who you are today. You see hurts, failures, successes, loves, sorrows, and joys. Every reflection shows you a place of rebirth; sometimes old, sometimes young, sometimes happy, sometimes sad, but always growing, changing, and evolving into the person that you are now.

At the end of the hallway, Niksa waits. He holds the cup of life, and the trident of death. He is courage in the face of fear, honor in the face of adversity, faith when all seems hopeless. He faces you with the consequences of your actions, be they great or sorrowful. He judges, he watches, he waits, and he returns to you what you have earned, whether you want it or not.

Niksa honors you for your bravery in making this journey. There are few who have the courage to meet him face to face. There are less who understand the secrets of death and rebirth. They shrink from his dark mysteries. They avoid his deep embrace.

Look upon Niksa and know that without pain there can be no pleasure, without adversity there can be no triumph, and without suffering there can be no love. Niksa offers you emotional fulfillment, love, peace, honor, gratitude, happiness, contentment, a sense of well-being, and a connectedness to spirit. He teaches you the secrets of intuition, initiation, how to navigate the waters of the subconscious, and to interpret the fluid messages of spirit.

He challenges your weaknesses to make you strong so that you can become who you were meant to be. He forces you to choose life or settle with death. He can be a powerful ally or a feared and hated enemy. He doesn't care how you feel about him, only that you feel something, that you do something. He wants you to transform, and grow, to become greater tomorrow than you are today.

He offers you the chalice, and you drink the potion within. You know it creates an emotional bond between you, an agreement from which you cannot escape. Niksa promises to be there, like the tide, always returning to you what you send out.

He points his trident at your third eye and releases a blast that sends you through a dimensional portal. You find yourself back on the edge of the water, where you began, left to think about the path that has lead you here, and the consequences of your actions. Take a moment to send a gentle thank you to the west.

When you are ready to come back to your body, take a deep breath, wiggle your toes, and open your eyes. Be sure to stretch and take the time to write down what happened in the space provided below, right now while it is fresh in your mind, before going on to the next element.

Calling Water

Stand facing west, in front of the water altar, think of Niksa and the alliance that you have made with him. Think of the emotional, transformational power of water and how it brings about growth and rebirth. Think of the pleasure and growth that love brings, and the welcoming, cleansing, renewing power of water.

Draw a blue invoking pentagram, calling this image forth as you do so, repeating the following incantation: *"Ye Lords of the Watchtowers of the West, Ye Lords of Water, Lords of Death and Initiation, I do Summon, Stir, and Call thee Forth to witness these rites and to guard this circle."*

Banishing Water

After you get through practicing, draw a banishing pentagram, and say *"Ye Lords of the Watchtowers of the West, Ye Lords of Water, Lords of Death and Initiation, I do thank thee for attending these rites, and ere you depart for your pleasant and lovely realms, I bid thee, Hail and Farewell."*

Air Element Meditation

Close your eyes and focus on your breathing. Breathe in to the count of 8, hold for the count of 8, and release to the count of 8.

You are sitting on a mountain, facing north. It is winter at midnight. The Wind is blowing in your face. The air is cold and the sky is black. You stare out into nothingness with only a few stars to light the night.

You are comfortably wrapped in a buffalo blanket. You hear the screech of an owl above. You are old. You have seen many years' come and go. You have learned much over the course of your existence. You have learned to temper passion with patience. You have learned to balance judgment with compassion, pride with accomplishment, justice with tolerance.

You have seen many things come and go, and you know that all things must change. You have learned to be flexible in the face of adversity, and strong in the

Second Heart Chakra Activation – Calling the Quarters

shifting sands. You know that all the pain and suffering you have ever experienced has either faded away, or one day will. There is no wound that time won't heal.

You look into the blackness of the future, dotted with the many stars in the universe, and you know that each star represents a promise, a hope, and an opportunity to renew and rejuvenate you. The choices you make today will determine how the stars will shine tomorrow.

Some of the stars are more appealing than others. Some are closer, some are brighter, some are very far away, and barely visible. You know that you will one day have experienced them all. But tonight you can choose only one.

You reflect on the choices of the past, and think clearly of the possibilities of the future. Ask for guidance and choose. When you have settled on one of the stars, stare at it.

All the stars begin to fly around and at first they appear to be fireflies. But, as your star flies straight at you, you can see that it is a Sylph; a bright yellow fairy that holds the seed-thought of your choices, hopes, and aspirations of the future.

The Sylphs fly around and through you, carrying thoughts back and forth through your consciousness like the drifting breeze. The one that has your chosen thought is hovering in front of you, waiting to imbed the thought into your awareness. Look at this creature of light. It loves to talk. Open your ears and listen to what it has to say. Give it permission to plant the seed in your mind.

As you feel the seed enter your being, the sylphs all gather around you fluttering in, out, and through you. They are so quick and light. As they flutter around, they begin to form a shape in front of you. A yellow glowing pentagram takes form, opening a gateway to a golden world of the future, suspended in the air.

A beautiful angelic being comes up through the opening and telepathically communicates with your energy field, temporarily altering your physical composition. Your body begins to glow and suddenly there is no more cold or darkness. You feel illumination, clarity, and a sense of purpose. All your senses are acutely aware, and you feel your physical body lift up into the air. You shed the heavy blanket, and float effortlessly towards the golden angelic being.

She smiles at you, and reaches out to pull you through the portal made by the Sylphs. As you float through the energetic field you feel the tingling sensation of so many thoughts formed together as one, and you realize that you are feeling the power of a group mind.

The angel holds you by the hand and you fly through the golden landscape. You can hear so many thoughts, that it is hard to tell which thoughts belong where. It is a little confusing, but you find that if you focus, you can tune in on any one line of communication or process several different ones at the same time.

As you enjoy the sights of the beautiful kingdom, you notice that all manners of technological development have been explored and utilized. The angel directs you to fly up. Way up high, floating in mid-air, you can see a magnificent, shining, golden castle. It looks like something out of a science-fiction movie, and you are amazed at the technology of this race of beings. You know this is where you will meet Paralda, the King of the Sylphs, and ruler of this realm.

You fly up and up, so quickly and effortlessly that you expect to loose your breath, but the air is sweet and crisp. You breathe deeply, and feel your wit sharpening with every moment that passes here.

As you enter the castle there are little Sylphs everywhere. Angelic beings are tending to large volumes of books, using computers, communicating, educating, and expanding their mind in many ways, using various, different gadgets and amazingly advanced equipment. This is a very technologically advanced place, and you imagine that Paralda must be a very wise and educated monarch.

As you drift into the throne room, a huge crowd gathers to witness this joyous occasion. They are all interested in the events of this meeting, wondering what will take place, comparing ideas, and discussing possibilities.

Paralda is seated on a huge, golden throne. His vibration is so high that you can see right through him. His presence crackles with electricity. His face is wise, kind, and welcoming. He greets you respectfully, but doesn't say a word. You can feel him inside your head. His thoughts are so powerful that it is difficult to tell whether they are his or your own.

There is no need to introduce your self to him. He already knows everything about you. He is aware of your intentions and your visions. He knows what you will do with the powers that he offers you. He has seen your future. He is aware of every word you will ever utter. His gifts are words of advice, prophecies of your destiny, and insights into what choices will lead you to the quickest and most joyous route. Be still close your eyes and listen to the voice of fate.

When Paralda is finished speaking, you find yourself back on the mountaintop. Your blanket is still wrapped securely around you, and the owl is still flying overhead, watching over you, and protecting you. The hoot of the owl echoes in the canyons below and you know it's the voice of Paralda reminding you of your greatness and the

Second Heart Chakra Activation – Calling the Quarters

path that will take you there. Take a moment to send a gentle thank you to the north.

When you are ready to come back to your body, take a deep breath, wiggle your toes, and open your eyes. Be sure to stretch and take the time to write down what happened in the space provided, right now while it is fresh in your mind.

Calling the Air

Stand facing north, in front of the air altar, think of Paralda and the connection that you have made with him. Think of the cool, detached, wisdom of air and how communication and education bring forth understanding and enlightenment, cooling the passions of conflict like a gentle breeze.

Draw a yellow invoking pentagram, calling this image forth as you do so, repeating the following incantation: *"Ye Lords of the Watchtowers of the North, Ye Lords of Air, Boreas, Guardian of the Northern Portal, Thy Powerful God, Thy Gentle Goddess, I do Summon, Stir, and Call thee Forth to witness these rites and to guard this circle."*

Banishing Air

After you get through practicing, draw a banishing pentagram, and say *"Ye Lords of the Watchtowers of the North, Ye Lords of Air, Boreas, Guardian of the Northern Portal, Thy Powerful God, Thy Gentle Goddess, I do thank thee for attending these rites, and ere you depart for your pleasant and lovely realms, I bid thee, Hail and Farewell."*

Moon – Mothers

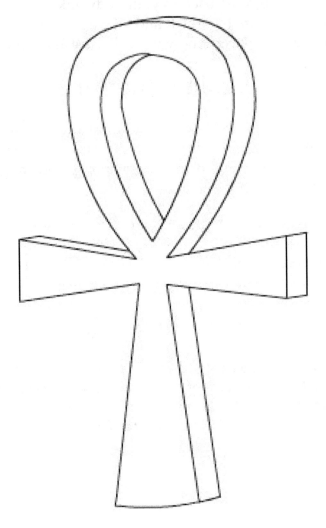

Color Me Green!

At the age of 21, the Sun has ruled his world with zeal and fervor. He has sought out perfection, and beauty. He has imposed his will on the world, and forced it into his perception of perfection. Yet, he is alone.

He has a full social calendar, and friends by the dozen. But, he is lonely in a crowd of loneliness. He feels an emptiness inside, that before he hadn't noticed. He hears her lonesome cry when he passes a reflected pool, or a mirror. When he looks up at the moon something inside him stirs his soul.

Oh, he has sexual partners. All he wants and them some, but none that capture his heart. None reflect the true, inner beauty that he seeks. Suddenly he becomes aware

Second Heart Chakra Activation - Moon - Mothers

of his superficial universe. Everything is measured at face value; there is no depth, no sentiment. How can his world be purposeful when it lacks meaning?

He knows what his outer world holds for him. He built it. But, now in seeking purpose he turns inward. As his vision is focused on the dark, depths of the missing piece of his soul, she rises. The Moon, Luna, awakens and emerges, a silent reflection, drifting dreamily through a starlight sky.

The Mother Moon levels her gaze across the landscape of glittering gold, and sees beneath the flattery, pomp and circumstance to the heart of the matter. She understands the darkest part of the human heart, and loves it unconditionally. She recognizes the emptiness in a life of glamoury and gives it a home. She is waiting at the end of the brilliant lights of the disco, at a nurtured hearth on a quiet, little street with a warm meal simmering on the stove, kids playing in the yard, and a mini van.

The Moon shows up interpreting all the deeds of the past, and reveals how shallow and unimportant all the silly, material values that you thought meant something, really are. She perceives reality in a completely different light, and nothing is accepted at face value.

She is unwilling to be reasonable, logical, on a time schedule, pigeon holed, stereotyped, or in any way go along to get along. Luna doesn't follow plans or guidelines. She laughs at your structure and hierarchy. She feels, and she is, and she does what she does, without regard to race, color, religion, sex, national origin, or any of the grand plans that you thought you had made.

Luna throws all to the wind. She falls in love with whom she will, for whatever reasons or none at all. She loves blindly, and sees a reality that is connected with emotional ties that bind us to each other in ways that only she can understand. She does not ask for facts or rational explanations. She knows what She feels, and reacts solely on that information. She bridges the physical and the astral worlds together, in a place inside yourself, to which only you can truly relate. Luna longs to be understood, and loved, not for any deed or attribute, but just because She exists.

Luna is the mirror of your world. She gracefully accepts what you have to offer, and sends it back in return. She teaches you to take only what you need, and to be grateful for what you receive. The Moon longs to be a part of the flow, but can't help but stand out. She shapes, guides, molds, and forms you to achieve your greatness, for she is the mother. She cares for those that do, rather than being the one who does.

She longs to be one with you, to experience all that you do. She nurtures, protects, and remembers every special moment of your life. She takes pictures, collects mementos, and neatly files them away in nostalgic scrapbooks. She keeps every card and letter, and cherishes every triumph as if it were her own success. Even if no one else ever does, she will love you always.

The Moon loves to nurture her children. She adores their innocence, and gently whispers hints to guide them in the right direction. She provides the right environment for their growth and success. She is caring, forgiving, and often misunderstood, silently drifting along the sidelines, cheering others on, sharing in their triumphs and caring in their sorrows.

She is Isis, Demeter, Luna, Hecate. She is intuition, emotions, and moodiness. She is unconditional love, and acceptance. But she is also wrathful when her gentle guidance is dishonored, scornful when potential is thwarted by laziness. She prompts and admonishes, cheers, and jeers. She is always on your side, even when you are wrong. Yet she is ever quick to point out your shortcomings, for she cares about your success far more than she needs your approval.

Second Heart Chakra Activation – Certification Requirements

Practice

Learn your incantations and practice calling quarters.

Look at different objects in your world and try to figure out which quarter they would go in.

Spend time communicating with the elementals. Make special places in your yard that will be undisturbed, for the elementals (fairie folk) to play.

Remember, practicing your quarter calls will invoke the elementals, always release them after you have finished practicing.

Certification Requirements

Perform elemental meditations. Write down personal experience, taking care to include as many details as you can remember. Explain what you learned, if anything.

Journal Entries

Record the results of your Elemental Meditations.

13
Second Throat Chakra Activation
The God and The Goddess

Blue

Color Me Blue!

There are many ways to look at God. Humans have been trying to solve the mystery of God for ages. All of them think they have it right, and none of them completely agree with anyone else. It's a complex issue... for humans.

Goddess on the other hand, is trying to figure out humans. Well, not really humans so much as just the whole, physical universe thing. Which is why she created the physical universe in the first place.

Goddess understands the vastness of many, many things, but learned these things through experiencing the connection with humans, just as humans learn about spirituality through connecting with Goddess. This is a polarity trying to achieve balance, a constantly, self-perpetuating, spiral journey, which leads to wholeness and enlightenment.

There are many philosophical theories that humans subscribe to. Goddess can manifest in any form that humans need Her. She just wants them to know Her. She is not attached to the physical interpretation of what she represents. She just wants to be represented.

As Her servant, it is important to be as flexible. It is important to recognize that everyone needs spiritual growth, just like everyone needs to eat. You need to eat three times a day. It would be nice if you could eat an organic, all natural, perfectly balanced diet, custom tailored to meet your nutritional needs, based on scientific analysis of your daily activities, lifestyle, body chemistry, etc. But, if that's not available you still need to eat something. If you don't eat you will die. So eat. Try to eat the best you can, but if nothing else is available just see to it that you eat something on a regular basis.

It is the same with spirituality. It matters not what way you are pursuing God, as long as it uplifts you and brings you closer to God. Christian, Hindu, Buddhist, Pagan, Jewish, whatever, all paths lead to the same place in the end. Let's not argue over who God is, let's just agree that It exists, and we want to connect with it, and let's do that.

A Priest or Priestess of the Goddess should be able to minister to anyone of any faith. This takes a theological understanding of religious principles. Once you understand the spiritual truth, you can listen to the cultural interpretation, and understand which truth they are trying to express. I have outlined the twelve main theological concepts, so you can relate them to your beliefs. The following definitions were taken from Webster's Dictionary © 1976 by Thomas Nelson Inc.

- ✓ Animism – attribution of conscious life to nature as a whole or to inanimate objects.
- ✓ Atheism – denying the existence of God.
- ✓ Buddhism - a philosophy of life aimed solely to liberate sentient beings from suffering.
- ✓ Confucianism - a way of life in which morality occupies a supreme

Second Throat Chakra Activation – The God and The Goddess

position.
- ✓ Hinduism – a body of religious beliefs and practices native to India, which believes the universe is one divine entity.
- ✓ Monotheism – a doctrine or belief that there is only one deity.
- ✓ Mysticism – the belief that direct knowledge of God or ultimate reality is attainable through immediate intuition or insight.
- ✓ Pantheism – a doctrine that equates God with the forces and laws of the universe.
- ✓ Polytheism – belief in or worship of many gods.
- ✓ Rationalism – the practice of guiding one's actions and opinions solely by what seems reasonable.
- ✓ Deism - 1. belief in the existence of a God on the evidence of reason and nature only, with rejection of supernatural revelation (distinguished from *theism*). 2. belief in a God who created the world but has since remained indifferent to it.
- ✓ Theism – 1. The belief in one God as the creator and ruler of the universe, without rejection of revelation (distinguished from *deism*). 2. belief in the existence of a god or gods (opposed to *atheism*).

In reading through these definitions, note which ones you do and do not subscribe to. You may find that you want to do some in-depth study on one or more concepts. The more you understand theology the easier you will find the underlying connectedness of all of them.

God is everywhere, everything, and everybody. We can focus on individual expressions of God/dess in our worship, but to honor one aspect does not exclude or invalidate any other expression of the spiritual perfection that makes up our universe.

The perfection of Goddess lies in Her adaptability, tolerance, patience, and the gentleness that She shows for us, Her children. There are many religions that attempt to define God. People want to find love, trust, happiness, and fulfillment in this life and the next, no matter with what religion they affiliate. Any opportunity you have to help people reach any measure of those things will be an act of ministering, in service of, and an expression of Goddess.

I see no reason why all of the twelve cannot be true in some form or another. Even Atheism has truth from certain perspectives. In interpreting true balance, it is interesting to realize that to achieve theological balance, a student of the mysteries would need to find the truth and lessons within each of these concepts. Of course, this would require deep searching, and would at first appear ridiculous and impossible, which is the reason why it would necessitate balance.

All gods are one, and the one has many faces. To put a single face on God/dess precludes the sacredness, omnipotence, and omnipresence of God/dess. To truly understand God/dess we must be flexible in our interpretation, as we know that our mind is limited in what we can comprehend. God/dess is without limitations, and far beyond our individual need to be validated in our separateness from Her and each other.

To truly know Goddess: pray and meditate. Speak to Her and She will listen. Listen for Her and She will speak to you. She is within and around you always, a part of you. There is nothing you need that She won't give you. There is no question that She will not answer. All you have to do is ask.

Balance and Polarity

Color Me Blue!

Balance promotes harmony. Harmony promotes health, wealth, happiness, and fulfillment. Every moment of discomfort originates from a lack of balance. Every moment of bliss is a moment when all things are balanced. If you are happy in an area of your life, then balance has been established there. Learning to achieve and maintain balance is one of the most overlooked lessons of the universe, but it is also one of the most important.

Polarity helps you begin to understand balance. If you can learn to balance two things that are opposite, you may then be able to learn how to balance three things that are all equally different. If you can do that then, you are ready to try to learn how to balance four things that are all equally different, then seven, then twelve, and twenty-four.

By learning to balance opposites, you find a way to expand your consciousness to empathize with and find value in both things at the same time. This is a very difficult concept for many humans. As we often find that the lesson never presents itself in a way that is easily identifiable.

For instance, if Goddess approached you and said, "How can you balance having enough to fulfill your needs, and still be able to share with everyone?" You would stop, put on your highest vibration and find a way to balance that out. But, if you came home and found that someone had stolen everything you had that you hadn't used in the last year, you probably wouldn't respond from your highest place.

It wouldn't really matter that you didn't use the TV, the juicer, the jewelry, or the chair in the upstairs bedroom that you never go in. It wouldn't matter that you still had all your food, clothes, computers, books, and everything that you use on a regular basis. You would be mad. You would feel violated, and you would look for someone to blame so you would have a target at which to direct your negative emotions.

Maybe, after you calmed down, you could look around and see that they didn't take anything that you needed. You could relax, and realize that you really didn't lose anything of importance. But, that won't get back the hours, days, weeks, months, or years it took you to get to that place. It won't recall all the hate and negativity that you generated during your healing process, and it won't shield you from receiving that negativity back.

The ability to find balance between men and women is the most obvious place to begin. We learn at an early age whether we are male or female, and all that it entails. Our clothes, our toys, our language, our disposition, our games, our employment, and many other things are often predetermined by our gender. As a species we have worked to raise our awareness about balancing those two roles, and have made remarkable progress.

If you watch any TV shows from the 50's and 60's you will see a marked difference in the gender roles. I remember when I was young, there used to be "Battle of the Sexes" themes all the time. Now, men and women fighting against each other, trying to prove which is the better gender, is a foreign concept to me.

We are working together, and we have learned that while some things are naturally easier for one gender or the other, it is possible for men and women to do any job that they are truly motivated to do. Relationships teach a person what is going on inside ones self. Your mate mirrors your strengths and weaknesses, in regards to the male/female balance within you. Brothers and sisters, mothers, fathers, co-workers, everyone in your life that causes you opposition, is giving you an opportunity to balance a situation where you have chosen a side, or a pole.

There is no opposition that you cannot balance with communication. Always remember the principles of Yin and Yang in an opposition. Do the opposite of whatever the other person is doing. If they are yelling, whisper. If they are screaming, just ground and let them get it out. They will eventually get tired, and then it will be your turn to talk.

If they are avoiding you, seek them out. If they are closed off show them you care about them by sharing your feelings. Remember always, if you want more, give more. If you want less, give less. The world will respond according to the laws of balance. When applying this concept you will emerge successful from every conflict, argument or confrontation.

Awakening Spirit – Freshman Course – www.WISESeminary.com

Mercury – Scholars

Color Me Blue!

Something really weird happens right about the age of 28. Saturn returns to the place where it was in your natal chart when you were born. A transition is made and The Fates spin the wheel of your life.

The first 28 years are all about your inheritance. You receive all the things you were fated to have in this existence, all the things that you need to complete your

Second Throat Chakra Activation – Mercury – Scholars

contract. The first 28 years are under the direction of the Spinning Goddess. Sometimes knows as Atropos, or Urdh, "that which is becoming".

The Spinner spins the thread of life. She pulls you out of the cauldron, spins you into existence, and provides all the right circumstances for you to get exactly what you need. She makes sure you learn your lessons, and have the appropriate resources available, before she turns you over to Verdandi.

At your first Saturn return, (about age 28) you are passed from Urdh, the Spinner, to Verdandi, the Weaver. She is "that which is coming into being". Verdandi weaves you into the fabric of life. Urdh has prepared you to live. Verdandi gives you the opportunity to actually do it.[15]

At the Moon's 28th birthday, all she knew about hearth and home, raising children, preparing meals, and all her dreams of domestic bliss, suddenly leave her feeling trapped, and unfulfilled. She doesn't resent the work she has done. She is just ready for more. She feels cut off from life, disconnected from the community, lost in the worlds of others.

She has become something to everyone else, but nothing to herself. She is someone's mom, someone's wife, someone's daughter, someone's sister, and someone's employee. She is watching everyone else have fun, and suddenly realizes that while she is enjoying the show, she is not taking part in it.

She longs to have friends, to be a part of things, and to rediscover her self. She has lost her youth in her motherliness, and her passion as well. She needs a makeover. She needs a new wardrobe. She needs a life.

Mercury awakens inside her and is just full of ideas. From ages 28 to 35, he will be showing her the hippest new dance moves, the trendiest places, and the coolest people in town. He is all ready to make her over and show her just how fabulous she still is. He has all kinds of ideas about self-improvement, and knows all the newest gimmicks. He knows how to make friends and influence people, and he is all about networking.

Mercury loves to try new things, and explore the wonders of the universe. Right at the elbow of the Sun, he has the young King's ear, and he knows just how to direct that powerful will in a way that will get just about anything accomplished.

He wants to change jobs, get a job, start a business, and do something different, something exciting. There's a whole world of people out there, and he wants to meet

---

[15] Z. Budapest – *Summoning the Fates*, Harmony Books 1988

them all. He loves to learn. He wants to share. He wants to be a part of things.

He knows there is a wealth of information out there, and he doesn't want to miss a penny of it. He pays close attention to detail. He notices everything. He is bent on self-improvement and he wants it right now.

Mercury finds that communication is where it's at, listening, speaking, sharing ideas, and sorting through information. He records every message, clearly, and files it away in a very specific place so that he will know exactly where to go when he needs that information again.

Mercury demands to be valued. He knows his worth, and you better know it too. He won't bother wasting the time of those who don't appreciate him. There are too many places he needs to go, too many things to experience, to bother with someone who isn't intelligent enough to know a good thing when they see it.

No, there won't be any big argument, or battle. He is not into confrontation. He would much rather just say his polite good-byes, and leave behind a friend. I mean good grief, there's no need to get all emotional and stuff. We're here to have a good time, let's not mess things up by getting feelings involved.

Mercury loves to fast, to purify, to excel, and to improve. He takes you on a fast track to a new realm where there are powerful people to admire, and intelligent people to learn from.

He will find a way for you to grow, be thinner, smarter, faster, stronger, wealthier, whatever. If you are lacking anywhere he will find it and make it right. He is not addicted, and there is no bad habit that he can't break. There is nothing on the physical plane that has more power over him than he does. He loves himself, and if it's not logical to continue doing something then he just won't do it anymore.

But, watch out, Mercury gets bored quickly, and he can easily manipulate you into any situation that amuses him. He is a master of disguise. If he doesn't want you to see him, you won't. He may be standing right beside you, but you will never know. He's a shape shifter, a chameleon. He can be whatever he needs to be at any given moment. He can see what motivates you and point you at all the shiny things, while he works his magic behind your back.

It's all done with smoke and mirrors, but darn he's good. You can't help but like him. He's charming, he's witty, he's flattering, and a great party guest. He has the world by the tail, and it has no idea Mercury is driving. It thinks Mercury is just hitching a ride, and welcomes the company… And that's just the way Mercury wants it.

Awakening Spirit – Freshman Course – www.WISESeminary.com

Practice

Work with balance and polarity this week. Notice the conflicts, and opposition in your life. Apply the principles of balance to find the source of imbalance within yourself, and find a way to restore balance both on the inner and outer worlds.

If you are not praying and meditating every day, set aside 10 to 15 minutes a day to do so. Talk to Goddess and then listen for Her to respond. Try to remain in that bridge state, in tune with spirit, always asking for direction and always listening for Her words.

Certification Requirements

Write a report that documents the magical and mundane properties of the following herbs. Include pictures. Document references.

Rosemary	☐ Peppermint	☐ Frankincense	☐ Myrrh
Sandlewood	☐ Chamomile	☐ Mugwort	☐ Lavender
Rose	☐ Eucalyptus	☐ Cinquefoil	☐ Apple

Journal Entries

List the imbalances in your life, explore how you can apply the principle of polarity to create balance.

14
Second Third-Eye Activation
Invoking Deity

Indigo

Color Me Indigo!

Invoking Deity often sounds like something scary, dark, and maybe manipulative from some points of view. Invoking is one of those buzz words that puts us on alert that someone is directing power, so these feelings are appropriate. You want to be alert and aware when someone is invoking deity, just as you want to be aware when anyone important visits you.

Let's explore the terminology of Invoking and Incantations, so that we can educate ourselves past the Hollywood programming that some of us have over these words.[16]

Invoke – 1. to petition for help or support 2. to appeal to or cite as authority 3. to call forth by incantation: conjure 4. to make an earnest request for: solicit 5. to put into effect or operation 6. to bring about or cause

Invocation – 1. supplication: a prayer at the beginning of a service 2. a formula for conjuring: incantation

Incantation – a use of spells or verbal charms spoken or sung as a part of a ritual of magic; also a formula of words chanted or recited in or as if in such a ritual

So, basically to Invoke Deity is to call them to attend your religious service, or spiritual working. An invocation is the prayer used to bring them. And an incantation is a recited prayer that is used over and over, such as The Lords Prayer. Of course, all of these things can be used to call positive, loving beings, or dark, negative, malevolent beings. The intent is up to you.

As we have discussed before, Incantations have power because they have been repeated and used by so many spiritually minded people. You can use an incantation, or write an invocation of your own. Both are very effective in different ways. You should do what you feel drawn to do for each situation. It is important to remain flexible in your practice.

The first thing one should do is identify the need. When you are doing any religious service; a sabbat, a moon, a hand fasting, or a working, the deity you call should support the working. You can call The Goddess, in general, or you could fine-tune your need by identifying which Goddess would be appropriate to support your working.

Researching deity and working with different ones is a fun part of your

---

[16] All three definitions stated are quoted from Webster's Dictionary, © 1976 by Thomas Nelson, Inc., Publishers

Second Third-Eye Chakra Activation – Invoking Deity

education as a Priest/ess. It's good to include a few reference books in your library that are dedicated to identifying and explaining the nature of the different Gods and Goddesses. Original texts on mythology as well as books explaining modern interpretations are very helpful in guiding you to your own personal understanding.

You should always research and know what a Deity is all about. What are their likes and dislikes? What are their customs, and traditions? What are they used to? How will they behave once they arrive? Kali is going to bring a very different vibration than Hera, or Venus. Pan will feel very different from Hades or Zeus.

It would not be wise to invoke Papa Legba without having rum and a cigar for him. It's a bad idea to invoke Kali to attack your enemies, or Ma'at to bring you justice, if you are not without blame. Their reaction will be to teach you to take responsibility for your own Karma, instead of attacking those whom you may be blaming. Nor would you want to call Venus for marital fidelity, as she is known for promiscuity.

The purpose of calling a certain God or Goddess is to focus your intention and layer power to your purpose. If you do not know the personalities, and proclivities of the God or Goddess, you may be undermining your purpose. Always follow up your intuition with education. Have a couple of nice reference books on hand just for the purpose of researching deity.

In your quarter incantations, the North quarter call does say "thy powerful God, thy gentle Goddess, we do summon, stir, and call thee forth to witness this rite and guard this circle". Therefore, without any extra work, you have called the God and Goddess to your circle.

But, it is customary for the Priest and/or Priestess to do a separate invocation to the God and/or Goddess, to whom you are dedicating the rite. The Priest and Priestess offer up their physical vehicle to be occupied by the Gods during the rite. This serves several purposes:

- ✓ To serve the Gods you have to know what the Gods want. To do that you must connect with them and listen to them often.

- ✓ To give the Gods an opportunity to speak to the group as a whole. Sometimes the Goddess has important messages to give to a person or group. The Priestess acts as Her voice in delivering Her messages.

- ✓ To bridge the worlds between astral and mundane. If you are doing a working to honor the Goddess, She does need to be there. It would be silly to have a birthday party for someone and not invite him or her. The same rule applies for rituals that honor the Gods.

- ✓ To deepen the connection between Goddess and Priestess, and bring them closer as one. The Priestess serves as a vessel of the Goddess. If you are a solitary practitioner, you are the bridge of that connection.

- ✓ If you are a member of a group, the High Priestess is the living representative of the Goddess. She has gained the experience, education, and practice to connect with and speak for the Goddess, as the embodiment of Goddess. That relationship must be respected, honored, and nurtured often to keep it clear, strong, and pure.

- ✓ To ensure that the rite is pleasing and appropriate to the Gods. We do our best to plan a ritual that will serve our purposes, in harmony with Goddess. But, once ritual starts and the Gods are invited, sometimes they take on a life of their own, and plans are thrown to the wind. It's like the saying goes, 'Men make plans, and the Gods laugh'.

When you are willing and able and it's important to those whom you are serving, the Goddess will come through in the proper intensity to do the work that needs to be done.

Possession is a more intense act of invocation, which comes with time and practice. It happens gradually as you get more in tune with channeling the Gods. As you learn to invoke, and begin to allow the Gods to speak through you, you slowly feel safer and safer giving up control of your being to the deity. When you are no longer concerned with the safety of your physical being or your need to be in control of it, you can be an open channel for the God or Goddess to occupy.

Many people are afraid that they will not be able to regain control, or that they will get lost. It isn't like you are an outsider, and someone or something else has total control. It is just like meditation or trance, you agree to what is going on, and at any moment, you can choose to take control back. You agree to listen to the person guiding your meditation, and follow along with what they are saying, and you can consciously choose to stop following along at any time.

Some religions teach that possession is a requirement of worship. In Wicca we do not prescribe to that philosophy. As a Priest or Priestess gets more comfortable with working with a deity, the relationship gets more and more intense, until eventually the invocation does allow the Priest/ess to be the physical channel for the Gods to speak through. But this isn't necessary to worship.

A Priestesses goal in invoking deity is to strengthen the relationship between her and deity, to be Her servant, Her voice, Her hands, Her eyes, and Her body. So that she can in turn serve her brothers and sisters, and improve the universe through healing,

Second Third-Eye Chakra Activation – Invoking Deity

and helping others.

Drawing Down the Moon

Color Me Indigo!

Drawing Down the Moon or Drawing Down the Sun is an energetic exercise that consciously pulls your connection with the divine down into your being. The effectiveness of this action deepens with practice. You will be able to feel a shift the first time you do it, but you may not be able to identify it as a presence of deity until you have become adept at the practice.

Your Transpersonal Point is a Chakra about 12 to 18 inches above your head. This is your direct connection to external God/dess, as opposed to the Sacral Chakra, which is your connection to your internal God/dess. Drawing Down is the act of charging that Chakra, expanding that energy, and pulling it down into your being.

Once you have drawn down, if you have done it correctly, you are in an enhanced state. You are connected with Goddess and become a vessel from where She can act, and administer. If you are calling a particular deity, time your incantation or invocation so that you will be finished speaking at the same time your hands stop moving.

- ✓ Stand with your feet about shoulder width apart.
- ✓ Ground and breathe with your diaphragm.
- ✓ Bring your arms up over your head and cup your hands, as though you were holding a softball, about 12 to 18 inches above your head, fingers together.
- ✓ See the Moon, glowing silvery, blue in your hands. (If you are connecting with the God see the Sun, glowing bright yellow in your hands.)
- ✓ Expand that energy and make the Moon or Sun bigger, and adjust your hands to

hold the bigger ball of energy.
- ✓ As you move your hands apart over your head, stay grounded.
- ✓ Continue to make the energy grow into a big huge ball that you lower over and into yourself, by bringing your hands out and down to your sides.

Using the Charge of the Goddess

Memorizing the Charge is a very important part of connecting with Goddess. She likes hearing it, and she will come every time you speak it with intent to call her. The way you use the Charge is to draw down first and then speak the Charge as though you are Goddess.

If you practice with this method and do it repeatedly, you will begin to feel the difference in your body. You will begin listening to yourself speak the Charge as if it is someone else's voice. Sometimes, I can feel physical changes in my body, such as my face will feel distorted, as though it has become someone else's face, or my body will lengthen, become more graceful, or stronger.

There are a great many mysteries in the Charge. I have had the Charge memorized for 14 years and I continue to gain new insights into it daily. This is a powerful tool that is well worth the time it takes to memorize it.

When calling the Goddess or God into your being it is a gentle, loving, empowering feeling. I have never felt invaded, cast aside, disrespected, or unappreciated for my efforts. I have never felt overcome with the urge to do evil, or unable to control my actions. I have never felt as though I could not immediately regain control, or that I was loosing control. There is a big difference between loosing control and releasing control.

Loosing Control is against your will. Think of how you choose to participate in a meditation, but at any time you can choose to quit meditating and come back to normal reality. It is the same way with invoking the Goddess, at any time you can choose to return to your natural state. Drawing Down is a partnership between Priestess and Deity. Either one can withdraw from the coupling at any time.

Saturn – Crones

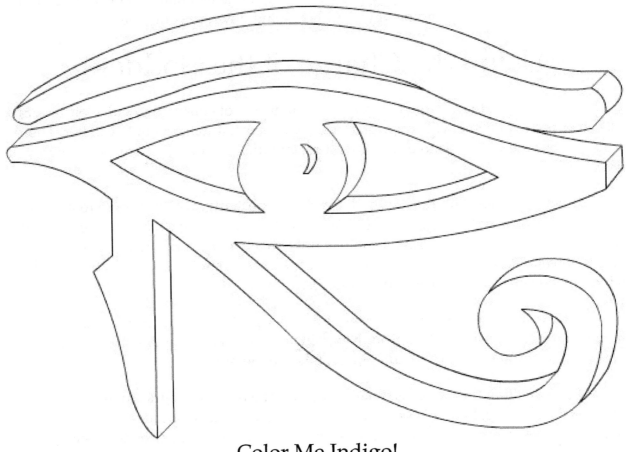

Color Me Indigo!

At age 35, a subtle, silent, almost unperceivable shift takes place within the being of the career minded, socially skilled, fast, and nimble, net-worker known as Mercury. A quiet maturation happens, without anyone's notice, without bells, or whistles. Without the need to do or say anything, Saturn awakens.

She has been known as Kali, Hecate, Sekhmet, Seth, Loki, and even Satan. She is feared by son-in-laws, and daughters alike. She notices everything. She sees it all. She knows not only what is happening, but why it is happening, as well.

Sometimes she is detached from outcome, and watches quietly from the sidelines, while others trip over each other learning their various lessons. Sometimes she becomes quite involved, and strengthens you by exposing your weaknesses in an embarrassing or painful lesson that you are not soon to forget.

She feels very comfortable being judge, jury, and executioner. She has no room

Second Third-Eye Chakra Activation – Saturn – Crones

for silly games, and immature temper tantrums. She knows what you're up to, and while she may not say anything, don't think you're getting away with it.

Grandmother Saturn eats energy. She takes in everything. She observes, scrutinizes, monitors, perceives, discerns, determines, detects, recognizes, judges, and adjudicates. She is discipline and direction. She shows the truth for what it really is, not sugar, no spice, just the facts. If you wanted them to be pretty facts, you should have made them that way. She is not responsible for how well you do or don't look under her penetrating gaze.

Hecate was who Zeus turned to for the facts, when settling the dispute between Demeter and Hades over Persephone's stay in the Underworld. Kali is who was called to bring evil to Justice. Sekhmet was invoked to remind mankind of its relationship to the Gods, when man forgot, and lost gratitude for the many blessings bestowed by Ra.

Loki laughs at your misfortune. Not because he's cruel, but because he told you it was going to happen, and you did it anyway. He finds your inept ability to screw up over and over again amusing. Seth provides the harsh lessons necessary for Horus to become the great ruler that he was destined to be. It would not have served humanity for Horus to ascend the coveted throne as the Supreme Ruler, were it not properly earned, and Horus not properly prepared.

Satan, as hated and misunderstood as he is, provides the lessons of adversity that force you to overcome the obstacles in your life and ascend to your greatness. He does so from the lowliest of places, shunned, hated and feared among all who recognize his name, discarded as a scapegoat by those who don't understand his place in the universe.

Grandmother Saturn rewards you for your deeds. She takes great delight in your successes, and announces your victories from every mountaintop. She has every reason to be proud, she was the one who kicked your butt across the finish line. She was the one who dragged you to training every day. She was the one coaching, cheering, admonishing, and administering. She orchestrated every lesson, and was there with you every time you failed.

The Crone wants your success. But, she is going to make you earn it. You can't fake it with her. Shallowness isn't in her gene pool. You better mean it. You better feel it. You better eat, breathe, and sleep it. Because, you're going to get it, one way or the other. She's ok with doing it the easy way. But, she's not afraid of doing it the hard way, either.

It doesn't matter if it takes you 57,000 tries and 450 lifetimes. She's got all the time in the world, and nothing better to do. She only cares that you keep trying. She brought you into this world, and if you give up, she can take you out.

Grandmother will continue to put choices in front of you that demand you make the right decision. She is the master of illusions. Is it a reward, or is it a test? Choose and see. She may be impressed that you gave the $5.00 mistake back to the clerk at the cash register, but what about that lie you told your child? Yeah, it's really great that you go to church every Sunday, but what good does that do, if you cheat your clients every other day of the week?

Being a good person doesn't matter, unless you mean it on the inside too. Making the right choices when everyone's watching doesn't count if you lie to yourself. Grandmother rules the hands of time. She can extend your life, or shorten it. She can promote your success or ensure your failure.

She wants you to win. But you will win fair and square, or you will face the consequences of your own weapon. She strongly believes if you live by the sword, you should die by the sword. You choose your fate, with your own actions. She can do her best to teach you. She can dole out karmic rewards only as fast as you earn them. But, it's up to you to appreciate all her hard work, or hate her for it. It doesn't matter to her. We can always try again tomorrow.

Honor dear Grandmother, and all those who serve you selflessly to teach you the painful lessons that bring about your greatness. She is a master of disguise and can appear anywhere. It is a great illusion that she manifests herself as your enemy, nothing could be farther from the truth. She is the Kingmaker. She is the teacher. She is committed to your success. She is the only one, who has the guts to be that which you hate the most, your Adversary.

It seems difficult to look into the face of your greatest adversity and know that love is looking back at you. But, just because it's difficult doesn't mean it's not true. Grandmother Saturn doesn't test you because you're bad. She only returns to you *exactly* what you have earned, no more, no less.

She can only put the puzzle pieces in front of you. You have to actually put it together. Find the patterns, the connections, the rewards and consequences of your actions. If you don't like what you are getting, do something different. If you don't like how that felt, make a change. All you have to do is change your actions, and you will change the world. Yes, it is an illusion, but only for those who aren't aware. Wake up. The answers are literally everywhere you look.

As your third eye opens, you see mankind for what it really is: petty, deceitful, shallow, base, greedy, and jealous. But, you also see the potential that lies within. The beautiful spirit struggling to be free from the fear that threatens to drag us down every day. You have compassion for those pure of heart, who truly struggle to do the right thing. You lose patience with those who continue to waste your time and energy on fruitless ventures, and empty debauchery.

You understand that anything worth having is worth working for, and you lose the desire for a meaningless existence. You understand temptation and sin results not in the judgment of a benevolent father god, and the withholding of a golden afterlife, but in an empty and pain based reality that is real, tangible, and bitterly mundane.

You learn to recognize that Grandmother, while old, and wrinkled, never tires of testing you; pushing you onward and upward, or backward and downward. You know that heaven or hell is of your own making, and while the devil is real, he is anything but a wicked, evil, little red tailed demon, who delights in your misery. She is but a little old woman, carrying a very big spindle, spinning your fate, as fast as you can create it.

Awakening Spirit – Freshman Course – www.WISESeminary.com

Practice

Practice Drawing Down, and incorporate it as much as possible in your workings. Remember that any relationship that is important to you needs nurturing. This is an important part of nurturing your relationship to Goddess.

Memorization

Learn the Charge of the Goddess, and say it at least once every day even if it's just while driving in your car. Say it over and over again until you can say it without thinking, like singing a song that you have known all your life.

I only repeat the Priestess part, since I am a Priestess. I think if you are saying it alone as a prayer or incantation, it works fine without the Priest's parts. But, if you have a working partner, saying it together as a couple is very spiritually intimate and a bonding experience.

The Charge of the Goddess[17]

Priest – *"Listen to the words of the Great Mother; she who of old was also called among men Artemis, Astarte, Athene, Dione, Melusine, Aphrodite, Cerridwen, Dana, Arianrhod, Isis, Bride, and by many other names."*

Priestess – *"Whenever ye have need of anything, once in the month, and better it be when the moon is full, then shall ye assemble in some secret place and adore the spirit of me, who am Queen of all the witches. There shall ye assemble, ye who are fain to learn all sorcery, yet have not won its deepest secrets; to these will I teach things that are as yet unknown. And ye shall be free from slavery; and as a sign that ye be really free, ye shall be naked in your rites; and ye shall dance, sing, feast, make music and love, all in my praise. For mine is the ecstasy of the spirit and mine also is joy upon earth; for my law is love unto all beings. Keep pure your highest ideals; strive ever toward it; let naught stop you nor turn you aside. For mine is the secret door which opens upon the Land of Youth. And mine is the cup of the wine of life and the Cauldron of Cerridwen, which is the Holy Grail of immortality. I am the gracious Goddess, who gives the gift of joy unto the heart of man. Upon earth, I give knowledge of the spirit eternal; and beyond death, I give peace, and freedom, and reunion with those who have gone before. Nor do I demand sacrifice; for behold, I am the Mother of all living, and my love is poured out upon the earth."*

Priest – *"Hear ye the words of the Star Goddess; she in the dust of whose feet are the hosts of heaven, and whose body encircles the Universe."*

---

[17] Eight Sabbats for Witches, Janet and Stewart Farrar, Phoenix Publishing, Inc., 1981

Priestess – *"I, who am the beauty of the green earth, and the white Moon among the stars, and the mystery of the waters, and the desire of the heart of man, call unto thy soul. Arise, and come unto me, for I am the soul of nature, who gives life to the universe. From me all things proceed, and unto me all things must return; and before my face, beloved of Gods and of men, let thine innermost divine self be enfolded in the rapture of the infinite. Let my worship be within the heart that rejoiceth; for behold, all acts of love and pleasure are my rituals. And therefore let there be beauty and strength, power and compassion, honor and humility, mirth and reverence with you. And thou who thinkest to seek for me, know thy seeking and yearning shall avail thee not unless thou knowest the mystery; that if that which thou seekest thou findest not within thee, thou shalt never find it without thee. For behold, I have been with thee from the beginning; and I am that which is attained at the end of desire."*

Certification Requirements

Read The New Wiccan Book of the Law. Rewrite each law in your own words.

Journal Entries

Don't forget to record your experiences with drawing down, and reciting The Charge.

15
Second Crown Chakra Activation
The Eight Paths of Power

Violet

Color Me Violet!

The Eight Paths of Power are the eight ways to raise energy, and are represented by this and variations of this symbol:

The Eight Paths of Power[18]

1. Meditation or Concentration
2. Chants, Spells, Invocations, Invoking the Goddess, etc.
3. Projection of the Astral Body, Trance, Journeying
4. Incense, Drugs, Wine, etc. Any Potion, which aids to release the spirit
5. Dancing, Drumming, Making Music
6. Blood Control, Use of the Cords
7. The Scourge
8. The Great Rite

Meditation or Concentration

When you visualize something different from what you have, either through meditation, imagination, concentration or any other effort of controlled thinking, you are putting energy in motion towards that thought. Your thoughts become a projective energetic outburst that affects any receptive pocket of energy in your universe.

This creates a ripple effect, which will in turn transform your universe and mirror your projected thought back to you. Your reality will be directly affected depending on what thoughts you focus your energy on. It is for this reason that those trained to work between the worlds, must monitor their thoughts and be sure to project into the universe only that which they wish to happen.

---

[18] *The Witches Bible Compleat*, Janet and Stewart Farrar, New York: Magical Childe, 1984.

Chants, Spells, Invocations, Invoking the Goddess, etc.

Speaking your magic into being is a powerful way to bring about change. Using visual props to focus your intent, or singing affirmations over and over again, fine-tune your will into discovering exactly what you wish to manifest. Thinking a spell through, writing it down, gathering the needed items and then performing it, sets your desires into motion and creates a boomerang effect that will bring about change in your reality.

Projection of the Astral Body, Trance, Journeying

Journeying is a method of raising power that sends you out into the cosmos. Your search for answers, understanding, and wisdom brings about internal shifts in your awareness that ripple out from you, causing changes in everything that you touch.

Internal transformations are an extremely effective and ethical form of magic.

Incense, Drugs, Wine, etc.
Any potion which aids to release the spirit

The use of drugs, alcohol, or potions has a long-standing controversy in the realm of the occult. It is argued that this form is dangerous, and a short cut for those wishing to serve ego. I agree that many have found this path has taken them to their detriment, but I do not discount it as a valid path to raise power.

I discourage any and all illegal activities, both for spiritual practice and in everyday life. Substance abuse of any kind is not a balanced position, and should be strongly avoided. However, there is no doubt that herbs, incense and potions have a powerful effect on energy and one can become more attuned to the movement of energy under controlled, and responsible use of mind altering concoctions.

I have also found that any wise Priest or Priestess will quickly learn the difference between controlled use of potions and chaos. I have seen many a powerful Priest or Priestess snap back to reality the minute the energy got out of hand. I trust their wisdom to handle their circle, and respect their demonstration of self-control. I have also seen those, who have lost control in a circle of magic, suffer for their carelessness.

As with anything, we either learn from our mistakes or lose our ability to continue making them. I find this method will make or break anyone wishing to perform magic. So, as with any method of power, respect it and use with caution.

Dancing, Drumming, Making Music

Physical movement to raise energy is an act that can be performed with very little understanding, discipline, or focus. One can easily slip into trance when dancing in a disco, or around a sacred fire. Moving energy up through your body is an intoxicating experience. If controlled and directed, it is as effective to create change as any other method.

It is important to monitor, blend, and direct the energy of a group of dancers and/or drummers, as each person acting in their own accord can cause the energy to quickly degenerate into chaos. Where as, someone blending the energy can take the exact same situation and maintain a harmonious, empowering, sacred and uplifting moment of spiritual bliss.

Blood Control, Use of the Cords

Demonstrating physical restriction by the use of cords invokes powerful feelings of vulnerability on the person being bound. It is an exercise in perfect love and perfect trust that cannot be denied. Giving up control of your self to another is something that many of us never have to consciously do. Bringing that vulnerability to the conscious mind releases powerful, deeply hidden emotions in even the most openhearted people.

Facing and releasing our fears of death, restriction, vulnerability, and distrust are ethical pursuits for any spiritual practitioner. Yet, putting postulants to the ancient test of the sarcophagus is frowned upon by society, as it smacks of ritualized torture and spiritual abuse. Blood control reduces the amount of blood in the extremities, which increases the amount of blood in the brain. This induces trance, and mind-altering experiences. This state of awareness can be easily and safely accomplished by sitting on ones legs in a kneeling position, without the risk of cords.

Forced immobilization does invoke an inner seeking that is extremely enlightening. A person cannot escape their thoughts if they cannot physically move. However, it can also bring forth fear and overwhelmingly powerful manifestations of pain and anger that can take a widdershins turn on the experienced and experimenter alike. Use with extreme caution.

The Scourge

The Scourge is used to symbolically bring forth an understanding of humility and the connection between suffering and spiritual growth. Letting your self be scourged by another is a difficult act for those, who are caught up in pride and ego.

The Scourge brings the blood to the surface of the skin making each strike more intense than the previous. It brings about awareness that it is through discomfort that we are driven to spiritual growth. Many ancient mystery schools have used scourging, and self-scourging has been used to purge the body of ego and heighten awareness. It should be used as a light gentle stimulation, that awakens the skin, and never to inflict pain or true suffering.

We are aware that suffering is a choice that one makes when one's ego is attached to outcome. Accepting the lessons of spirit and releasing our attachment removes our desire, and brings us into acceptance.

The Great Rite

Always a powerful moment, the Great Rite brings together the polarity of God and Goddess, forging them into one combined force of strength and power. Whether symbolic or actual, the Great Rite holds reverence within the magic circle.

Two people merging as one, connecting with each other spiritually, physically, emotionally, mentally, and intellectually, in perfect love and perfect trust, is the first real step towards connecting, and merging with the divine.

Consensual sex between two already sexually active partners, in a private circle is a powerfully, spiritually moving experience. Those who are adept at energetics, and can keep their thoughts focused on both the lovemaking and the intent of the working, find the Great Rite a very effective tool to raise energy and bring about intense change.

However, Sex is inappropriately demeaned in our society. There are many cultural hang-ups about it. These cultural implants are not easy to overcome, and therefore, it is almost impossible to ensure that any group of more than two people can perform a sexual act inside a magic circle and maintain the reverence and sacredness of the Great Rite.

Sex is often used to sensationalize, titillate, control, and dominate others. The Great Rite can be symbolically performed with as much reverence and power as the actual act. No one should ever be asked to perform the Great Rite against their will for purposes of initiation, to demonstrate their dedication, for the good of the group, or any other reason.

There are certainly those who try anything to entice others to commit sexual acts in the name of religion, the Goddess, or spiritual enlightenment, for their own gain. I have seen rituals written that used the Charge of the Goddess, repeating the phrase "all acts of love and pleasure are my rituals" over and over, while calling for ridiculous sexual acts, which are obviously designed for personal gratification.

Demoralizing the sacredness of the sexual union of a priest and priestess joined together in a committed, spiritual partnership is bad enough. Committing sexual crimes on those impressionable enough to be willing to do it is deplorable. Do not be a victim to this type of exploitation.

Using the Power

Any combination of these elements can be combined to increase the effectiveness of your intent. Any path can be used to the good of all, or the detriment of any, the direction lies within the intent of the practitioner.

Second Crown Chakra Activation – Raising Energy and Directing Power

Raising Energy and Directing Power

Color Me Violet!

After you get your circle cast, the quarters called, and the Gods invoked, it's time to get down to the body of the ritual. You have called the mighty ones and have their attention. Now it's time to get down to work.

There are many ways to raise and direct energy, as we have discussed. Identifying your need and then finding a way to ritualize it to the Gods is what you are intending to do.

When we do ritual, we take our needs, wants, and desires, and send them to the Gods. If our desires, wants and needs are not in conflict with our highest good, the Gods will return that which we have requested.

A good ritual is one that keeps you focused, entertained, excited, and interested. Anyone standing around bored causes the ritual to loose its effectiveness. Magic is done on the subconscious level. The subconscious looses interest quickly. Therefore, long periods of silence, waiting, standing, etc, are to be avoided. There are many ways to get a point across. Analogies are an effective tool because you can explain a spiritual concept in a way with which people can identify. However, the analogy must make sense, and be simple.

When raising energy you want everyone in circle to be focused, energetically invested, and to have the same intent. It is imperative to identify what that intent is, and to have everyone in agreement that it is what is important at the time.

You can choose any variation of the eight paths to build power and focus your intent. The general idea is to *raise it* and then *direct it*. How you do that is as varied as there are people on the planet.

If you were doing a dedication to Cerridwen; you could invoke Cerridwen with a Chant, blend an incense just for Her, and lead a pathworking, where you journey to meet Her, which involves drinking a potion from Her cauldron. That provides 5 different ways of raising the energy of Cerridwen.

When energy is raised you can feel a prickling sensation on your skin and giddiness. You could yawn, get a chill, or a warm sensation. There are many ways that you can tell energy has been raised. How you identify with it is something you will learn over time as you develop your practice.

Once you find Her, what are you going to do? That is directing the energy. You want to meet Cerridwen, then what? Do you want to ask Her something, give Her something, or learn something? Once you arrive at your destination you should have something to accomplish.

If you were brewing a potion, you may want to focus and sing an affirmation over the potion while it was boiling. If you desire money, you could do a candle spell, focus and chant, as you light it. You should feel the energy moving up and through you, just like you feel it when you ground and shield. Always ground first, so that you can be plugged into your power source and then bring the energy up, spin it, channel it, move it out through your hands, however you want to use it.

Second Crown Chakra Activation – Raising Energy and Directing Power

If you can visualize it, you can make it happen. It is very easy for children to move energy because they are use to using their imagination, and have not lost the ability to believe in magic. But, most adults have to work at it.

Here are some exercises that you can do to help you remember how to work with energy (remember – ALWAYS ground first):

Put the palms of your hands together, and rub your palms against each other back and forth vigorously for about 30 seconds. Then hold them apart, with the palms facing each other. Relax your hands and hold them gently around the ball of energy that has now formed in your hands. Your hands should be tingling with the energy that you have stimulated. If you move your hands back and forth gently pressing in on the ball of energy you will be able to feel a subtle pressure between your hands.

Play your favorite song, sing and dance to it. Notice the difference in your mood after you sing and dance.

Hold your hands down by your side with your palms facing towards the floor. Pull energy up with your hands, *up, up, up, up,* keep doing it for about 1 minute, pulling as much energy up from the earth as you can hold. Then suddenly let it all go. Feel the difference in how heavy you feel holding the energy and how much lighter you feel after you let the energy go.

Now do the same thing with your hands above you, reaching up for the sky. Reach up, pull yourself up, feel yourself lightening up, floating into the air, reaching up. Then let it all go and feel yourself sink back down to the earth.

Get a ball (like a tennis ball or something that size) and toss it up into the air, every time you catch it, add energy to it, until you can feel yourself tossing a ball of energy. The ball will gain weight and feel tingly when you touch it.

Playing with energy is fun, and it increases your ability to understand, raise, move, and direct it. Don't be too serious with it. You are supposed to get giggly when you play with energy. Allow yourself to have fun with it, laugh out loud, and be silly.

Jupiter – Holly Kings

Color Me Violet!

Grandmother Saturn begins to mellow around the age of 42. She has given a good seven years to perfection, immortality, hard work, and perseverance. She has had her nose to the grindstone, and has clawed her way through every obstacle between her and her goal. She has raised her children, upheld tradition, and passed on a legacy. She has earned what she has, and deserves every reward for a job well done.

She is so ready to relax. But she can see that there is still much to be done. She has made much progress, but there is always more to do. Just about the time she begins to understand that there will never be a time when her work is finished, Jupiter drops in for a visit.

He has a million dollar smile, and a pocket full of money. He is wearing an Armani suit, has a limo waiting in the driveway, reservations at the finest restaurant and tickets to the hottest show in town. Jupiter, if nothing else, knows how to relax, enjoy life, and have a good time.

He is a grand king, with every amenity that you would expect, and no question within himself that he deserves every bit of it. He knows he earned it, and by goodness, he's going to enjoy it. No pretensions here, just flat out, unadulterated, innocent and irreverent fun.

Jupiter says, "YES"! Yes, to more money, more fun, more stuff, more knowledge, more freedom, just more and better and more of the better. He loves the good life, and he knows how to enjoy it. He's a traveler, philosopher, healer, compulsive gift-giver, and the original social-butterfly.

Society itself, was Jupiter's idea, along with religion, universities, and all manner of structured institutions that help us define who we are in relation to the universe around us. Why without those things, how else would we know he is king?

He's not trying to impress you with his great mansion, beautiful clothes, impeccable dinner china, and fancy automobiles. This is just how he likes to live his life. Don't you?

He wants to share. Don't get caught up in your issues. He's not thinking about your skimpy little paycheck or other idiosyncrasies. He just wants to have a good time, and this is how he likes to do it. Enjoy, or go home, he has plenty of other friends, who are more than happy to accept his gracious generosity.

What's your hang-up, anyway? No don't tell him, he will just change the subject. It's not that he doesn't care. He just can't hear you over the music and merry-making. It's such a drag to dwell on misery, when there are so many fun things just waiting to be experienced. He will be happy to refer you to a good psychologist. But, for now, why not just forget about that silly stuff, and enjoy the moment.

Better yet, he is the king, he will just banish your pain from his kingdom. No misery allowed, only beautiful people, happy children, delicious delectables, and glittering toys allowed here. Thank you; come again when you're feeling better.

Jupiter is the father king. He has a big, fat bank account, and all he really wants to do is spend money on, and time with the people he loves. His heart is as big as the planet that represents him, and he hasn't a care in the world. He can't be bothered with worrying right now, he promised to wrestle on the floor with his grandchildren today.

What he does have time for is to revel in the beauty of his kingdom. He delights in seeing his children and loved ones squeal with delight from his gifts on Christmas morning. If he had it his way, it would be Christmas every day of the year.

He won't waste a moment on work. Why in the world would anyone want to do that? He spends his days on his passions and hobbies; dressing up his favorite toys, shining up his pretty car, getting all his clothes nice and clean and ready for him to wear.

He wouldn't dream of leaving his prized possessions lying around. They each have a special place in his perfect kingdom, and he has all the time in the world to enjoy putting all his nice things exactly where he wants them to go.

He loves to shine, fix, organize, beautify, admire, and take care of all his fantastic treasures. You call that work? Really? That's just another day of playing with all his cool stuff to him. You should really take a look at changing your reality about that. After all, why have all those nice things if you don't love them enough to treat them like the treasures they are. Wow, you mean you don't see the world as one big game board? How boring for you.

Oh well, he's off to the mall. He needs a new wardrobe for his trip to Rome. He has a private appointment at the Vatican with the Pope. He's curious and wants to ask a few questions about the nature of the universe. Then he has to stop by and check out that new amusement park he put in at the orphanage, and take lunch to the homeless guys in the park.

Be a dear on your way out, and remind his secretary to book a trip to Jerusalem, Egypt, and Greece, and make sure none of it conflicts with his annual camping trip in the Nevada desert with that Navaho Shaman, or his reservations to spend the week at Maccu Piccu on the Solstice.

And don't forget to pick up a copy of his newest book, "God Just Wants to have Fun". Who knew his journal would end up making the bestseller list? What a lucky guy!

Thanks for stopping by. It's been fun. Let's do lunch. He'll have his people call your people.

Ciao, Baby!

Awakening Spirit – Freshman Course – www.WISESeminary.com

Certification Requirement

Explain your favorite way to raise power, and how you know you have done it.

Journal Entries

Don't forget to record the results from your energy games, you will want to look back on your notes later.

16
Second Transpersonal Chakra Activation
Letting the Magic Work

Color Me!

Magic works in your life through a series of changes. These changes sometimes happen quite suddenly, but most materialize gradually over time. When you give birth to a thought form, or you move energy, a series of energetic waves are set into motion.

We move energy deosil to bring things into being, we move widdershins to banish, or dissolve energetic thought forms.

Once you have put the energy in motion, you have to get out of its way and let it work. It takes faith, and patience to let your magic work for you. It is best to just put it out of your mind altogether.

Don't talk about it. Don't tell your friend about the cool working you just did. Don't even ask someone if you did it right. Talk about it before you do it, if you need to. But, once it's done, it's sacred, and should be kept private.

If you keep dwelling on the thought, wondering if your magic is going to work, you put energy into the possibility that it will not work, which makes it harder for it to work. If you do this enough, you can completely counteract any magical working that you do, which then invalidates that you have any ability to positively affect your reality at all.

Fear is a powerful destroyer. It will undermine every positive step that you try to take for yourself, if you allow it to. We are told "it is better to fall upon your blade, than to enter the circle with fear in your heart". This is because amplifying your fear will lead to your ultimate destruction.

You cannot practice positive magic if you are fearful, because you are already convinced that the world is not a safe, and loving place. If any affirmation you repeat will follow with a silent thought in your head that it's just not true, you cannot make a positive change, because your subconscious is programmed to work against you.

The wonderful thing about our fears is that they tell us where the negative energy is invested. If you have a fear of heights, you can work on that, because you have recognized the fear. If you have a fear that people won't love you, it's difficult to find that seed-thought. You end up looking all around it, and blaming all kinds of different problems in your life, but eventually you will find it, if you keep looking.

We find all kinds of ways to disguise our fears: fear of money, fear of poverty, fear of success, fear of failure, fear of being loved, fear of not being loved. We will refuse to allow someone to love us, so that we won't have to face the possibility that they may end up leaving us in the end. We somehow justify that it is better to have no love in our life, than to have loved and lost.

We are sometimes so afraid of success that we will doom ourselves to failure, which is much easier to deal with, because we knew we weren't good enough all along, and now at least we feel validated. We complain that we have no money, and refuse to see the treasures that are littered at our feet. We refuse rewards that are offered to us,

Second Transpersonal Chakra Activation – Letting the Magic Work

and then complain that nobody appreciates us. It's a vicious cycle, and a really silly one too.

So pay attention when you are planning to do a money spell, because you *know* you aren't going to make the rent. If you *know* you aren't going to make the rent, a money spell is not going to help you. You have already ordained that you will not make the rent. I suggest making a plan to deal with that inevitable future, or ordain a different one.

Notice that when someone disrespects you, they are only treating you the way you have shown them you expect to be treated. If you treat yourself differently, so will they. Recognize that what you dislike in someone else, you dislike about yourself, and they are just being nice enough to hold a mirror for you. Take note, when you hear yourself speaking into being the very thing that you don't want. Such as, "I can't walk into a grocery store without gaining weight." Or, "I can never pay my bills on time." Do you really want to create that?

Think twice when you send out that curse at the driver that just pulled over in front of you, or when you call your mother to complain about what a crappy husband (or wife) you have. Why would you do that? Do you really want to validate to your mother that your spouse is less than wonderful? Wake up and notice all the little things that you do that undermine you. Journal, meditate, pray, and pay attention every day.

Remember that you are the perfect you. No one can be you better than you can. There is no one on the planet that you can be better than you. So focus on being the best you can be, don't compare yourself to anyone else. Find out what you are good at. Don't compete with others. They can't possibly serve your purpose better than you can. It only causes you to separate yourself from love.

Try to be the best you, you can be, everyday, and tomorrow try to be better than that. Do all you can to empower yourself, and those around you. Share loving, uplifting thoughts every chance you get. Dwell on all the good things, and just let the bad stuff fade away like a forgotten memory that you don't need anymore. Focus on the positive.

Learn your lessons gracefully. Find the truth within the lesson, and choose to release suffering. Be in the love, and focus on what you want. Then get out of the way, and open yourself to receiving all the abundance, love, and wonderful gifts the universe has to offer you. It will be more than you can possibly imagine.

Cakes and Wine

Color Me!

    Cakes and Wine are traditionally partaken of at the end of a ritual. The feminine elements ground and seal the working we have done, as well as bring us back into our physical awareness. Eating is an act of bonding between family members. It creates the magical ties that bind us to each other, both on the mundane and astral realms. Drinking together connects us to each other emotionally, creating camaraderie, and

Second Transpersonal Chakra Activation – Cakes and Wine

friendship.

We often overlook the magical bonding that takes place when a family sits down to share a meal, or when we spend time sharing drinks with our friends. We complain that we don't have natural rituals in our lives. But, it's not a matter of not having them. It's a matter of not recognizing the magical implications of our daily actions. We eat, bathe, sleep, work, spend time with each other, celebrate special occasions, give birth, get married, and die. These are all natural rituals, which we take for granted.

Raising your awareness about the energy exchanged in the daily routines of your life will help bring the sacred closer to you. Eating and drinking is an important part of these daily rituals. We should express gratitude for that which we consume. Something was sacrificed for everything that we consume. You may not be sacrificing an animal, but you are sacrificing money, which was earned by someone, who sacrificed time and energy away from other things they wanted to do, to earn it.

To bless the cakes, draw a pentagram over the plate with your athame, speaking a prayer from the heart. Consider the relationships that you have to the others in circle, and bless the cakes to strengthen the ties of family, and each one of you individually. Then feed a bite of the cake to the person standing deosil from you while saying the blessing, "May you never hunger", to which they should respond, "Blessed Be".

When blessing the wine, insert the athame into the chalice and say, "As the athame is to the God, so the Chalice is to the Goddess, Joined together they bring blessedness". If you have a man to hold the chalice and a woman to bless the wine, this act is known as the Great Rite. It brings Goddess and God together as one, reinforcing that when we come together in cast circle, we come together as one being, with our thoughts focused and our hearts beating as one.

When a Priest holds the Chalice and a Priestess holds the Athame, they represent polarity in harmony. The Athame inserted into the Chalice joins Priest and Priestess, God and Goddess, as one, and thus joins us all. This is a very intimate blessing, and should be done with the same reverence and respect that you would approach any sexual union. The Great Rite fertilizes your working, and blesses it as a sacred seed planted in the womb of the Goddess.

After the wine is blessed offer the cup to the person standing deosil from you while saying the blessing, "May you never thirst" to which they should respond, "Blessed Be".

Banishing a Cast Circle

When you are finished with cakes and wine, it is time to release the circle. We discussed releasing the quarters in the Initial Heart Chakra Activation, Lesson 4, so I will not go back over the details. But, at this time you should go to each quarter and release the elements, thanking them for their attendance, and help. I consciously pick up the circle with my athame when I am releasing the circle by myself. When the group is doing it, we see the whole circle dissolving away with each quarter being released.

I start in the east and move deosil releasing each quarter as I go. I have heard arguments that since you are banishing you should banish widdershins. It is my belief that you should try new ways, if for no other reason than to validate that you like your way better, and I have tried that. But, I feel the widdershins movement somehow undoes or takes the energy out of my working. So I stick with deosil movement, and banishing pentagrams, which works perfectly for me.

If you use the standard circle incantations provided in this text, you will automatically thank the God and Goddess at the end, and are completely finished, with nothing else to do. However the following is a nice incantation that was brought to our circle by Lady M'hira Nightsky, which she originally learned as a member of Serpent Stone. We like it, and as extended members of the Serpent Stone family, we include it in our rituals as well. All hold hands and say together:

"Now, as we leave this place, between the worlds, to walk once more upon the ordinary ground, remember; what we have done here is ever a part of us. We are power. We are change. Our circle is open, but never broken. Merry Meet, Merry Part, and Merry Meet Again."

Banishing

Banishing negativity from you is an important part of releasing our fears. As we banish negative energy from our world, we create a void, which is an opportunity waiting to be filled. Fill that void with positive energy, so that the negative energy doesn't manifest itself again. For example, it's easier to go on a diet with a list of all the things that you *can* eat rather than listing all the things you *can't* eat.

There are many ways to banish. I find it most easy to banish something by just drawing a banishing pentagram in its direction, as soon as I recognize the negative energy. I try to immediately move onto something positive, so that the void is filled with love. Be aware, if you draw a banishing pentagram, and then talk about how negative and heinous the energy was, you are recreating it as you speak.

Another way to banish negativity is with candle magic. Place the negativity in a black candle, and burn it. As the candle burns, the negativity will be reduced to nothingness. You can also freeze negativity into ice, and then take the ice outside and let it melt into the ground. As the ice melts, the negative energy is carried back to the mother where it can be recycled. Or just put it in a glass of water and pour it down the sink. It doesn't have to be hard, and ugly, just ask Goddess to help you let it go. And then let it go......

Any way that you can imagine getting rid of energy will work, as long as you can visualize it happening. Remember that energy is tangible, if you can move it, you can work magic.

Try to avoid bindings, as you bind the negativity to yourself, and ask for a binding in return. Remember that no matter what others are doing, it somehow serves spirit, and although you may not understand, you don't have to. Let others reap the rewards of their karma, and just move out of their sphere of influence, rather than trying to stop them, fix them, or somehow change their behavior. Learn your lesson and move on. Keep in your mind and heart the understanding that you can choose to see the beauty or misery of any situation. It is up to you to channel your thoughts towards love.

You have too many things to think about in this lifetime to dwell on past unpleasantness or what might have been. Get on with the business of living life today, while you still have it. Make it a wonderful experience that is filled with love, joy, laughter, and abundance. That is what Goddess wants for you. Remember to want it for yourself, and make room in your life to receive your gifts.

Awakening Spirit – Freshman Course – www.WISESeminary.com

Pluto – Priest Kings

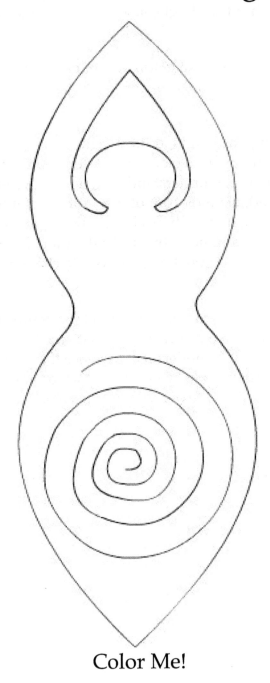

Color Me!

Always, just outside of you, lurking over your shoulder, watching you from the shadows is the ever-ominous presence of Death. It is the not-so-gentle reminder that life is precious, and should be savored, never wasted.

Death pays no attention to age, and you may embody it at any time. It is the black pit that you dance around, sometimes close to the edge, sometimes far from it. But, always the awareness is there, and never do you forget that a wrong step could send you plummeting to destruction.

Pluto can be very scary. It is the epitome of the unknown, and that incites your fear. It is the embodiment of Darkness, and that invites terror. It is the illusive demon taunting you that you cannot see to fight. It is the immortal, omnipotent reminder that Death is only one wrong step away from consuming you. Doesn't it make you feel alive!

Change is inevitable. Go ahead and cling to your misery, it will only bring you closer. Death's bliss lies within the knowing that, that which you fear most is the one thing that will carry you to rebirth, and life. Your fear doesn't threaten it. It knows it is the key to unlock the mysteries of your transformation.

It desires to connect with you, to experience you, and to reveal to you the mysteries of your potential. You are going to come face to face with it, whether you are spiraling widdershins or deosil. You call it a demon of pain and death in your fear, but in your enlightenment you will look back and recognize it as an angel of transformation and rebirth.

Pluto will encourage your drug addiction, and when you hit the bottom, it will be the one who reveals the mystery of your denial, that allows you to embrace healing. It will drive you to the seedy, red-light district, to meet your sexual depravity face to face. When your responsibilities and commitments catch you in the act, it will be the one to show you how to find true fulfillment in the monogamous depth of connectedness with your soul mate. It will make up your lies, and help you tell them, only so you can find that integrity and self-respect is so much more empowering than manipulating others to cover your shame.

Pluto is not afraid to die to be reborn. It will rip out your heart and show it to you, and then put it back in a way that works much better. It will laugh as it kicks your crutches away, to watch you fall on your face in humiliation, all for the purpose of revealing to you that you had wings all along.

It seems to be the Dark God to those gripped in their fear. But, when you face it with courage, and honor, it returns the favor with wisdom, guidance, spiritual epiphany and sacred connectedness with divinity.

Pluto's home is on the edge of your being, not within you. It reveals your shadow, so that you can shine light on it. It is the friend that always gets you into trouble, but whom you don't have strength, or sense enough to stay away from. You are the moth to its flame, as it presents you with the irresistible, delectable delights of carnal pleasure, depravity, and debauchery.

Shhhh, don't tell, no one will know.... It won't tell anyone. Go ahead, you know you want it. Never mind that your conscience will eat at you until you reveal yourself, your pain, your embarrassment, and your secrets, at the most inopportune time, exactly when it can do the most damage to yourself. That's part of the fun, isn't it?

Oooops, I wasn't supposed to tell you about that part, as it laughs behind its hand, with its fingers crossed behind its back hoping that you will choose to do the right thing this time, but content to continue to play this game for another few thousand millennia, if that's what you choose.

For all Pluto's secrets, mysteries, scary masks, and life threatening illusions, death and transformation is the path that will lead you to love, truth, enlightenment and life. Pluto loves purity. It longs to see it emerge from within you. It will do all it can to drag it out of you, if you will only reach for it.

You are never alone in your darkness. Just ask. It's waiting. It wants to help you. It feels your pain. It knows how bad it is. But, although it is your constant companion, and will leave you hints and clues, it can't interfere unless you reach for the answers. Those are the rules. It's learned to live with it. It's hoping someday soon, you will too.

Finishing Up

You now have all the elements to completely cast sacred space. You understand who, when, why and how the process works, and with practice you should be able to confidently cast your own circle whenever you wish to.

Learn your incantations and practice. Nothing will take the place of knowing the words, and working with the energy. Reading from text will never be as powerful as speaking from memory, there are no short cuts to memorizing, and no substitutions for a well cast circle.

Do the work and enjoy the rewards that come with it.

Certification Requirement

Choose topic of private study and write a 1,000-word essay paper on said topic. Include personal thoughts, footnotes and a biography.

Journal Entries

Continue recording your magical journey. Who knows where your path may lead. Your journal may be someone else's sacred text in 2000 years.

First Year Certification Requirements

Awakening Spirit if the textbook for the Freshman Course in the WISE Seminary. On-line completion of this course enrolls you as a student of Wiccan Clergy in the WISE Tradition as a WISE Practitioner. It is a path of personal discovery and growth, and an excellent body of work to present to any Priestess, who may consider you for formal training and/or admittance to a coven.

The First Year Program academically prepares an individual for dedication into a coven or study group. It is an excellent course to do alone, or with a group. Individual counseling is available on-line for those who seek it. Many chapters have graphics, animations and other tools on-line for you to view free of charge. Utilize the website with the book to get the greatest benefit from both. For more information about receiving your First Year Certification, please see www.wiseseminary.com on the World Wide Web.

The following is a checklist compiled from the individual assignments given throughout the text.

Chapter 1 - Complete each grounding meditation, and record results.

Chapter 2 - Write a one-page biography about an historical Wiccan.

Chapter 2 - Write your story of how you came to Wicca.

Chapter 3 - List some boundaries that you have established in your life that you defend at all costs, and how these boundaries serve you. Example – "I don't drink and drive, because I don't want to hurt someone or go to jail."

Chapter 3 - List some boundaries that you would like to be more established, and how these boundaries could serve you.

Chapter 4 - Collect wood and light a sacred fire, either inside or outside, without using man made accelerants. Tend fire and keep burning for 24 hours. Record your experience.

Chapter 4 - List the names of Gods and Goddesses that stand out to you and why.

Chapter 5 - Record your answers to the Chakra and Color exercises.

Chapter 6 - Record two past life journeys.

First Year Certification Requirements

Chapter 7 - Plant seeds at Imbolc, follow seeds through the wheel of the year to harvest. Document your experience. Relate how the magically charged plants interconnect with your goals.

Chapter 7 - Write and perform, or attend each sabbat celebration for one year. Write your personal experience about each one, and what you have learned from it.

Chapter 8 - Write and perform, or attend each moon celebration for one year. Write your personal experience about each one, and what you have learned from it.

Chapter 8 - Perform the 12 spells included in Chapter 8. Record your results.

Chapter 9 - Create an Altar. Explain the symbolism of everything on your altar. Note the history behind each magical tool, and explain why you chose to include it on your altar. Include Pictures.

Chapter 9 - Create your own incense. Explain the magical intent of the incense and why you chose each specific herb. Include Recipe.

Chapter 10 - Collect your tools and consecrate each one. Write your consecration ritual down, including necessary details. After performing the consecration, meditate with each tool, work with its energy, and ask it to speak to you. Write about your experience during the rituals.

Chapter 10 - Prepare a record of magical tools to keep within your Book of Shadows, a tool log. Include every magical tool you posses. Document with pictures, a short description of item, where or whom you obtained it from, the date you received it, any history behind it, and the rituals you performed to consecrate it. Other pertinent items to include may be the receipt or gift card, a tag, instructions, etc.

Chapter 11 - Record your experience with casting circle.

Chapter 12 - Perform elemental meditations. Write down personal experience, taking care to include as many details as you can remember. Explain what you learned, if anything.

Chapter 13 - Write a report that documents the magical and mundane properties of the following herbs. Include pictures. Document references.

| Rosemary | Peppermint | Frankincense | Myrrh |
| Sandlewood | Chamomile | Mugwort | Lavender |

Awakening Spirit – Freshman Course – www.WISESeminary.com

Rose   Eucalyptus   Cinquefoil   Apple

Chapter 14 - Read "The New Wiccan Book of the Law" by Lady Galadrial, published by White Light Pentacles www.wlpssp.com. Rewrite each law in your own words.

Chapter 15 - Explain your favorite way to raise power, and how you know you have done it.

Chapter 16 - Choose topic of private study and write a 1,000-word essay paper on said topic. Include personal thoughts, footnotes and a biography.

About the Cover

The Cover like the rest of the book came about in a strange way. Goddess guided me, often with much resistance, every step of the way in this book. There were so many times that I just had to stop and smile, and realize that even though I couldn't see them, I was not the only person in the room. A piece of paper would fall in the wrong spot, or I would print a wrong page, only to find that there was something important on that page that I needed to address. It's truly been a blessed experience.

I had something completely different in mind for the cover. I had enlisted Keslevar to draw up a picture of me with all my totem animals, and tools, and certain symbols, etc. I wanted it all on a multicolor background. It was a beautiful picture. All we needed was the background. Jason Plum and I sat down and began to pull color across the page in a paint program, to make a rainbow, chakra color effect, starting with red and going up from there. We finally finished, and saved our background. Jason began to close the program, and a picture popped up from a different window. It was a beautiful picture of the Goddess, manifested in the middle of all that color we had been working on.

I gasped. Where did it come from? We had been working in a completely different window. As soon as I looked at it, I noticed the transpersonal point, formed like the Dove of Venus at the top center of the page. Then looking down I noticed the Red and Orange Yin & Yang, rising up together, prominently displaying their polarity in balanced unity. Then as the yellow caught my eye, I saw the rising shield of ego giving way to a pathway leading through a mountain range, to a great Goddess in a blue dress looking down on the path as she swirls everything into existence. I see a smiling pair of blue eyes, as the God becomes the sky, earth, and ocean.

I see the colors of the chakras teaching the same lesson of the rainbow, the lesson that starts at the red, center of our earth, and extends into the inky, blackness of space. I see the self, enfolded in the rapture of the infinite.

I don't know where the picture came from, but I am grateful to have been blessed with it.

Bibliography

Adler, Margot – *Drawing Down the Moon: Witches, Druids, Goddess-Worshippers & Other Pagans in America Today*, (The Viking Press, 1979)

Andrews, Ted – *Animal Speak, The Spiritual & Magical Powers of Creatures Great & Small*, (Llewellyn Publications, 2000)

Andrews, Ted – *Enchantment of the Faerie Realm, Communicate with Nature Spirits & Elementals*, (Llewellyn Publications, 1993)

Aswynn, Freya – *Leaves of Yggdrasil* (Llewellyn Publications, Minnesota 1994)

Brennan, Barbara – *Hands of Light* (Bantam Books, 1988)

Buckland, Raymond – *Buckland's Complete Book of Witchcraft*, (Llewellyn Publications, 1986)

Budapest, Z – *Summoning the Fates, A Woman's Guide to Destiny* (Harmony, New York 1998)

Burk, Kevin – *Astrology – Understanding Your Birth Chart* (Llewellyn Publications, Minnesota 2001)

Circle – *Circle Guide to Wiccan/Pagan Resources* (Circle Publications, annual)

Cunningham, Scott – *Magical Herbalism, The Secret Craft of the WISE*, (Llewellyn Publications, 1990)

Farrar, Janet and Stewart – *Eight Sabbats for Witches* (London: Robert Hale, 1981)

Farrar, Janet and Stewart – *The Witches' Way: Principles, Rituals, and Beliefs of Modern Witchcraft* (London: Robert Hale 1984)

Farrar, Stewart – *What Witches Do* (2nd Edition, Capel Books, Dublin, 1983, and Phoenix Publications, Custer WA)

Fortune, Dion – *The Mystical Qabala* (Rider, London, 1954)

Galadriel, Lady – *The New Wiccan Book of the Law*. (Grove of the Unicorn. PO Box 13384, Atlanta, GA 30324: Moonstone Publications, 1992)

Bibliography

Gardner, Gerald B. – *Witchcraft Today* (Rider, London, 1954)

Goodman, Linda – *Linda Goodman's Star Signs* (St. Martin's Press, New York 1987)

Graves, Robert – *The Greek Myths*, two volumes, revised edition (Penguin, London, 1960)

Guttman, Ariel & Johnson, Kenneth – *Mythic Astrology, Archetypal Powers in the Horoscope,* (Llewellyn Publications, 1998)

Hall, Manly – *The Secret Teachings of All Ages*, (The Philosophical Research Society, Inc., 1988)

Hamilton, Edith – *Mythology* (Little, Brown and Company, New York, 1942)

Hickey, Isabel M. – *Astrology, A Cosmic Science*, (CRCS Publications, 1992)

Jordan, Michael – *Encyclopedia of Gods* (Facts on File, 1993)

Joy, W. Brugh – *Joy's Way*, (Jeremy P. Tarcher/Putnam, 1974)

Judith, Anodea & Vega, Selene – *The Sevenfold Journey, Reclaiming Mind, Body & Spirit Through the Chakras* (The Crossing Press, Freedom, CA 1993)

Judith, Anodea & Vega, Selene – The Sevenfold Journey, (The Crossing Press, 1995)

K, Amber – *Coven Craft* (Llewellyn Publications, Minnesota 1998)

Leland, Charles G. – *Aradia: the Gospel of the Witches*, (C.W. Daniel Co., London, 1974)

Mathers, S. Lidell, MacGregor (translator and editor) – *The Key of Solomon the King (Clavicula Salomonis)*, with foreword by Richard Cavendish (Routeledge & Kregan Paul, London, 1972)

Miller, Susan – *Planets and Possibilities, Explore the World of the Zodiac Beyond Just Your Sign*, (Warner Books, 2001)

Murray, Margaret A. – *The Witch-Cult in Western Europe*, (Oxford University Press, London, 1921)

Murray, Margaret A. – *The God of the Witches*, (Daimon Press, Castle Hedingham, Essex, 1962)

Ovid – *The Metamorphoses*, Translated and with an introduction by Horace Gregory, (Penguin Putnam, Inc., New York, 1958)

Redfield, James – *The Celestine Prophecy, The Tenth Insight*, (Quality Paperback Book Club, 1996)

Starhawk – *The Spiral Dance: A Rebirth of the Ancient Religion of the Great Goddess* (San Franscisco: Harper & Row, 1979)

Valiente, Doreen – *An ABC of Witchcraft Past and Present* (Robert Hale, London, 1973)

Valiente, Doreen – *Witchcraft for Tomorrow* (Robert Hale, London, 1978)

Woolfolk, Joanna Martine – *The Only Astrology Book You Will Ever Need*, (Scarborough House, 1982)

Woolger, Jennifer Barker and Woolger, Roger J. – *The Goddess Within, A Guide to the Eternal Myths that Shape Women's Lives*, (Ballantine Books, 1989)

CPSIA information can be obtained
at www.ICGtesting.com
Printed in the USA
FFHW011247061119
56005153-61863FF